RENEWALS 458-4574
DATE DUE

GAYLORD			PRINTED IN U.S.A.

Additional praise for Performance Management: Integrating Strategy, Execution, Methodologies, Risk, and Analytics

In his most recent book, Gary Cokins shows he has successfully been able to expand his base thinking into a contemporary and useful read. In recognizing the importance of enterprise risk management to today's organizations–and integrating it into the broader content message–this books makes a leap forward for 21st century business practices.

—Ellen M. Heffes, editor-in-chief,
Financial Executive; Financial Executives Institute

Gary Cokins has cracked the code to improving performance by producing a comprehensive body of knowledge which focuses on the implementation of the strategy. A unique feature of Gary's work is that he provides an integrated framework that incorporates Governance, Risk, and Compliance, as well as Customer Value Management. This is a must read for every executive who intends to show performance growth.

—V. Kumar, Ph.D., Richard and Susan Lenny
Distinguished Chair Professor of Marketing, and Executive Director,
Center for Excellence in Brand & Customer Management,
J. Mack Robinson College of Business, Georgia State University
Author of *Managing Customers for Profit*

Gary Cokins is one of those gurus who not only is a recognized expert but truly gets it. He is the first expert to truly link performance management to customer value management in a way that makes sense for the 21st century. Because of that, mark my words here, this book will make a serious difference to the conduct of business in the workplace.

—Paul Greenberg,
President, The 56 Group, LLC; and Managing Partner/CCO: BPT Partners
Author of *CRM at the Speed of Light*, 4th edition.

Cokins' writings on Performance Management represent valuable contributions to better understand why and how performance management is essential in managing in a dynamic business environment. The book enables today's managers and executives to take another critical step forward in realizing the potential operating and strategic improvements that can be derived from a well structured and implemented Performance Management system.

—Lawrence Maisel,
Managing Partner, DecisionVu LP

Gary's latest work on Performance Management continues his thought leadership on the topic. He crystallizes the broad array of performance measurement tools into a holistic approach to better and higher level performance management. His emphasis on learning from others, behavioral change, making choices, focusing, and using reliable fact-based data are all sound pieces of advice that should help organizations deal with tough times and keep on the winning track.

—Christopher T. McKittrick, CPA,
Director of Members in Business, Industry & Government,
American Institute of Certified Public Accountants (AICPA)

Gary Cokins has been a proven thought-leader ever since he was the lead author of the popular *An ABC Managers' Primer* published in the early 1990s. With each of his successive books, Gary has raised the bar to help practitioners with concepts and implementation issues related to managerial accounting and performance management. This book is written in a lighthearted way that anyone can understand and describes the integration the many possible solutions that an organization can use to improve their performance and also avoid implementation pitfalls.

—Steve Vieweg,
President and CEO, CMA-Canada

Gary Cokins has succeeded in creating a must have resource for anybody either in the midst of or even just considering a performance management project. This book contains valuable content from the basics to advanced performance management 2.0 capabilities. Gary's book will be helpful for first time analysts trying to jumpstart their initiative to seasoned project management experts looking to advance their knowledge-base to a higher level.

—John Colbert, Vice President,
Research and Analysis,
BPM Partners

Gary's performance management expertise comes to light with increasing clarity in his newest book, *Performance Management: Integrating Strategy Execution, Methodologies, Risk, and Analytics*. His writing style is direct. His examples and predictions are colorful and often uncomfortably true. On a personal note, readers will appreciate Gary's accessibility and his willingness to help when needed.

—Ron Powell, Editorial Director,
Business Intelligence Network

Despite knowing Gary for some 20 years, I continue to be amazed at the depth and clarity of his thoughts and arguments. This book presents a vision for performance management and how that discipline integrates with other key management processes. But most importantly for readers, Gary tells us how to achieve this, not just what and why, and that makes this book that much better.

—Robert Torok, Executive Consultant,
IBM Global Business Services

Many organizations attack the parts. In this book Gary, a consensus thought leader in the performance management community, shows how to align organizational gears for maximum effectiveness.

—Steve Player, Managing Director,
The Player Group
Program Director, the Beyond Budgeting Roundtable
Co-author of *Cornerstones of Decision Making:
Profiles of Enterprise Activity-Based Management*

Gary Cokins offers powerful insights and practical counsel for all who are seeking to manage effectively in these turbulent times.

—David A.J. Axson; Founder, Sonax Group Inc.
Author of *Best Practices in Planning and
Management Reporting*

Performance Management provides a bridge between high-level strategies and practical implementation. Gary's book is required reading for all executives serious about building shareholder value. Think of it as a survival guide for managing in these tough times.

—Dr. Stephen G. Timme, President, FinListics Solutions
Adjunct Professor, Georgia Institute of Technology

Gary Cokins has been pioneering performance management endeavors. His new book shows that he's still not only following but leading thought processes when it comes to further developing performance management strategies. It's a must-read for everyone who wants to learn about how to improve organizational performance."

—Christoph Sporleder, Managing Partner,
Echô Advisors GmbH, Germany

As always, Gary sheds light on a vast array of complex issues with an ease that I always found amazing. In particular, his effective use of analogies draw great parallels with the many points he is bringing across. Just as an example, his use of the brain to illustrate the distinct contributions of transactional systems versus BI and performance management information is simply brilliant.

—Daniel Dubé, M.Sc., FCMA,
Founder and former CEO of Synerma Inc.
Professional Practice Manager,
Raymond Chabot Grant Thornton,
Montreal Canada

Improving and organizing performance requires the right balance of quantitative and qualitative decision making. Gary Cokins' past writings have explained in easily understood language how to achieve the right balance of the quantitative and qualitative. In this book, Gary educates, entertains, and inspires readers who are interested in improving their organizational decision making.

—Michael D. Shields,
Schaberg Endowed Chair in Accounting,
Broad College of Business,
Michigan State University

Performance measurement and management are at the center of current corporate concerns. Gary Cokins has been a global leader in this field for decades and this new contribution provides an integrated approach that is a must read for corporate leaders interested in improving business performance.

—Marc J. Epstein,
Distinguished Research Professor of Management,
Jones Graduate School of Management,
Rice University

Cokins' uses a holistic, action-oriented approach to explain performance measurement. His framework calls for managers to conduct measurements to support strategy implementation. Thus alignment with strategy defines the performance measurement process and its role in the managerial decision-making process.

—F. Asís Martínez-Jerez,
Associate Professor, Harvard Business School

It takes a lot of experience and wisdom to discuss a comprehensive business concept such as enterprise performance management in a conversational way, which Gary does in his new book. He has strong opinions, with which you may agree or disagree, but reading this book will make you reflect on your own beliefs.

—Frank Buytendijk,
author of *Performance Leadership*

Gary Cokins has been at the forefront of championing one of the most comprehensive visions of performance management in the industry for many years. *Performance Management: Integrating Strategy Execution, Methodologies, Risk, and Analytics* is the culmination of this vision and will join his long list of writings that are mandatory reading for anyone in the field who wishes to understand state of the art in current thinking on this topic. Heartily recommended!

—Nenshad D. Bardoliwalla,
Vice President, Technology,
Business Performance Optimization,
Office of the CTO, SAP AG

Performance Management provides invaluable insights into what it takes to achieve outstanding organizational performance by taking a very broad view of what "performance management" really means. Going well beyond the establishment and monitoring of metrics, Gary Cokins successfully links topics such as strategic planning, cost management, predictive analytics, business intelligence, enterprise risk management, and organizational change management. Whether you are new to the topic of performance management, or a well seasoned practitioner looking for new insights, this book is a "must read."

—Douglas Webster, Chief Financial Officer,
U.S. Department of Labor
Co-author of *Chasing Change:*
Building Organizational Capacity in a Turbulent Environment

Gary has moved the dials of the evolving architecture of performance management. A brilliantly landscaped mosaic. The chips of the performance management fitting into a circuit of a visionary class.

—A.N. Raman, Central Council Member,
ICWA of India

Organizations have been struggling for decades, arguably for centuries, on how to improve their performance. Gary Cokins is an internationally recognized thought leader on this topic and active contributor to professional societies such as my organization. With this book and its deep and rich insights, Gary has set a high-level mark that other experts will be challenged to exceed.

—Ashok G. Vadgama, President,
Consortium for Advanced Management - International (CAM-I)

In a very important chapter on customer value management, Gary Cokins rightly views the customer as a business entity with an asset life value and a dedicated profit and loss (measure). Gary addresses the real cost to serve the customer with an activity-based management approach that is essential to maximize the business performance of critical customers.

—Bernard Quancard, President and CEO,
Strategic Account Management Association (SAMA)

Gary Cokins' clear writing is derived of clear thinking about performance management. Performance management is about nothing less than how to run an enterprise. Gary cuts through the jargon and explains what performance management is, why it is important and how to do it. This book is invaluable for any businessperson.

—Neil Raden, Founder of Hired Brains Inc.

Gary is always focused on how technology can help manage and improve an organization's performance–not just measure or monitor it. Performance management the way Gary describes it in this new book provides the essential linkage between corporate strategy and operational decision-making. Gary's brand of performance management should be on every executive's to-do list.

—James Taylor, Author of *Smart (Enough) Systems:*
How to Deliver Competitive Advantage
by Automating the Decisions Hidden in Your Business

Using company strategy as a point of departure, Gary clearly articulates the "strategy as hypotheses" connections between business functioning and the intelligence/analytics measurement/feedback loop. This scientific approach to measuring and managing business performance, a logical but important extension to the Balanced Scorecard, provides a clear (though not necessarily simple) prescription for businesses that wish to be managed nimbly from evidence and facts.

—Steve Miller,
President, OpenBI, LLC

Gary writes with a seldom encountered clarity that is conversational and collegial, but that also has a distinct tone of challenge and urgency for the reader to "get it". With a complex subject, he consistently engages you to work out the challenge of PM in all its implications and potential rewards. His central notion that many organizations are "over-managed, but under-led" is one that should keep many executives up at night. A thoroughly stimulating read.

—Peter Traynor, Editor in Chief,
Dashboard Insight

An excellent book whose insights into cost control and performance management are more relevant than ever in light of current economic conditions. Gary Cokins has spent a career focusing on how companies can improve performance and cost management without simply resorting to cost cutting. This both fun and serious book continues his numerous contributions to the study of performance management.

—Jack Fingerhut,
President, SmartPros Ltd.

Our working association with Gary Cokins spans more than two decades, including his invaluable services as Advisory Board member for the journal, *Cost Management*. Several times, Gary could have made the choice to rest in "emeritus" status. Instead, his uncanny talent for targeting the next developments in performance and cost management–subjects covered in this volume such as sustainability effects on CFOs and social and environmental performance management–drives forward both the professional discipline as well as its receptive practitioners. Gary's inability to remain satisfied with the immature aspects of current practice has made him both reviled (to the immature) and revered (by those ready to receive his message). In these times, we opt for maturity.

—Joe and Catherine Stenzel,
Editors in Chief, *Cost Management*

Gary has done a terrific job of pointing out that Performance Management is about Performance Improvement rather than just Performance Measurement. His emphasis that Performance Management consists of a variety of methods that must be integrated in order to successfully execute strategy is critical. His focus on predictability rather than after-the-fact reporting is exactly what every organization needs to do.

—John Antos consultant
Co-author of *ABM for Services, Government,
Nonprofits* and *Driving Value Using
Activity-Based Budgeting*

Gary's years of experience, expertise, knowledge, and creative personality flow in this new book like a torrent! Gary's insights and use of humor get better all the time, this new book is like having a chance to peek inside the mind of Yoda, really! A smartly written book with loads of examples and experiences for leaders and managers at all levels.

—Bob Paladino, CPA
Managing Partner, Bob Paladino
& Associates, LLC
Author of *Five Key Principles of Corporate
Performance Management*

Once in a while there emerges from a cloud of conflicting three letter acronyms, poor definitions and misconceptions a ray of light that makes everything so much clearer and as a consequence so much more useful. Gary's book on Performance Management burns away the mists. His emphasis on strategy execution over strategy formulation–in other words actually moving the business forward–is supported by his advice that Performance Management has to change from monitoring the dials to actively moving them and thereby improving performance.

—Brian Plowman, Managing Director of Develin
& Partners, Cost Management Consultancy

Gary Cokins is the consultants' consultant for performance management. His detailed knowledge of the subject and its role in the management of the enterprise, combined with comprehensive coverage, creates an invaluable reference guide for those in pursuit of performance improvement.

—Peter B.B. Turney, Ph.D.;
President and Chief Executive Officer, Cost Technology
Author of *Common Cents: How to Succeed with Activity-Based Costing and Activity-Based Management*

Concise and backed by real life expertise! The idea of integrating hindsight (BI) and foresight (predictive analytics) is a powerful approach to Performance Management for organizations. We have always found Cokins' inputs, value adding to our solutions and service offerings on Performance Management.

—Prem Swarup, Practice Manager
Pawan Kumar, Vice President,
Business Intelligence & Information Management,
Wipro Technologies, Bangalore, India

No one can explain performance management concepts better than Gary Cokins and that has never been truer than in this compilation of his recent articles and blogs. The format and conversational style of the book not only make it an enjoyable read, but they enable Gary to present the issues in a variety of ways and from many different perspectives. This book is a must for anyone who really wants to understand performance management.

—Douglas T. Hicks,
President, D. T. Hicks & Co.
Author of *Activity-Based Costing: Making It Work for Small and Mid-Sized Companies*

I've had the pleasure of knowing and working with Gary for over 20 years. During that time I know of no one that has been in better position to observe, document, and refine best practices in the arenas of ABC and business performance management. In this book he deals with the much more subtle, and equally important, ways in which we accomplish the many faceted challenges of management to support these practices.

—Jack Haedicke,
Founder, Arena CG

Gary Cokins does in this book what he does so eloquently each time I see him–makes it startlingly obvious just how extensively performance management weaves through the most important systems and processes of moving an organization from where it is to where it's planned to go. He boldly and honestly admits that the field of performance management is broad and relatively immature, and tackles this daunting fact head on with a collection of practical and insightful articles that do what I've seen no other work in this field do: give performance management a complete, clear, and compelling identity, above and beyond the individual notions of scorecards, dashboards, budgeting, performance appraisals, and the rest. This book is every performance management facilitator's reference manual.

—Stacey Barr, -,
Director of Stacey Barr Pty Ltd.

Having known Gary since his first book, having travelled and seen him present throughout Europe for years, I have grown to respect Gary's endurance of spearheading and constantly re-inventing his views on performance management. Until this book, people unfamiliar with Gary, have only read his serious side. Those of us who have enjoyed him present know, however, that Gary sometimes promotes his ideas by pinches of humor in the manner his latest book now does it. The future will tell if some of those stories of this book will become industry classics?

—Juha Jolkkonen, Sales Director,
Cox Consulting Oy; Helsinki, Finland

Leaders should *not* promise change. Change can either be good or bad. Instead, organizations need improvement. Gary Cokins' book is loaded with practical principles and methods every manager can use to improve their organization.

—Tom Pryor; Growth Coach,
Texas Manufacturing Assistance Center
Author of *Using Activity Based Management*
for Continuous Improvement

Gary is a gifted communicator and in this book he brings together decades of practical experience and scholarly expertise. The book is a useful starting point for managers grappling with modern challenges of performance management. It is also a valuable resource for the experienced manager; integrating recent advances in diverse management disciplines (e.g., strategy, marketing, operations and accounting systems) to present an integrated view of performance management.

—Shannon W. Anderson; Associate Professor of Management,
Jesse H Jones Graduate School of Management, Rice University

For many years, Gary Cokins has been a globally-recognized thought-leader that translates complex management concepts into understandable insights that help managers drive breakthrough results. His latest book distills the principles of performance management into practical nuggets of wisdom that will guide managers in fulfilling their most important responsibility—strategy execution.

—Dr. Peter C. Brewer, Professor of Accounting,
Miami University of Ohio
Co-author of the market-leading college textbook *Managerial Accounting.*

Gary Cokins, a renowned consulting expertise, has just added a brilliant piece of work to his already long list of accomplishments. His new book provides conceptual frameworks and operational guidelines for a fully integrated performance management, which are much needed for a company to 'intelligently' perform.

—Joonho Park; Associate Professor,
School of Business, Hanyang University
Former Chairperson of Accounting & Audit Committee,
Korea Communications Commission

Gathering reams of information has no value. Information only has value when it is used to support decision-making aimed at increasing shareholder value. This is the major lesson to be learned from (my long-standing colleague) Gary Cokins' new book on performance management. Gary has drawn upon his many years of experience to provide the reader with practical frameworks for deciding what information is meaningful to collect and how it can be leveraged to drive improved customer value and business performance.

—Larry Lapide, Ph.D., Director,
Demand Management, MIT Center for Transportation & Logistics

Gary's book is a thoughtful work on performance measurement and management. He is an author with deep experience in the accounting arena. Written in a very accessible writing style.

—Dr Eva Labro; Reader in Management Information,
London School of Economics

This text combines a sound and original critique on the contemporary performance management discussion with a constructive and practical summary of some essential of its concepts. The format and content of the book provides the reader with a variety of perspectives on performance management. Together these form a rich and much needed addition and even alternative to some of the 'generally accepted performance management principles' found elsewhere.

—Prof. Dr. Frank Hartmann; Management Accounting & Management Control,
Rotterdam School of Management, Erasmus University

Already a proven author, Gary has done it again. The engaging style with which Gary handles the various concepts will give this book an appeal well beyond the consultants and practitioners who help design and implement performance management systems. In fact, I could easily see his material having a place in graduate business education.

—Paul E. Juras; Professor of Accountancy, Wake Forest University

During my professional marketing and academic activity, the Performance Management domain has become critical, not only regarding customer and market value, but also in the holistic vision of execution, strategy monitoring and Return on Marketing Investment. Gary Cokins' work has become obligatory reading regarding Activity Based Management. His skills and knowledge are a reference for leveraging and increasing my business vision and my marketing performance

—Luis Bettencourt Moniz,
Marketing Director, ESRI Portugal

Gary Cokins who is well known in practitioner circles around the world outlines the strategic importance of performance management and the methodologies to provide executives and managers the basics and insight to adapting their organizations and management to reach their full potential.

—Mark Smith, CEO and EVP Research, Ventana Research

Gary Cokins brings to light the fact that performance management goes well beyond a set of software toward the convergence of change management and the execution of corporate strategy. With his first person examples and use of satire, this book reads like a novel, making it an enjoyable read and accessible to everyone interested in making performance management a reality within their organizations.

—Lyndsay Wise, President and founder, WiseAnalytics

Gary Cokins is a solid and visionary thought leader in the field of Performance Management. Through his deep research and field experience, he has generated perspectives that are guiding this sector forward. Decision teams exploring ways to take Performance Management to the next level should pay close attention to the ideas in this book.

—Britton Manasco, Principal, Manasco Marketing Partners

Gary's brings Performance Management all together in this book and is a must read for those responsible and accountable for managing the performance of their organizations. By Gary's definition, that's all of us.

—John Miller, Director, Arkonas Corp

From my first encounter with Gary more than 10 years ago, he has had an incredible knack of making difficult concepts appear simple. This is again demonstrated in this book, this time, demystifying Performance Management. Organizations in Asia will gain tremendously from his insights which effectively clear up their misperceptions about performance management.

—Andrew Lim, Co-founder & CEO, Balanced Scorecard Solutions, Singapore

'When you are driving with a GPS instrument and you make a wrong turn, the GPS's voice chimes in to tell you that you are off track—and it then provides you with a corrective action instruction . . . the performance management framework includes a GPS." This is just one example of Gary Cokins use of simple analogies to cut through the jargon and buzz-words which surround the various methodologies that make up performance management. The result is a very readable and useful book for anyone interested in implementing all or any of these methodologies as part of an integrated performance management system.

—Jim Doorly, B.Comm.,
FCA, ABC/M Implementation Specialist
former partner at KPMG

Gary has created what is sure to be an important book on performance management. Well illustrated, and often very entertaining, he provides deep insights into the interrelationships of performance management tools. I will be adding Gary's *Performance Management* to the select list of books that we recommend to our seminar attendees on this topic.

—John L. Daly, President, Executive Education
Author of *Pricing for Profitability*

Any book in these times with the title *Performance Management''* and a subtitle that touches ALL the key bases including *Integrating Strategy Execution, Methodologies, Risk, and Analytics''* deserves a look. When it's authored (humorously, no less) by someone with the savvy and vision of Gary Cokins, you should consider buying it. When he promises "It *is* possible to tame an organization's dysfunctional behavior," buy it.

—Alan Dybvig,
Dybvig Consulting in partnership with INSIGHT, Inc.

Read this book to learn how a performance measurement framework can help your organization build value by digging deeper and acting sooner than the competition.

—Bill Hass, CEO, TeamWork Technologies
Co-author *The Private Equity Edge*
past chairman of the Turnaround Management Association

Strategies are useless if an organization can't execute them, and most organizations can't. Gary Cokins' *Performance Management* will teach you how to improve your organization's ability to execute its strategies. I recommend this book because my firm's performance has improved significantly as a result of what I learned from Gary.

—Bruce Pounder, CMA, CFM, DipIFR (ACCA),
President, Leveraged Logic

Gary does a great job in this book of showing the key role of performance management in the execution of an organization's strategy. This is a timely book that effectively brings together and explains clearly the emerging features of performance management, including topics such as strategy maps, predictive analytics, rolling financial forecasts, and customer value management. And the book is enjoyable to read.

—Professor Edward Blocher, Kenan-Flagler Business School,
University of North Carolina at Chapel Hill

Organizations are confused about what enterprise performance management is. Most view it as too narrow. Gary Cokins does an excellent job clarifying what it is, its purpose, and its benefits.

—Carsten Rohde, Ph.D., Professor,
Department of Accounting and Auditing,
Copenhagen Business School; Copenhagen, Denmark

Gary's ideas, covered in this book, will inspire you to reexamine your Performance Management perceptions and initiatives. His performance management framework provides a complete business picture with key insights that are suitable for both my business students and industry clients.

—Alan See, Associate Faculty, Business & Management,
University of Phoenix

Performance Management

PERFORMANCE MANAGEMENT

Integrating Strategy Execution, Methodologies, Risk, and Analytics

GARY COKINS

WILEY

John Wiley & Sons, Inc.

Published by John Wiley & Sons, Inc., Hoboken, New Jersey.
Published simultaneously in Canada.

For general information on our other products and services, or technical support, please contact our Customer Care Department within the United States at 800-762-2974, outside the United States at 317-572-3993 or fax 317-572-4002.

Wiley also publishes its books in a variety of electronic formats. Some content that appears in print may not be available in electronic books.

For more information about Wiley products, visit our web site at www.wiley.com.

Library of Congress Cataloging-in-Publication Data:

Cokins, Gary.
  Performance management: integrating strategy execution, methodologies, risk, and analytics/Gary Cokins.
      p.   cm. — (Wiley and SAS business series)
   Includes index.
   ISBN 978-0-470-44998-1 (cloth)
  1. Performance—Management.   2. Risk management.   3. Organizational effectiveness. I. Title.
   HF5549.5.P35C65   2009
   658.4'013—dc22

                                                                    2008048208

Printed in the United States of America

This book is dedicated in memoriam to Robert A. Bonsack—friend, mentor, and craftsman in the field of performance improvement

Contents

About the Author

Gary Cokins is an internationally recognized expert, speaker, and author in advanced cost management and performance improvement systems. He received a B.S. in Industrial Engineering/Operations Research from Cornell University in 1971 and was a member of both the Tau Beta Pi and Alpha Pi Mu honor societies. (At Cornell he also played varsity football as a linebacker with Ed Marinaro for the *Hill Street Blues* TV fans.) He received his MBA from Northwestern University's Kellogg School of Management in 1974 and was a member of the Beta Gamma Sigma professional society.

He began his career as a strategic planner with FMC Corporation. With FMC's Link-Belt Division Cokins served as Financial Controller and then Production Manager, which exposed him to the linkages between cost information, strategy, operations, performance measurements, and results. In 1981 Cokins began his management consulting career with Deloitte. There he was trained by Eli Goldratt and Robert Fox and implemented Theory of Constraints (TOC) OPT software. Cokins then joined KPMG Peat Marwick, where he implemented integrated business systems and ultimately focused on cost management systems, including activity-based costing (ABC). At KPMG Peat Marwick, Cokins was trained in ABC by Professors Robert S. Kaplan of the Harvard Business School and Robin Cooper. Next, Cokins headed the National Cost Management Consulting Services for Electronic Data Systems. In 1996 he joined ABC Technologies, a leading ABC software vendor that was acquired in 2002 by SAS, a global leader in business intelligence, analytics, and performance management software.

Cokins was the lead author of the acclaimed *An ABC Manager's Primer* (1992), sponsored by the Institute of Management Accountants and the Consortium for Advanced Management International (CAM-I). In 1993 Gary received CAM-I's Robert A. Bonsack Award for Distinguished Contributions in Advanced Cost Management. His second book was *Activity-Based Cost Management: Making It Work* (McGraw-Hill, 1996), was judged by the Harvard Business School Press as "read this book first." His 2001 book, *Activity-Based Cost Management: An Executive's Guide* (John Wiley & Sons, 2001) regularly ranked as the #1 best-seller by book distributors of over 150 books on the topic. In 2004 he authored *Performance Management: Finding the Missing Pieces to Close the Intelligence Gap* (John Wiley & Sons, 2004). Gary is a coauthor of the textbook, *Cost Management: A Strategic Emphasis* (McGraw-Hill, 2008).

Cokins is certified in Production and Inventory Management by the Association for Operations Management. He serves on several committees of professional societies, including CAM-I, the Supply Chain Council, and the Institute of Management Accountants (IMA). He was the coeditor of CAM-I's 2001 *Glossary of ABC/M Terms* and is a member of the Journal of Cost Management Editorial Advisory Board.

Cokins resides in Cary, North Carolina, with his wife, Pam Tower. He has two stepdaughters, Jennifer and Kristin, and two grandsons, Conor and Brodie. He can be contacted at garyfarms@aol.com or gary.cokins@sas.com.

Preface

In the preface of my book *Activity-Based Cost Management: An Executive Guide* (John Wiley & Sons, 2001), I stated:

> Sometimes luck beats planning. I have been fortunate in my professional career—a career that began in 1973 as an accountant and continued into line operations management and management consulting. Without realizing it—through this series of different jobs and management consulting assignments—I somehow earned a reputation as an internationally recognized expert in activity-based cost management (ABC/M). In truth, I am always learning new things about how to build and use managerial systems. I'm not sure that any expert in ABC/M exists. I'm just fortunate to have been formally working with ABC/M since 1988 when I was introduced to ABC/M.

Since 2001, I have expanded my understanding of how management works. I learned that cost management must be done in a much broader context—enterprise risk-based performance management. This is because one must consider time, quality, cost, risk, service level, resource capacity planning, innovation, customers, and suppliers as an integrated framework.

My university education in the late 1960s was in industrial engineering and operations research, and I attribute to that foundation my thinking during my work career about how organizations work as a set of intermeshed systems—like linked drive-gear teeth in a machine. In some ways, I am glad that, for a while after I graduated from my university, operations research was not broadly practiced and computers were not yet sufficiently powerful to process and store data. Otherwise, my career might have been narrowly focused on solving interesting problems appreciated only by mathematically trained specialists. Instead, as I was exposed to the deficiencies of traditional managerial accounting and performance measurement practices, I realized that these were challenges that were important to all managers around the world and that I could potentially contribute in a way to make a difference.

As a management consultant in the 1990s, my work assignments began to weave in strategy and nonfinancial performance measures. That initially led me to realize that cost management must occur in a broader context—that being performance management. My 2004 book on this topic reflected my observations from my work experiences and from some exceptional people I have been fortunate to interact with.

Since 2004, I have annually averaged visiting roughly 30 international cities, presenting seminars on enterprise performance management, meeting with commercial and public sector executives, and dialoging with management consultants. I have been so fortunate. I am a careful observer of what I see, and somehow I developed a knack for explaining complicated things in a way that people can understand them.

HOW THIS BOOK DIFFERS FROM MY 2004 BOOK ON PERFORMANCE MANAGEMENT

This book is different from my 2004 book on performance management. In that book, I explained with a serious tone the basic concepts of the various methodologies that, when integrated, comprise the performance management framework, such as strategy maps, balanced scorecards, and activity-based cost management. This book is more light-hearted but hopefully more insightful in explaining what it will take to successfully implement the *full vision* of the performance management framework. Here, I expand performance management to include the dimension of risk management.

This book is a compilation of media articles and blogs that I have authored since publishing my 2004 book. I have grouped the 35 chapters into 10 parts. Several of the articles, edited for this book, were posted in my monthly column that I write for the Web portal InformationManagement.com. I am grateful to the editors at InformationManagement.com (previously DMReview.com) for having provided me the platform to write about enterprise risk-based performance management, which I refer to in this book simply as *performance management*. My writing style for media articles is that of conversing with the reader; I hope that becomes apparent as you read this book.

LINKING STRATEGY TO OPERATIONS WITH THE ABILITY TO RESPOND

I have some concerns with misperceptions about what performance management is. One misperception, in which performance management is viewed far too narrowly, is that it is just a bunch of dashboard measurement dials plus better financial reporting. It is much broader than that and includes robust integration of typically disconnected information technology (IT) systems. A Forbes.com article described this as "The old model of the enterprise was purely financial, focused on costs.... The modern practice of performance management has replaced this outmoded process with the equivalent of a corporate nervous system that shows what is happening right now in a company and can avert problems in the future." (By Dan Woods, 8/25/08, available at http://www.forbes.com/2008/08/22/cio-performance-management-tech-cio-cx_dw_0825performance_print.html)

Another concern is performance management's name—it is really about performance *improvement*; this implies the need for analytical support for better decisions—another distinction of performance management. Finally, although performance management's scope is broad, my belief is that its main purpose is strategy *execution* rather than strategy *formulation*. Executives are quite competent with the latter, strategy formulation, and they often engage consultants like McKinsey to assist or validate their strategy. Executives' frustration and challenge comes in successfully implementing and managing their strategy. This requires greater linkage of strategy to operations in the top-to-bottom direction and the alignment of the work and priorities of the workforce in the reverse, bottom-to-top direction.

There is no need to list here all the external commercial market or public sector government pressures and forces that are placing stress and demands on leadership teams. Almost every conference PowerPoint presentation begins with that almost-obligatory slide of a circle with arrows pointing into the circle—each arrow representing a pressure. Performance management is about helping executives to understand how to react to these pressures and then to select and take necessary actions. Selecting the right actions and then completing them is the tough part of management.

To complicate matters, transforming an organization is somewhat like having heart surgery while running a marathon (except there is no finish line). The goal of sustained long-term improved performance is a balancing act of many dimensions. One aspect is balancing pursuit of the short-term goals demanded by external bodies, such as capital market investors, with long-term strategic objectives.

External forces are producing unprecedented uncertainty and volatility. The speed of change makes calendar-based planning and long-cycle-time planning with multiyear horizons unsuitable for managing. Pursuits in both time frame horizons involve change:

- *Short-term goals* require agility to maintain linkage of a constantly adjusting strategy with operational execution while complying with and meeting aggressive performance level expectations of stakeholders (e.g., quarterly financial earnings reports). Stakeholders can include customers, taxpaying citizens, investors, and government regulators.
- *Long-term strategic objectives* require continuous innovation, foresight of risk and opportunity, relentless process improvement, an eye on recruiting and retaining a motivated workforce, and leveraging partnerships and alliances of all kinds for interdependent mutual benefits.

Executives are gradually shifting their perception from a common acceptance that their reengineered processes should be sturdy and resilient to a new view that they must be flexible and agile. Along with this change in perception comes one involving an economic structural shift wherein their view of their organization's cost structure, including its employees, as being highly fixed relative to volume is changing to a view that its capacity is variable—that capacity is adjustable in the short term. With uncertainty and volatility rising, there is little choice to think otherwise.

FIVE CRITICAL MANAGERIAL AREAS

I believe advances in five managerial areas will help organizations concurrently pursue both time frame horizon goals:

1. *The rising role of analytics, particularly predictive analytics.* An educated workforce with analytical skills and supported by powerful information technologies is converging with increasingly complex problems. In addition, all decisions involve trade-offs that result from natural conflict and tension, such as customer service level objectives and budgeted cost (i.e., profit) objectives. It is essential to balance the overall enterprise's performance with better trade-off decision making, rather than allow political self-interests of individual departments to preside.

2. *A chief performance officer.* Progressive organizations are realizing that strategy execution is too important to be a part-time job of the chief operating officer. New job titles like *chief performance officer* (CPO) or departments such as the office of strategy management are evolving to ensure that the executive team's formulated strategy is executed and that the various performance management methodologies are phased in and integrated. Measurements drive behavior, and the CPO's role is tasked to assure alignment of many dimensions, including capacity, the work of employees, and the fiscal budget to achieve the enterprise's strategy. A strategy is never static—it is dynamic. It is adjusted as external factors change and new things are learned. A CPO is needed to ensure that executives are continuously modifying the strategy and that its adjustments are quickly linked and cascaded to those who execute the strategy.

3. *Enterprise governance, risk, and compliance management.* The observation "If you cannot measure it, then you cannot manage it" can be applied to risk. Techniques to recognize and measure risk are emerging, which positions risk for the subsequent step—the need to control risk through risk mitigation. Governance is the executive team's ability to formulate and execute its strategy. Compliance is abiding by the law with tracking capabilities to know who touched a transaction, what was changed, and why a change was made.

4. *Customer value management.* Power is shifting from suppliers to buyers. The Internet is one factor causing the shift. Suppliers and service providers must be judicious in determining where and how much to spend to get the highest yield by offering differentiated services to various customer microsegments.

5. *Collaboration.* Collaboration is much more than just e-mail and conference telephone calls. The information technologies embedded in a performance management framework provide capabilities for commentaries, dialogs, data tagging, and search features. Proximity to a problem or an opportunity is critical for being proactive, and collaboration through communication via information technology is a key enabler. Collaboration assures alignment of workforce behavior all the way from the vision at the top desk (i.e., the chief executive officer) to the actions at the desktops.

Admittedly, other critical shifts such as continuous innovation of products, services, and processes are necessary, but I view these five areas as the game-breakers that will propel performance management to top-of-mind for all organizations.

ORGANIZATIONAL TRANSFORMATION: HOW TO GET FROM HERE TO THERE

As I describe in Part One, the source of any organization's return on financial spending is the shifting from tangible assets, like equipment, to intangible assets, like *information* and *people*.

Regarding *people*, most notably employees (although contractors and partners matter, too), the personnel and human resource functions in organizations are increasingly improving their ability to better recruit, grow, and retain human capital by leveraging evolving workforce analytical solutions.

When it comes to *information* and the technologies that produce it, most leaders and managers are realizing that having had their upgraded software systems installed in anticipation of the Y2K (year-2000) meltdown scare, they are in much better shape. They have now sufficiently automated their daily transactional data systems, such as with enterprise resource planning or customer relationship management (CRM) software, to achieve proficient operations typically involving the order fulfillment core process that is universal to all organizations. The *better-faster-cheaper* productivity gains—both low- and high-hanging fruit—have been already substantially realized. However, now the shift is also to working *smarter*. This means that the future financial yield lift for organizations, whether public sector government or commercial, will come from transforming the treasure trove of transactional data into meaningful information to be combined with knowledge and intelligence for better planning and to make superior decisions.

Organizations complain they are drowning in data but starving for information, and this is where the confusion between software vendor business intelligence (BI) and performance management solutions comes into play. In the 1990s, BI was viewed as more of a software tool purchased by information technology (IT) to provide basic query, drill-down, and reporting for a few employees. In contrast, since 2000, the narrow view of performance management as bolt-on software tools was requested more by the financial function. The broader view of performance management tools, such as for customer intelligence, was requested by marketing and sales functions.

To differentiate BI from performance management, performance management can be viewed as deploying the power of BI, but the two are inseparable. Think of performance management as an application of BI. Performance management adds context and direction for BI. BI provides a platform of transactional data and its partial conversion into useful information. Then the integrated performance management applications, built on top of the BI platform, provide the various methodologies as solutions, each embedded with analytical capabilities, to turbo-charge the potential in the BI platform.

The good news is that the 1990s hype that information technologies are the ultimate solution is finally matching reality. That is, with BI and performance management software, organizations can actually do what they have always wanted to do—anticipate, react, and respond. Today, the reality of IT matches the promise of the past. In the past, executives and managers viewed deficiencies in their IT systems as impediments to improving performance. Those excuses are disappearing. Today, data collection, cleansing, and transformation into usable information are feasible. What is next needed is *people engagement*—concentrating on overcoming the natural hesitancy of employees and managers to shift from the status quo and apply BI and performance management information for better decision making. Today organizations can architect and customize their IT solutions to their pain points and opportunities. But convincing managers and employees to use the IT solutions is another matter.

PERFORMANCE MANAGEMENT 2.0

Performance management 2.0 is being referenced by some IT research firms as an advance over performance management 1.0. Does the designation performance management *2.0* simply mean it is *better and broader* (e.g., more inclusive and integrated) than the traditional performance management 1.0 view of being simply a chief financial officer–driven initiative of financial reporting, budgeting, and dashboard dials? In my opinion, performance management 2.0 is the *integration* of the methodologies I frequently mention in this book, such as balanced scorecards, strategy maps, budgets, activity-based costing, forecasts, CRM, and resource capacity planning.

Of course, a reference to performance management as having discrete version numbers like software releases is a bit of a gimmick. (My colleague Frank Buytendijk, a performance management author like me, asked me two questions: Should he refer to his second wife as wife 2.0? If so, what would be wife 2.1?). Performance management 2.0 is a clever way to imply that the implementation of the performance management framework goes through stages of maturity and phases, with each expansion providing something *better and broader* with more powerful benefits.

Performance management 2.0 places more emphasis on strategy execution. Its purpose is not just better reporting and *monitoring* dashboard dials, but *moving* the dials—*improving* performance. For commercial organizations, performance management 2.0 includes the shift in focus from products to customers—and particularly to customers with more economic value potential for the investors and shareholders. For public sector and government organizations, performance management 2.0 enables the *more-for-less* and *value-for-money* approaches to serving citizens, taxpayers, and military personnel.

However, performance management 2.0 places greater emphasis on more areas than just strategy management and customer value management. An additional feature is analytical tools, such as for segmentation or statistical correlation analysis, that can be seamlessly embedded within all of the various methodologies to accelerate and improve decision making and risk management. What performance management 2.0 provides is the capability to go beyond just reporting and querying historical data. Performance management 2.0 leads to the right actions and decisions to improve—and to increase the certainty that manager and employee decisions will lead to improvement. Performance management 2.0 is all about improvement—synchronizing improvement in the value of customers with economic value creation for stockholders and owners.

There will be many terms used to describe performance management 2.0—*optimized, unified, integrated, holistic,* and *synchronized,* for example. What matters more than what we call it is what it accomplishes. With today's patchwork quilt of independent IT systems, with the many spreadsheet reports patched in, it is difficult for an organization to truly model the flow and impact of information across the entire enterprise in order to respond to it or to proactively cause decisions to be made quickly. But performance management 2.0 makes this vision possible.

MY PERSONAL POSITION STATEMENT

As an author, I believe it is an obligation to share with the reader where my ideas are coming from. In addition to the points I just described to you, my basic beliefs are simple and few:

- *The discipline of managing is embryonic.* Unlike the fields of medicine, law, or engineering, which through codification have advanced their learning decade by decade, managing is more comparable to an apprenticeship program. We learn from observing other managers, whether their habits are good or bad. The introduction of performance management, with an integrated suite of tools and solutions, can make managing a discipline on par with the other mature fields. And managing with reliably calculated risks can convert managers into leaders.

- *We substantially underestimate the importance of behavioral change management.* Each year that I work, I increasingly appreciate the importance of change management—considering and altering people's attitudes and behavior to overcome their natural resistance to change.

- *Strategy is of paramount importance.* Strategy is all about choices and focus. Given limited resources, executives must get the most from them. However, the most exceptional business processes and organizational effectiveness will never overcome a poor strategy. Strategy execution is where performance management fits in.

- *It is critical to operate with reliable, fact-based data.* For example, organizations need visibility of accurate costs, but most receive flawed and misleading cost information from arbitrary cost allocation methods. They do not receive visibility into their hidden costs of marketing and sales channels. With the facts comes a better understanding of what drives results and costs. Without agreed-on, reliable facts and an understanding of if-then causality, the organization can stumble, lacking the ability to build strong business cases for ideas.

I ask that the reader patiently absorb my description of the interdependencies of the various aspects of an organization. Learn from this book how methodologies like forecasting demand, measuring performance, measuring segmented profits and costs, and planning for resource levels can themselves be integrated.

My hope is that reading this book will instill an increased sense of confidence that complex organizations can finally see clearly—that employees within such organizations can find the pervasive fog lifted and see how their organization truly operates. There is hope. It *is* possible to tame an organization's dysfunctional behavior, despite how prevalent it seems.

OVERVIEW OF THE BOOK

Part One, the Introduction, begins with one of my favorite pieces involving tongue-in-cheek satire about how to ensure that an organization is poorly managed. It includes a lengthy chapter that describes the broad vision of enterprise performance management and concludes with a chapter examining an even broader vision—enterprise risk-based performance management.

Part Two provides the reader with insights on how important the behavioral and change management issues are. It includes a chapter on human capital management, and it concludes with describing the importance of leadership. Part Three explains the difference between business intelligence and performance management with the emphasis that decision support is the primary purpose of the performance management framework. Part Four tackles the thorny questions related to how to successfully implement and integrate the various methodologies of performance management.

Part Five, on strategy maps and balanced scorecards and dashboards, is the first of the five parts that drill down into the key methodologies that comprise performance management. Part Six is on managerial accounting and budgeting (that evolves into rolling financial forecasts), and Part Seven deals with measuring and managing customer profitability and future value. Part Eight links customer value management with shareholder wealth creation by capital market companies and private equity holdings in particular. Part Nine reveals how governance and social responsibilities for the environment (i.e., going green with sustainability) and for people can be addressed using the same performance management methodologies that are used to improve an individual enterprise's economic performance.

Part Ten concludes the book with a vision of what enterprise risk-based performance management might be in the future, including my Christmas letter to Santa Claus and year-2015 diary postings by the executive team of a fictitious organization.

SOME READER INSTRUCTIONS

This book does not need to be read cover to cover. I see it more as a reference guide or manual. I encourage readers to initially scan the table of contents, thumb through the chapters, and glance at the many illustrations with the purpose of marking which book chapters are of most interest to possibly read in greater detail later. (Chapter 2, "Performance Management: Myth or Reality?" provides a good summary of the entire book.) Remember that the main idea is not to examine organizational improvement methodologies in isolation but rather to view them as an integrated solution set. Also remember that strategy-aligned performance measurement and measuring resource-consuming costs are the underpinnings for the core solutions of performance management.

I would like to thank my many coworkers, current and past, and other individuals who reviewed chapters of this book and gave me valuable feedback. I would like to thank those special people from whom I garnered the nuggets of insight that I have distilled and synthesized into this book. I would also like to honor, in memoriam, Robert A. Bonsack—friend, mentor, and craftsman in the field of performance improvement, who twice hired me (Deloitte and EDS). Having a true mentor can be a once-in-a-lifetime experience, and I was fortunate to benefit from that experience.

Finally, I am forever grateful to my wife, Pam Tower, who, for the year I was writing this book, allowed me to balance—and occasionally misbalance—my job and family.

Gary Cokins
garyfarms@aol.com (I welcome your e-mails.)

Part One

Introduction

A man's mind stretched by a new idea can never go back to its original dimensions.

—Oliver Wendell Holmes,
U.S. Supreme Court Justice, 1897

Sometimes a little satire is an effective way to better understand what performance management is all about. I begin this book with a tongue-in-cheek description of an organization that is doing the wrong things to pursue a performance management culture. Chapter 2 is the longest chapter of the book, because it is describes the broad view of performance management that all the subsequent chapters relate to. Chapter 3 boldly hypothesizes that predictive analytics may be comparable in impact to the major management breakthroughs of the past century.

Chapter 4 describes enterprise risk-based performance management—the comprehensive view that combines governance, risk, and compliance with performance management. Risk management is a top-of-mind concern for executives. It is important not to isolate risk from performance management but to explain how they are connected.

Chapter 1

Rules for Ensuring Poor Performance

In 1773, Benjamin Franklin, one the founding fathers of the United States, wrote a pamphlet aimed at the royalty of England, titled *Rules by Which a Great Empire May Be Reduced to a Small One*. Satire is one way to get your point across. I apply my own style of satire in this chapter to appeal to organizations to cease their hesitation and skepticism and embrace the benefits of performance management. I apologize in advance if I offend anyone, but sometimes there is truth in humor.

* * *

Imagine I took over the management of a poorly performing organization and wanted to keep it that way. For example, I might not want it to grow so quickly that it would leave me less time to pursue my hobbies. What steps would I take?

First, I would ensure that all of the managers and employees are totally ignorant of the executive team's strategy. That way, no one will understand how the work they do each week or each month contributes to successfully achieving the strategy. Next, I would figure out ways to ensure that managers and employees do not trust one another. I would discourage dissent and debate. It would be tricky to preserve some level of harmony by not allowing healthy conflict among managers who are already distrustful of each other, but I think I could do it.

Next, I would avoid holding anyone accountable. That would be fairly easy, because I would disallow reporting of performance measures. Anyone mentioning the phrase "the balanced scorecard" would be summarily fired. I would allow employees to measure their local processes and results in dashboards. After all, I do not want the organization to go bankrupt; I just want poor performance. But I would restrict any measures from being key performance indicators because we would not want to monitor our progress toward any targets that are strategic. I would try to disallow setting of targets, but some managers have a nasty habit of liking them. I think those managers believe that if they could make it appear that they are better performers than others, then I would reward them with a "pay-for-performance" bonus system. If I allow people to be motivated this way, performance might improve. I am not going to fall for that trick.

I would freeze our managerial accounting system to remain in its archaic state. It probably was designed in the 1950s, but our external financial auditors would always be giving us an *OK* grade. I would allow managers to hire more support overhead to manage the resulting complexity, but I would preserve the primitive overhead cost allocations to processes and products using those distorting and misleading broad averages, such as product sales volume or number of units produced. Most employees would already know that these cost allocations cause big cost errors, but I would want to keep them guessing about which products make or lose money and what it actually costs to perform our key business processes. I do not think my financial controller will correct this, but I need to keep a watchful eye because my accountants are getting much smarter about how to improve operations and serve as strategic advisors to me.

We would need to be careful about how much information we collect and report about our customers. Obviously, we would report their sales volume data, but I would not segment our customers into any groupings. I would keep sales reporting at a lump-sum level. I do not want anyone asking questions such as "Which types of customers should we retain, grow, acquire, or win back from competitors?" To keep our company from tanking, I would encourage sales growth by putting big signs in the marketing department saying "More sales at any cost!" I would prevent my chief financial officer from harboring any thoughts of measuring customer profitability. That would be easy, because our arcane cost accounting system would not be capable of calculating that information. The marketing people typically spend their budget with a spray-and-pray approach, anyway. Targeting specific types of customers and getting a high-yield payback from our marketing spend would be beyond their level of thinking. I would maintain our advertising spending as the black hole that no one understands.

I would, of course, implement an enterprise resource planning system. I would not want to be at a cocktail party with other executives and admit I do not have one. That would be too embarrassing, like a teenager without an iPod. Luckily, ERP systems alone will not improve performance; they produce mountains of transactional data for daily control, but not meaningful information from which anyone could make wise judgments or good decisions.

Our budgeting system would be another way to ensure our poor performance. Since the budget numbers are obsolete a couple of months after we begin the fiscal year, assembling the budget for six months during the prior year would provide a great distraction and prevent anyone from working on more important things. Plus, I would love to send the budget back down a few times to be redone to lower the budgeted costs. Everyone would moan. I would be very stingy about giving managers any budget for one-time projects. When those kinds of initiatives sneak in, companies always get a jolt of productivity improvement, which is counter to poor performance.

We would squeeze our suppliers. We could *talk* about partnering and collaboration, but any attempt to actually do so would be squashed immediately. Never trust a supplier. If you drive one out of business, you can always find another.

I do not think I could stop employees from using spreadsheets. They are contagious. But since every department would have its own spreadsheets, it would be like a Tower of Babel. Employees would waste a lot of time trying to make their numbers match. I might allow a few departments to purchase a common database to warehouse their information. Fortunately, there would be lots of incorrect input data in it, so that bad experience would burst their bubble. Those employees with spreadsheets might want to use them for forecasting and planning. I would put a stop to that by calling it *gambling* and promote our company as being conservative. Gambling is for fools, so I would set a policy forbidding risk taking.

I know that operating a poorly performing business is an extremely difficult job, but I think I would be up to the task. Suppressing the efforts of all those employees and managers who want to think, contribute, and make the business successful requires constant vigilance. The business world is full of subversive ideas that could hamstring my efforts to keep the business floundering aimlessly.

I am particularly concerned about this new concept called *performance management*. Whatever it is, I will stop it from happening. I believe that with hard work and dedication, I could keep any company from reaching its profit-making potential.

Chapter 2

Performance Management: Myth or Reality?

There is confusion in the marketplace about the term *performance management*. Just Google the term and you will see what I mean.

The confusion begins with which phrase we should use to refer to *performance management*. This confusion in part is due to semantics and language. We often see in the media the acronyms *BPM* for business performance management, *CPM* for corporate performance management, and *EPM* for enterprise performance management. But just as the words *merci, gracias, danke schön*, and *thank you* all mean the same thing, so do these acronyms. Fortunately, information technology (IT) research firms like IDC and Gartner are accepting the short version, and simply calling it *performance management*.

Additional confusion is that the term *performance management* is perceived by many as far too narrow. It is often referenced as a bunch of measurement dashboards for feedback and better financial reporting. It is much, much more. More recent confusion comes from the term being narrowly applied to a single function or department, such as marketing performance management or IT performance management.

Historically, *performance management* referred to individual employees and was used by the personnel and human resources function. Today, it is widely accepted as enterprise-wide performance management of an organization as a whole. Clearly the performance of employees is an important element in improving an organization's performance, but in the broad framework of performance management, human capital management is just one component.

Most new improvement methodologies typically begin with misunderstandings about what they are and are not. Perhaps that is why the famous business management author, Peter Drucker, observed that it can take decades before a new and reliable management technique becomes widely adopted. Misunderstandings are typically not a result of ignorance, but rather inexperience. The latest buzzphrase, *performance management*, is predictably laden with misconceptions due to the lack of experience with it. That is now changing.

One purpose of this book is to remove the confusion and clarify what performance management really is, what it does, and how to make it work. We begin by discussing a major reason why there is such high interest in performance management.

EXECUTIVE PAIN: A MAJOR FORCE CREATING INTEREST IN PERFORMANCE MANAGEMENT

It is a tough time for senior managers. Customers increasingly view products and service lines as commodities and place pressure on prices as a result. Business mergers and employee layoffs are ongoing, and inevitably there is a limit that is forcing management to come to grips with truly managing their resources for maximum yield and internal organic sales growth. A company cannot forever cut costs to prosperity. There is evidence that it is also a tough time to be a chief executive. Surveys by the Chicago-based employee recruiting firm Challenger, Gray & Christmas repeatedly reveal increasing rates of involuntary job turnover at the executive level compared to a decade ago.[1] Boards of directors, no longer having a ceremonial role, have become activists; and their impatience with chief executive officers (CEOs) failing to meet shareholder expectations of financial results is leading to job firings of CEOs, chief financial officers (CFOs), and executive team members.

In complex and overhead-intensive organizations, where constant redirection to a changing landscape is essential, the main cause for executive job turnover is executives' failure to execute their strategy. There is a big difference between formulating a strategy and executing it. What is the answer for executives who need to expand their focus beyond cost control and toward sustained economic value creation for shareholders and other more long-term strategic directives? Performance management provides managers and employee teams at all levels with the capability to move directly toward their defined strategies.

One cause for failures in strategy execution is that managers and employee teams typically have no clue as to what their organization's strategy is. Most employees, if asked, cannot articulate their executive team's organization strategy. The implication of this is significant. If managers and employee teams do not understand their organization's strategic objectives, then how can the executives expect employees to know how what they do each week or month contributes to the achievement of the executives' strategy? That is, employees can effectively implement a strategy only when they clearly understand the strategy and how they contribute to its achievement. The balanced scorecard (see Chapter 17, "The Promise and Perils of the Balanced Scorecard") has been heralded as an effective tool for the executive team to communicate and cascade their strategy down through their managers and employees to improve strategy attainment.

A balanced scorecard is designed to align the work and priorities of employees with the strategic objectives that comprise an organization's defined mission. But there is confusion with this methodology. Many organizations claim to have a balanced scorecard, but there is little consensus as to what it is. Worse yet, very few have designed a strategy map from which the scorecard is intended to be derived as its companion. The strategy map is orders of magnitude more important than the scorecard itself—the latter of which should be viewed as merely a feedback mechanism.

Is it enough to have a strategy map and its balanced scorecard with visual at-a-glance dashboards that display key performance indicators (KPIs)? Or do these provide merely one component needed for delivering economic value creation through achieving the strategy?

Ultimately, an organization's interest is not just to *monitor* scorecard and dashboard dials of measures but, more important, to *move* those dials. That is, reporting historical performance information is a minimum requirement for managing performance. Scorecards and dashboards generate questions. But beyond answering "What happened?" organizations need to know "Why did it happen?" and, going forward, "What could happen?" and ultimately, "What is the best choice among my options?"

WHAT IS PERFORMANCE MANAGEMENT?

Performance management is all about *improvement*—synchronizing improvement to create value for and from customers with the result of economic value creation to stockholders and owners. The scope of performance management is obviously very broad, which is why performance management must be viewed at an enterprise-wide level.

A simple definition of *performance management* is "the translation of plans into results—execution." It is the process of managing an organization's strategy. For commercial companies, strategy can be reduced to three major choices:[2]

1. What products or service lines should we/should we *not* offer?
2. What markets and types of customers should we/should we *not* serve?
3. How are we going to win—and keep winning?

Although performance management provides insights to improve all three choices, its power is in achieving choice #3—winning by continuously adjusting and successfully executing strategies. Performance management does this by helping managers to sense earlier and respond more quickly and effectively to uncertain changes.

Why is responding to changes so critical? External forces are producing unprecedented uncertainty and volatility. The speed of change makes calendar-based planning and long-cycle-time planning with multiyear horizons unsuitable for managing. As a result, strategies are never static; rather they are dynamic. Executives must constantly adjust them based on external forces and new opportunities. Strategies and the operational plans and decisions to execute them are never perfect. Imagine if employees at all levels—from executives to frontline workers—could answer these questions every day:

- "What if my plan or decision is wrong?"
- "What are the consequences if I am wrong?"
- "If I am wrong, what can I do about it?"

Performance management helps answer those questions. It can be summed up by stating that it gives an organization the capability to quickly anticipate, react, and respond. If executives were given the choice between two scenarios—one with relatively more precise information over the next three months with relatively less precision and more uncertainty over the next two years, and the other choice the opposite—I believe most executives would select the first one. Performance management helps anticipate problems earlier in the time cycle.

IS PERFORMANCE MANAGEMENT A NEW METHODOLOGY?

The good news is that performance management is not a new methodology that everyone now has to learn; rather, it tightly integrates business improvement and analytical methodologies that executives and employee teams are already familiar with. Think of performance management as an umbrella concept. It integrates operational and financial information into a single decision-support and planning framework. This includes strategy mapping, balanced scorecards, costing (including activity-based cost management), budgeting, forecasting, and resource capacity requirements planning. These methodologies fuel other core solutions, such as customer relationship management (CRM), supply chain management, risk management, and human capital management systems, as well as lean management and Six Sigma initiatives. It is quite a stew, but everything blends together.

Performance management increases in power the more these managerial methodologies are integrated, unified, and spiced with all flavors of analytics—particularly predictive analytics. Predictive analytics are important because organizations are shifting away from managing by control and reacting to after-the-fact data, toward managing with anticipatory planning so they can be proactive and make adjustments *before* problems occur. Unfortunately, at most organizations, performance management's portfolio of methodologies is typically implemented or operated in a silo-like sequence and in isolation from each other. It is as if the project teams and managers responsible for each of the methodologies live in parallel universes. We know there are linkages and interdependencies among them, so we know they should all somehow be integrated. These components are like pieces of a tabletop jigsaw puzzle. Everyone knows the puzzle somehow fits together—but the picture on the box cover is missing!

Performance management provides that picture of integration both technologically and socially. Performance management makes executing the strategy everyone's number-one job—it makes employees behave like they are the business owners. It is the integration of the methodologies spiced with analytics that is the key to completing the full vision of the performance management framework.

CLARIFYING WHAT PERFORMANCE MANAGEMENT *IS NOT*

As mentioned earlier, performance management is sometimes perceived as a human resources and personnel system for individual employees. It is much more encompassing. It embraces the methodologies, metrics, processes, software tools, and systems that manage the performance of an organization as a whole. Also, performance management should not be confused with the more mechanical "business process management" tools that automate the creating, revising, and operating of workflow processes, such as for a customer order entry and its accounts receivable system. Also, performance management is not just performance measurement. Metrics and indicators are simply a piece of the broad performance management framework.

To minimize confusion, there is no single performance management methodology, because performance management spans the complete management planning and control cycle. Hence, performance management is not a process or a system. There are substantial interdependencies among multiple improvement methodologies and systems. In a sense, everything is connected, and changes in one area can affect performance elsewhere. For example, you cannot separate cost management from performance as increases or decreases in expense funding generally impact performance results. For performance management to be accepted as the overarching integrator of methodologies, it must meet this test: Will performance management prove to be a value multiplier?

Think of it as a broad end-to-end union of integrated methodologies and solutions with three major purposes: collecting data, transforming and modeling the data into information, and Web-reporting it to users and decision makers. Performance management is also not software, but software is an essential enabling technology for any organization to achieve the full vision of the performance management framework. I view performance management as originating with the C-level executives and cascading down through the organization and the processes it performs. Performance management goes all the way from the top desk to the desktop.

Primitive forms of performance management existed decades ago. These forms were present before performance management was given a formal label by the IT research firms and software vendors. Performance management existed before there were computers. In the past, organizations made decisions based on knowledge, experience, or intuition; but as time passed, the margin for error grew slimmer. Computers reversed this problem by creating lots of data storage memory, but this led organizations to complain they were drowning in data but starving for information—thus distinguishing the word *information* as the transformation of raw data, usually transactional data, into a more useful form. In the 1990s, with the speedup of integration with computer technology, both at a technical level of database management and at a business level of user-friendly software applications for all employees, the term *performance management* took root.

WHAT HAS CAUSED INTEREST IN PERFORMANCE MANAGEMENT?

Admittedly, there is ambiguity and confusion about what performance management really is. Regardless of how one defines or describes it, what is more useful is to understand the answers to these two questions: (1) What does performance management do, and (2) what business forces or pressures have created interest in it among executives?

Seven major forces have caused interest in performance management because it resolves these problems:

1. *Failure to execute the strategy.* I have already mentioned this. Although executive teams typically can formulate a good strategy, their major frustration has been failure to implement it. The increasing rate of involuntary job turnover of CEOs is evidence of this problem. A major reason for this failure is that most managers and employees cannot explain their organization's strategy, so they really do not know how the work that they do each week or month contributes to their executives' strategic intent. Strategy maps, balanced scorecards, KPIs, and dashboards are the components of performance management's suite of solutions that address this issue.

2. *Unfulfilled return on investment (ROI) promises from transactional systems.* Few if any organizations believe they have actually realized the expected return on investment promised by their software vendor that initially justified their large-scale IT investment in major systems (e.g., CRM, enterprise resource performance [ERP]). The chief information officer (CIO) has been increasingly criticized for expensive technology investments that, although probably necessary to pursue, have fallen short of their planned results. The executive management team is growing impatient with IT investments. Performance management is a value multiplier that unleashes the power and payback from the raw data produced by these operating systems. Performance management's analytics increase the leverage of CRM, ERP, and other core transactional systems.

3. *Escalation in accountability for results with consequences.* Accelerating change that requires quick decisions at all levels is resulting in a shift from a command-and-control managerial style to one where managers and employees are empowered. A major trend is for executives to communicate their strategy to their workforce, be assured the workforce understands it and is funded to take actions, and then hold those managers and employee teams accountable. Unlike our parents' workplaces, where they retired after decades with the same employer, today there is no place to hide in an organization anymore. Accountability is escalating, but it has no teeth unless it has consequences. Performance management adds teeth and traction by integrating KPIs from the strategy scorecard with employee compensation reward systems.

4. *Need for quick trade-off decision analysis.* Decisions must now be made much more rapidly. Unlike in the past, where organizations' employees could

test-and-learn or have endless briefing meetings with upper management, today employees often must make decisions on the fly. This means they must understand their executive team's strategy. In addition, internal tension and conflict are natural in all organizations. Most managers know that decisions they make that help their own function may adversely affect others. They just do not know who is negatively affected or by how much. A prediction of impact of decision outcomes using analytics is essential. Performance management provides analytical tools, ranging from marginal cost analysis to what-if scenario simulations, that support resource capacity analysis and future profit margin estimates.

5. *Mistrust of the managerial accounting system.* Managers and employees are aware that the accountants' arcane "cost allocation" practices using noncausal broad-brushed averaging factors (e.g., input labor hours) to allocate nondirect product-related expenses result in flawed and misleading profit and cost reporting. Some cynically refer to them as the *"mis*allocation" system! Consequently, they do not know where money is made or lost or what drives their costs. Performance management embraces techniques such as activity-based costing (see Chapter 25, "How Profitable to Us Is Each Customer Today . . . and Tomorrow?") and lean accounting (which arguably are similar techniques) to increase cost accuracy and reveal and explain what drives the so-called hidden costs of overhead. It provides the cost transparency and visibility that organizations desire but often cannot get from their accountants' traditional internal management accounting system.

6. *Poor customer value management.* Everyone now accepts how critical it is to satisfy customers to grow a business. However, it is more costly to acquire a new customer than to retain an existing one. In addition, products and standard service lines in all industries have become commodity-like. Mass selling and spray-and-pray advertising are obsolete concepts. This shifts the focus to require a much better understanding of channel and customer behavior and costs. This understanding is needed to know which types of existing customers and new sales prospects to grow, retain, acquire, or win back using differentiated service levels—and how much to spend on each type of customer that is worth pursuing. It requires working backward by knowing each customer's unique preferences. Performance management includes sales and marketing analytics for various types of customer segmentations to better understand where to focus the sales and marketing budget for maximum yield and financial payback. *Return on customer* is an emerging term.

7. *Dysfunctional supply chain management.* Most organizations now realize it is no longer sufficient for their own organization to be agile, lean, and efficient. They are now codependent on their trading partners, both upstream and downstream, to also be agile, lean, and efficient. To the degree their partners are not, then waste and extra unnecessary costs enter the end-to-end value chain. These costs ultimately pass along the chain, resulting in higher prices to the end consumer, which can reduce sales for all of the trading partners. Sadly, there have been centuries of adversarial relationships between buyers and

sellers. Performance management addresses these issues with powerful fore-casting tools, increasing real-time decisioning and financial transparency across the value chain. It allows trading partners to collaborate to join in mutually beneficial projects and joint process improvements.

8. *The broken budgeting process.* The annual budget process is often viewed as a fiscal exercise by accountants that is disconnected from the financial executive team's strategy and does not adequately reflect future volume drivers. Many budgets are often scorned as being obsolete soon after they are produced or biased toward politically muscled managers who know how to sandbag their requests. Though some organizations revert to rolling financial forecasts, these projections may include similarly flawed assumptions that produce the same sarcasm about the annual budgeting process. What is the solution? Entrepre-neurs know the adage, "You need to spend money to make money." In other words, excessive belt-tightening can jeopardize an organization's success. Rather than evaluating where costs can be cut, it is more prudent to take a dif-ferent view: Ask where and how the organization should spend money to in-crease its long-term, sustained value.

PERFORMANCE MANAGEMENT FRAMEWORK FOR VALUE CREATION

One of the most ambiguous terms in discussions about business and government is *value*. Everybody wants value in return for whatever they exchanged to get value. But whose value is more important and who is entitled to claiming it? Customers conclude that they receive value if the benefits they received from a product or service meet or exceed what they paid for it (including time, investment, cost, etc). If shareholders' and stakeholders' investment return is less than the economic return they could have received from equally or less risky investments (e.g., a U.S. Treasury bill), then they are disappointed. Value to employees is another issue altogether, usually tied to compensation and job satisfaction.

Three groups believe they are entitled to value: customers, shareholders/ stakeholders, and employees. Are they rivals? What are the trade-offs? Is there an invisible hand controlling checks and balances to maintain an economic equili-brium so that each group gets its fair share? Are some groups more entitled to receiving value than others?

Exhibit 2.1 illustrates the interdependent methodologies that comprise perform-ance management for a commercial organization. Before I describe how the dia-gram represents performance management, first look at the exhibit and ask yourself which box in it has the most important words. The answer depends on who you are in the organization.

If you are the CEO and executive team, the answer must be the "Strategy/ Mission" box. That is the CEO's primary job—to define and constantly adjust organizational strategy as the environment changes. That is why CEOs are paid

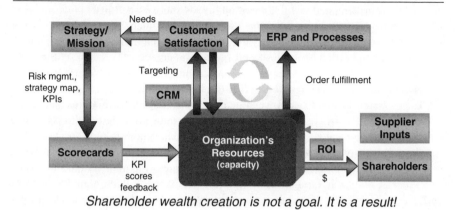

Shareholder wealth creation is not a goal. It is a result!

Exhibit 2.1 Performance Management Is Circulatory and Simultaneous
Source: © Gary Cokins. Used with permission.

high salaries and reside in large corner offices. However, after the strategy defini-tion is complete and maintained through adjustments to be current, then the core business processes take over, with competent process owners held accountable to manage and improve each process.

You might have answered that "Customer Satisfaction" is the most important box in the exhibit. With businesses' increasing focus on customers, many will agree with you. Customer satisfaction encompasses four customer-facing trends:

1. *Customer retention.* A recognition that it is relatively more expensive to acquire a new customer than to retain an existing one.
2. *Source of competitive advantage.* Gaining an edge by shifting from commodity-like product differentiation to value-adding service differentiation apart from the product or standard service-line.
3. *Microsegmenting of customers.* A focus on customers' unique preferences rather than mass selling. Spray-and-pray marketing days are nearing an end.
4. *The Internet.* The Internet is shifting power, irreversibly, from suppliers to customers and buyers.

It is easy to conclude that a customer focus is critical.

To explain Exhibit 2.1, focus on the three counterclockwise arrows at its center, starting and ending with the "Customer Satisfaction" box and passing through the "ERP and Processes" box. All three arrows represent the primary universal core business processes possessed by any organization, regardless of whether they are in the commercial or public sector: Take an order or assignment, and fulfill that order or assignment. These two processes apply to *any* organization: Orders, assignments, or tasks are received, and then organizations attempt to execute them.

These two processes combined are commonly called "Order fulfillment," and it is the most primary and universal core process of any organization. An example in healthcare is that a hospital admits patients and then treats and heals them. The IT support systems needed to fulfill these two core processes represented by the three arrows are called *front office* (i.e., from the customer) and *back office* systems (i.e., to the customer). This is the realm of "better, faster, and cheaper."

The customer-facing, front office systems include customer intelligence and CRM systems. This is also where targeting customers, marketing campaigns, sales processes, and work order management systems reside. The back office systems are where the fulfillment of customer or work orders, process planning, and operations takes place—the world of ERP and lean/Six Sigma quality initiatives. The output from this "ERP and Processes" box is the delivered product, service, or mission intended to meet customer needs. To the degree that customer revenues exceed all of an organization's expenses, including the cost of capital, then profit (and positive free cash flow) eventually accumulates in the shareholder's box in Exhibit 2.1's lower right.

PERFORMANCE MANAGEMENT AS A CONTINUOUS FLOW

Exhibit 2.1 should be viewed as a circulatory flow of information and resource consumption similar to your body's heart and blood-vessel system. As mentioned, organizational performance management practices existed for decades before the advent of computers. Think of how widening the constrictions and speeding the flow will increase throughput velocity and yield from the organization's resources. *More with less*; *value for money*—these are the phrases associated with performance management.

Exhibit 2.1 is dynamic. The starting point of the diagram is the "Customer Satisfaction" box. The need to satisfy customers is the major input into senior management's box in the exhibit's upper left: "Strategy/Mission." As the executive team adjust their organization's strategy, they continuously communicate it to employees with their strategy map and its companion balanced scorecard. With strategic objective adjustments they may abandon some KPIs intended to align work behavior with the outdated strategy. In those cases, KPIs associated with outdated strategies, while not unimportant, are rather now less important. The team may also add new KPIs or adjust the KPI weightings for various employee teams. As the feedback is received from the scorecards, all employees can answer the key question: "How am I doing on what is important?" The power of that question is in its second half: to focus everyone on what is most important. With analysis for causality, corrective actions can then occur. And note in the exhibit that the output from scorecards does not stop at the organization's boundary, but it penetrates all the way through to influence employee behavior which resides inside the "Organization's Resources (capacity)" box—the increasingly important intangible assets. This in turn leads to better execution.

Continuing on, the upward arrow from the "Organization's Resources (capacity)" box to the "Customer Satisfaction" box represents how the organization's marketing and sales functions can better target which existing and potentially new customers to retain, grow, acquire, and win back—and the optimal amount to spend on each one with differentiated service levels, deals, or offers.

Finally comes the order fulfillment loop as previously described. Take orders and efficiently fulfill the orders.

As this circulatory system is streamlined and digitized with better information and decisions, and more focused and aligned employee work, the result is faster and higher yield of shareholder wealth creation. Remember, shareholder wealth creation is not a goal—it is the result of addressing all of the methodologies in the flow. In the end, performance management is about "better, faster, cheaper, and smarter." The smarter comes not only from process improvements but from facilitating the executive team's strategic objectives.

Where is the box for innovation in the exhibit? It is not there, because it must be *inside* every box and arrow in the diagram. Innovation is as mission-critical today as achieving quality was in the 1980s. It is assumed to be a *given*—an entry ticket to even compete. I do not dwell on innovation, because innovation and its associated breakthrough thinking is so critical that I leave it to other authors to devote entire books to this most important topic.

The best executive teams do not consider any of the components in Exhibit 2.1 to be optional—they are all essential. The best executive teams know the priorities of where in the flow to place emphasis to widen constrictions as well as how to improve all of the other methodologies in the flow, even if it is with rapid prototyping and iterative remodeling, to learn things previously unknown that will evolve into permanent and repeatable production reporting and decision support systems. The key is to integrate, because much can be learned from addressing the lower priorities, such as implementing a higher-level activity-based costing model for customer segment profitability reporting. These quick-start approaches reveal findings that can contribute to altering strategic objectives formulated in the beginning of the circulatory flow.

AUTOMOBILE ANALOGY FOR PERFORMANCE MANAGEMENT

As mentioned, organizations were doing performance management well before it was labeled as such. It can be argued that on the date each organization was first created, it immediately started managing (or attempting to manage) its enterprise performance by offering products or services and fulfilling sales orders with some sort of strategy.

Imagine the organization in Exhibit 2.1 as a poorly tuned automobile. Include in your imagination cog gears in the engine where some of the gear teeth are broken, some of the gears have moved apart and are disengaged, some of the gears are made of wood and are crumbling, and where someone threw sand in the gears. Further, imagine unbalanced tires, severe shimmy in the steering wheel, poor timing of engine pistons, thickened power-steering fluid, and mucky oil in the crankcase. These collectively represent unstable, imbalanced, and poorly operating methodologies of the performance management framework. Take that mental picture and conclude that any physical system of moving parts with tremendous vibration and part-wearing friction dissipates energy, wasting fuel and power. The car's fuel efficiency in miles per gallon (or kilometers per liter) would be low.

At an organizational level, the energy dissipation from vibration and friction with lower fuel efficiency translates into wasted expenses, where the greater the waste, the lower the rate of shareholder wealth creation—possibly leading to wealth destruction. In a different case, you may find a car that seems perfect in the mind of the customer in every way, but is not priced to make a profit, making the shareholders unhappy. In another case, the focus may be on producing an automobile at the lowest cost to the point of undermining customer satisfaction.

Now replace that vision and imagine that same automobile with an engine having finely cut high-grade steel cog gears spinning at faster revolutions per minute. Imagine its tires finely balanced and its moving parts well lubricated and digitized with internal communications. The performance management framework (i.e., the automobile's frame) remains unchanged, but shareholder wealth is more rapidly created because there is balance in quality, price, and value to all. There is no vibration or friction. The higher fuel efficiency translates into a higher rate of shareholder wealth creation. That is how good performance management integrates its portfolio of multiple methodologies and components and provides better decision analysis and decision making that aligns work behavior and priorities with the strategy. Strategic objectives are attained, and the consequence is relatively greater shareholder wealth creation.

One can take this analogy further, with the strategy map and its derived target measures serving as the automobile's risk-mitigating global positioning system (GPS). When you are driving with a GPS instrument and you make a wrong turn, the GPS's voice chimes in to tell you that you are off track—and it then provides you with a corrective action instruction. With most organizations' calendar-based and long-cycle-time reporting, there is a delayed reaction. However, the performance management framework includes a GPS.

WHERE DOES MANAGERIAL ACCOUNTING FIT IN?

Note that managerial accounting does not appear in Exhibit 2.1. That is because the output of a managerial accounting system is always the input to someplace where decisions are made. The primary purpose of managerial accounting is *discovery*—to ask better questions. Although not in the exhibit, it supports every box and arrow.

Managerial accounting (including activity-based costing [ABC] data) is a key component in performance management. Its information permeates every single element in this scenario to help rebalance these sometimes-competing values. By including managerial accounting as a foundational component of the performance management framework, we involve the language of money to support decision making and build better business cases.

Managerial accounting itself is not an improvement program or execution system like several other systems in the exhibit. Its information, such as from ABC, serves as an enabler for these systems to support better decision making. For example, ABC links customer value management (as determined by CRM systems) to shareholder value creation, which is heralded as essential for economic value management. The tug-of-war between CRM and shareholder wealth creation is the trade-off of adding excessively more value for customers at the risk of reducing wealth to shareholders.

Ultimately, businesses will discover that customer value management by targeting the marketing spend to different customer microsegments is the *independent* variable in the economic value equation. This equation then solves for the *dependent* variable for which the executive team is accountable to the governing board: shareholder wealth creation. Performance management provides the framework to model this all-important relationship.

Is Exhibit 2.1 the best diagram to represent of the performance management framework? I do not know. Professional societies, management consultants, and software vendors have their own diagrams. Perhaps a business magazine or Web portal can have a contest where diagrams are submitted and voted on by readers. But the key point is that performance management is not narrowly defined as dashboards with better budgeting and financial reporting. Clearly, performance management is much broader and balances competing values.

PERFORMANCE MANAGEMENT UNLEASHES THE RETURN ON INVESTMENT FROM INFORMATION

There is a shift in the source from which organizations realize their financial ROIs—from tangible assets to the intangible assets of employee knowledge and information. That is, the shift is from spending on equipment, computer hardware, and the like to knowledge workers applying information for decision making.

Exhibit 2.2 displays across the horizontal axis the stages that raw transactional data passes through to become the knowledge and intelligence to make better decisions, which successful organizations will eventually experience. The vertical axis measures the power and ROI from transforming that data and leveraging it for realized results. The ROI increases exponentially from left to right.

The three bubbles on the left side are the location of transactional data for daily operations and reporting. The three bubbles to the right are where business intelligence (BI), the performance management framework of methodologies, and analytical software of all flavors lift the ROI.

Most organizations are mired in the lower-left corner's first two bubbles, hostage to raw data and standard reports. When the feared year-2000 (Y2K)

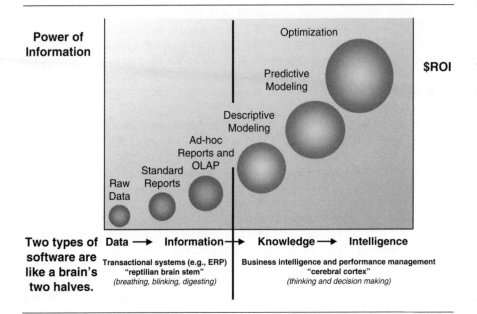

Exhibit 2.2   Intelligence Hierarchy

Source: © Gary Cokins. Used with permission.

meltdown approached, many organizations replaced their homegrown software applications with commercial transactional software, such as from the vendors Oracle and SAP. In some organizations, the chief information officer and IT staff allowed some managers to use basic query and reporting online analytical processing (OLAP) tools to drill down to examine some of that data. But this data restricts and confines workers to knowing only what happened in the past.

The power of BI, performance management, and analytics begins with the fourth bubble—descriptive modeling. As an example, ABC models the conversion of expense spending into the calculated costs of processes, work activities and the types of outputs, products, service-lines, channels, and customers that consume an organization's capacity. Costing is modeling. As another example, a strategy map and its associated performance indicators is a model of how an organization defines its linked strategic objectives and plans to achieve them. Data has been transformed into information. At this stage, employees can know not only *what* happened but also *why* it happened.

The fifth bubble passes from historical information, to which organizations are reactive, to predictive information, such as what-if scenarios and rolling financial forecasts, to which organizations are proactive. As mentioned earlier, organizations are shifting their management style from after-the-fact control based on examining variance deviations from plans, budgets, and expectations to an anticipatory management style where they can adjust spending and capacity levels as well as projects and initiatives before changes in work demands arrive. Information is used for knowledge. At this stage, employees can know not only *what* happened and *why* it happened, but also *what can* happen next.

The sixth and final bubble in the upper-right corner of Exhibit 2.2 is the highest stage—optimization. At this point, organizations can select from all of their decision options examined in the prior stage and conclude which is the best decision and action to take.

IT transactional systems may be good at reporting past outcomes, but they fall short on being predictive for effective planning. Given a sound strategy, how does the organization know whether its strategy is achievable? What if pursuing the strategy and its required new programs will cause negative cash flow or financial losses? Will resource requirements exceed the existing capacity?

TWO TYPES OF COMPUTER SOFTWARE: TRANSACTIONAL AND DECISION SUPPORT

Exhibit 2.2 is not intended to imply that the ERP and CRM transactional software vendors are of low value. Just the opposite is true. These vendors are excellent—at what their computer code is architected and designed to do. But the real ROI lift comes from applying information in the context of solving problems and driving the execution of strategy.

To simplify an understanding of computer software, it comes in two broad types: transactional and decision support. These two types can be thought of as similar to the two broad halves of the human brain. In the back of one's head above the spine is the reptilian brain stem evolved from early stages of life. It controls the most basic elements of life, such as breathing, eye blinking, digesting, and sleeping. In the front of one's brain is the cerebral cortex, from which thinking, learning, and decision making occurs.

The transactional software is essential. One must have it operating well. The better its condition, the better the BI, performance management, and analytical software can leverage it. But the real power and lift of ROI comes from the right side of Exhibit 2.2. The ROI lift from the performance management framework illustrated in the exhibit demonstrates that the upside potential is enormous. Its purpose is to robustly analyze and understand one's own organization, customers, suppliers, markets, competitors, and other external factors, from government regulators to the weather.

MANAGEMENT'S QUEST FOR A COMPLETE SOLUTION

Many organizations jump from improvement program to program, hoping that each new one may provide that big, yet elusive, competitive edge like a magic pill. However, most managers would acknowledge that pulling one lever for improvement rarely results in a substantial change—particularly a long-term sustained change. The key for improving is integrating and balancing *multiple* improvement methodologies and spicing them with analytics of all flavors—particularly predictive analytics. In the end, organizations need top-down guidance with bottom-up execution.

Operating managers and employee teams toil daily in making choices involving natural tension, conflicts, and trade-offs within their organization. An example is how to improve customer service levels and cost-saving process efficiencies while restricted to fixed, contract-like budget constraints and profit targets. The classic conflict in physical product–based companies is this: The sales force wants lots of inventory to prevent missed sales opportunities from stockout shortages; in contrast, the production group wants low in-process and finished goods inventory so they can apply the proven just-in-time production methods rather than continue with the less effective batch-and-queue production methods of the 1980s.

Organizations that are enlightened enough to recognize the importance and value of their data often have difficulty in actually *realizing* that value. Their data is often disconnected, inconsistent, and inaccessible, resulting from too many non-integrated single-point solutions. They have valuable untapped data that is hidden in the reams of transactional data they collect daily.

How does performance management create more value lift? One fundamental thing performance management does is it transforms transactional data into decision-support information. For example, employee teams struggle with questions such as "How do we increase customer service levels, but without increasing our budget?" or "Should we increase our field distribution warehouse space 25% or instead have our trucks ship direct from our central warehouse?" How can employees answer these questions by examining transaction data from a payroll, procurement, general ledger accounting, or ERP system? They cannot; those systems were designed for a different purpose—short-term operating and control with historical reporting of what happened.

Unlocking the intelligence trapped in mountains of data has been, until recently, a relatively difficult task to accomplish effectively. Performance management is a value multiplier to the substantial investments organizations have made in their transactional software systems and technology (e.g., ERP systems), which are often viewed as falling short of their expected returns.

Fortunately, innovation in data storage technology is now significantly outpacing progress in computer processing power, heralding a new era where creating vast pools of digital data is becoming the preferred solution. As a result, there are now superior software tools that offer a complete suite of analytical applications and data models that enable organizations to tap into the virtual treasure trove of information they already possess, and enable effective performance management on a huge scale that is enterprise-wide in scope. Performance management is the integration of these technologies and methodologies. The performance management solutions suite provides the mechanism to bridge the business intelligence gap between the CEO's vision and employees' actions.

ECONOMIC DOWNTURNS AND PERFORMANCE MANAGEMENT

The financial crisis the world experienced in 2008 and beyond required a focus on what distinguishes true *economic* value realization from *artificial* creation, such as financial derivatives and credit default swaps. Citizens of the world now understand that the 2008 financial crisis resulted from a breakdown in governance and antiregulatory advocates that allowed opportunists to let their personal greed dominate the interests of the people of the earth—from all countries.

Since the crisis began, there has been a movement by global leaders to apply new laws, governance, and government regulation to place reins on unbridled capitalism. Lessons that have been learned are that it is not always true that the market knows best, that government hampers markets, and that market problems will automatically fix themselves.

For many executives, particularly younger ones, the economic crisis was a lifetime learning event. Most had only experienced a period of continuous sales growth. True career fullness comes from living through the complete economic cycle. In the corporate world, many organizations responded to the economic downturn with a knee-jerk reaction's: budget cuts, reductions in force, layoffs, reduced financial guidance, asset sales, bankruptcies, and so on. These organizations adopted a sort of bunker mentality to face the threat. As a result, many overreacted by cutting beyond the fat and into the nerve tissue and bone and thereby weakened their enterprise for the future.

While cutting costs may please Wall Street in the near term, this sort of short-term, tactical approach is detrimental for a company's future. In contrast, the prudent organizations carefully analyze the risks and threats from an economic downturn, develop what-if scenarios for the future, and create suitable short- and long-term plans. This forward-thinking approach allows management to proceed strategically, with an eye to the future, but still grounded in the present.

How can performance management help during an economic downturn? It does so as it would at any time in the economic cycle of growth, prosperity, decline, and recovery that will always be perpetual due to human nature. It provides managers and employee teams with the methods, tools, technologies, information, and analytics to react more quickly and to drive relatively higher economic value than they would otherwise achieve without them. As organizations accelerate the rate at which they create value, similar to a garden or forest, then healthy growth for everyone—including the planet—is the result.

NOTES

1. Alan Webber, "CEO Bashing Has Gone Too Far," *USA Today*, June 3, 2003, p. 15A.
2. Alan Brache, *How Organizations Work* (Hoboken, NJ: John Wiley & Sons, 2002), p. 10.

Chapter 3

What Will Be the Next New Management Breakthrough?

Since the 1890s, there have arguably been only a few major management breakthroughs with several minor ones. What will be the next big tsunami in management that can differentiate leading organizations from also-rans lagging behind them? I suggest one possibility at the conclusion of this chapter.

HISTORY OF MANAGEMENT BREAKTHROUGHS

Where does one draw the line between major and minor management breakthroughs of innovative methodologies that can provide an organization with a competitive edge? I am not sure, so the following list is somewhat of a blend:

- *Frederick Winslow Taylor's Scientific Management.* Taylor, the luminary of industrial engineers, pioneered methods in the 1890s to systematically organize work. His techniques helped make Henry Ford wealthy when Ford's automobile company applied these methods to divide labor into specialized skill sets in a sequential production line and to set stopwatch-measured time standards as target goals to monitor employee production rates. Production at rates faster than the standard was good while slower was bad. During the same period, Alexander Hamilton Church, an English accountant, designed a method of measuring cost accounting variances against predetermined standards to measure the favorable and unfavorable cost impact of faster or slower production speeds compared to the expected standard cost.

- *Alfred P. Sloan's Customer Segmentation.* Henry Ford's pursuit of a low unit cost for a single type of automobile (i.e., the Model T) was countered with an idea championed by Alfred P. Sloan, who became president of General Motors in 1923. Sloan advocated expansion of product diversity in style, quality, and performance with increasingly more expensive features in car models as a staircase for higher-income consumers to climb—starting with the Chevrolet and ultimately peaking with the Cadillac. It revealed the power of branding to retain customer loyalty.

- *Harvard Business School's Alfred D. Chandler Jr.'s Organizational Structure.* In 1962, Professor Chandler's pathbreaking book, *Strategy and Structure*, concluded that a factor explaining why some large companies fail or succeed involved how they learn about customers and how they understand the boundaries of their competencies to focus their strengths.

- *Harvard Business School's Michael E. Porter's Theories of Competitive Advantage.* It is hard to believe that prior to Porter's 1970 book, *Competitive Strategy: Techniques for Analyzing Industries and Competitors*, very few organizations had a formal strategic planning department. Today, they are commonplace. Conglomerates comprised of many diverse businesses were becoming numerous in the 1960s, when Porter introduced his *four forces* approach for individual businesses to assess their strengths and opportunities. His message was that strategy is about making tough choices.

- *Total Quality Management from Edward Deming, Joseph Juran, and Phil Crosby.* The total quality management and continuous quality improvement programs of the 1970s were a response to Japanese manufacturers grabbing market share as they progressed from making cheap products to high-quality ones. During the same period, Shigeo Shingo and Taiichi Ohno, of Toyota Motors, introduced *pull-based just-in-time* (JIT) production systems that were counter to traditional large batch-and-queue production management economic lot-size thinking. JIT provides faster throughput with less inventory. In the 1990s, at Motorola, Mikel Harry introduced a TQM refinement called *Six Sigma*, which recently has merged with lean management techniques.

- *Peter Senge and Organizational Learning.* In 1990, Professor Senge of MIT, recognizing that many industries were increasingly dependent on educated knowledge workers, published his book *The Fifth Discipline: The Art and Practice of the Learning Organization*. Senge concluded that a differentiator going forward between successful and unsuccessful organizations is not the amount, but the *rate*, of organizational learning.

- *Michael Hammer's Business Process Reengineering.* In the early 1990s, Hammer recognized the importance of focusing on and satisfying customers. He observed that stovepiped and self-serving organizational departments were inefficient at serving customers and that the best way to improve service, particularly given the rapid adoption of computers, was not to modestly improve business processes, but rather to radically reengineer processes through redesign, as if you were starting with a clean sheet of paper.

- *Peppers and Rogers's Customer Relationship Management.* In 1994, Martha Rogers and Don Peppers authored the book *Customer Relationship Management: One-to-One Marketing*, which announced the eventual death of mass selling and faith-based spray-and-pray marketing. It described how computers could track characteristics and preferences of individual customers.

- *Kaplan and Norton's Strategy Maps and Balanced Scorecard.* In 1996, Professors Robert S. Kaplan and David Norton published the first of a series of related books, *The Balanced Scorecard*. They recognized that executives were failing not due to poor strategy formulation but rather due to lack of success in implementing it. They advocated for executives' communicating their strategy to employees using visual maps and shifting performance measures from month-end financial results to nonfinancial operational measures that align work and priorities with the strategy.

WILL PREDICTIVE ANALYTICS BE THE NEXT BREAKTHROUGH?

Performance management, by applying its broad definition as the integration of multiple managerial customer, operational, and financial methodologies spiced with all flavors of analytics, embraces all of the above advances. Performance management integrates methodologies and their supporting systems to produce synergy not present when they are implemented in isolation from each other.

Professor Tom Davenport of Babson College authored a January 2006 *Harvard Business Review* article proposing that the next differentiator for competitive advantage will be predictive analytics. He has coined the phrase *competing on analytics*. His premise is that change at all levels has accelerated so much that reacting after-the-fact is too late and risky. He asserts that organizations are shifting their managerial style from control (e.g., analyzing variances from targets) to planning. He builds a strong case that organizations must anticipate change to be proactive and that the primary way is through robust quantitative analysis. This is now feasible due to the combination of massive amounts of economically stored business intelligence and powerful statistical software that can reveal previously undetected patterns and provide reliable forecasts.

In a recent study sponsored by the technology companies SAS and Intel, Davenport and two colleagues researched 32 organizations leveraging analytical activity.[1] They observed that the highest performers captured and managed lots of transaction data, combined it with other public domain data, and had a culture of fact-based decision making. These organizations follow a test-and-learn approach to business changes. As an example, Capital One, the credit card company, conducts more than 30,000 experiments a year to identify desirable customers and price credit offers.

As another example, customers can be finely microsegmented in multiple combinations, such as age, income level, residence location, and purchase history, and patterns can be recognized that can predict which customers may defect to a competitor, thereby providing time to attend to such customers with a deal, offer, or higher service level to increase retention levels. As an additional example, minute shifts in customer demands for products or services can be real-time monitored and projected to speed or slow actions and to manage various types of sales and marketing expenses to induce customer behavior.

POWER OF QUANTITATIVE ANALYSIS AND PERFORMANCE MANAGEMENT

Davenport's research validates that substantial benefits are realized from systematically exploring quantitative relationships among performance management factors. Those respondents using predictive analytics reported double the rate of innovation, competitive advantage, and agility compared with those respondents not leveraging predictive analytics. This should not be surprising. When the primary factors that drive an organization's success are measured, closely monitored, and predicted, the organization is in a much better position to adjust in advance and mitigate risks. That is, if a company is able to know—not try to guess—which nonfinancial performance variables directly influence financial results, then it has a leg up on its competitors.

Advanced organizations have realized that predictive analytics may likely be their future primary source for a competitive advantage. Consider the application of statistical regression and correlation analysis applied to the cause-and-effect arrow linkages within an organization's strategy map. Within each arrow are the strategic projects, core processes, and key performance indicators that contribute to accomplishing other strategic objectives the arrows connect to. With analytical software embedded in the strategy map and its companion scorecard, the thickness and color of the arrows between the map's strategic objectives can be programmatically calculated. This additional information compared to just uniform arrows visually reveals to the organization how the impact of an improvement (or decline) in one area affects results in another area. In some cases, there can be interference where improving something beyond a certain point adversely affects another process. Leading indicators have an impact on lagging indicators. By understanding the degree of correlation, organizations can evaluate the appropriateness of their current indicators and select potentially better ones to optimize the selection of all their performance measures.

Quantitative analysis of this type is way beyond traditional reporting of routine information at regular intervals. At a minimum, it allows managers and employee teams to customize their own reports and includes drill-down into what lies below high-level summary data to understand trends, patterns, or outlier abnormal results. It can signal alert messages when results are reported outside of preset upper- and lower-limit boundaries.

The real power kicks in when predictive analytics are applied. After all, the focus of most reporting, financial or nonfinancial, looks back at history,—not forward to the future. Predictive information provides early warning of potential problems and early indications of the successful realization of a plan. As organizations create statistical models of cause-and-effect relationships, they will build correlation or regression statistics models that connect an assortment of nonfinancial variables to their financial variables. Doing so obviously allows them to influence or control the variables that will significantly impact financial performance. This draws attention to the key variables and creates a test-and-learn laboratory approach to investigating which of the possible next additions or reductions of effort will yield the highest incremental impact on enterprise performance. The benefits are obvious. If they were to measure what truly matters, management's job would become less stressful.

Performance management does not mean merely better management of performance; it means improving performance. Integrating systems and information is a prerequisite step, but applying predictive analytics based on an explanatory quantitative model of performance may be the critical element to achieve the full vision of performance management.

NOTE

1. Thomas H. Davenport, Don Cohen, and Al Jacobson, "Working Knowledge Research Report: Competing on Analytics," Babson College, May 2005, www.babsonknowledge .org/analytics.pdf.

Chapter 4

The Future: Enterprise Risk-Based Performance Management

Enterprise performance management is now more correctly being defined in terms of the much broader umbrella concept of *integrated methodologies*—much broader than its previously misconceived narrow definition as simply being dashboards and better financial reporting. What could possibly be an even broader definition? My belief is that enterprise performance management is merely part—but a crucial, integral part—of how an organization realizes its strategy to maximize its value to stakeholders, both in commercial and public sector organizations. This means that enterprise performance management must be encompassed by the overarching concept of *enterprise risk management* (ERM).

A popular acronym is *GRC* (governance, risk, and compliance). From the performance management view described in this book, one can consider governance (*G*) as the stewardship of executives in behaving in a responsible way, such as providing a safe work environment or formulating an effective strategy, and consider compliance (*C*) as operating under laws and regulations. Risk management (*R*), the third element of GRC, is the element most associated with performance management.

Governance and compliance awareness from government legislation such as Sarbanes-Oxley and Basel II is clearly on the minds of all executives. Accountability and responsibility can no longer be evaded. If executives err on compliance, they can go to jail. As a result, internal audit controls have been beefed up. (My personal opinion is that today there is too much *C* in GRC. Its substantial administrative effort has become a distraction, keeping organizations from focusing on organizational improvement.)

The *R* in GRC has characteristics similar to performance management. The foundation for both ERM and performance management is built on two beliefs:

1. The less uncertainty there is about the future, the better.
2. If you cannot measure it, you cannot manage it.

RISK AS OPPORTUNITY OR HAZARD?

ERM is not about minimizing an organization's *risk exposure*. Quite the contrary; it is all about exploiting risk for maximum competitive advantage. A risky business strategy and plan always carries high prices. For example, what investment analysts do not know about a company or the uncertainty or concerns they have will result in adding a premium to capital costs as well as the discounting of a company's stock value. There can be uncertainty regarding accuracy, completeness, compliance, and timeliness; uncertainty also can be a prediction or estimate that can be applied to a target, baseline, historical actual (or average), or benchmark.

Effective risk management counters these examples by being comprehensive in recognizing and evaluating all potential risks. Its goal is less volatility, greater predictability, fewer surprises, and most important, the ability to bounce back quickly after a risk event occurs.

A simple view of risk is that more things *can* happen than *will* happen. If we can devise probabilities of possible outcomes, then we can consider how we will deal with surprises—outcomes that are different from what we expect. We can evaluate the consequences of being wrong in our expectations. In short, risk management is about dealing in advance with the consequences of being wrong.

Risk can be viewed as an opportunity that can be beneficial in the future in addition to being viewed as a hazard. For example, a rain shower might be a disaster for artists at an outdoor art fair while being a huge break for an umbrella salesperson. What risk and opportunity both have in common is that they are concerned with future events that may or may not happen, their events can be identified but the magnitude of their effect is uncertain, and the outcome of an event can be influenced with actions.

Exhibit 4.1 conveys that risk always exists, but how one interprets it—as hazardous, uncertainty, or opportunity—depends on what one is trying to achieve.

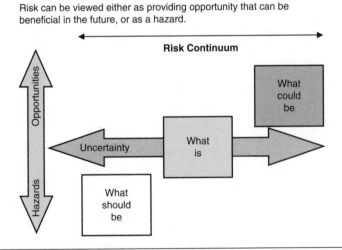

Risk can be viewed either as providing opportunity that can be beneficial in the future, or as a hazard.

Risk Continuum

Opportunities

Hazards

Uncertainty

What is

What could be

What should be

Exhibit 4.1   Risk Mitigation for Hazard Prevention and Benefit Gain

For any individual or organization at a particular moment in time, the starting point in the exhibit is the middle box, "What is." Uncertainty to some degree is everywhere. The exhibit suggests that one can mitigate risk to prevent hazardous outcomes on the left side and to exploit opportunity on the right side.

Risk is usually associated with new costs, because they may turn into problems. In contrast, opportunity can be associated with new economic value creation, such as increased revenues, because they may turn into benefits.

Most organizations cannot quantify their *risk exposure* and have no common basis to evaluate their *risk appetite* relative to their risk exposure. Risk appetite is the amount of risk an organization is willing to absorb to generate the returns it expects to gain. The objective is not to eliminate all risk, but rather to match risk exposure to risk appetite.

ERM is not simply contingency planning. That is too vague. It begins with a systematic way of recognizing sources of uncertainty. It then applies quantitative methods to measure and assess three factors:

1. The probability of an event occurring
2. The severity of the impact of the event
3. Management's capability and effectiveness to respond to the event

Based on these factors for various risks, ERM then evaluates alternative actions and associated costs to potentially mitigate or take advantage of each identified risk.

TYPES OF RISK CATEGORIES

Given the potentially hundreds of risks that may be identified, dealing with them may seem daunting. Consequently, ERM can be better understood by categorizing various risks. For example, identified risks could be grouped as being strategic, financial, operational, or hazard. Or they could be grouped as external or internal and controllable or uncontrollable. Another example is financial or nonfinancial and insurable or noninsurable.

An alternative risk categorization that I like is made up of these six types:

1. *Price risk*. The risk that an increasing product or service offering supply or an aggressive price reduction from competitors will force lower prices and consequently lower profits.
2. *Market risk*. The risk that customer preferences and demand might quickly change. (For banking professionals, this is the risk from trading financial instruments.)
3. *Credit risk*. The risk of not meeting obligations, such as a customer who fails to pay for her purchases, a mortgage holder who defaults on his loan, or an entity that fails to settle a legal obligation.
4. *Operational risk*. The risk of loss resulting from inadequate or failed internal processes, people, and technology, or from external events.

5. *Strategic risk.* The risk of poor performance resulting from poor strategy selection and execution.
6. *Legal risk.* This can be a mixture of risks. There is the financial risk that banks refer to as *liquidity risk* from insufficient net positive cash flow or from exhausted capital equity-raising or cash-borrowing capability. There is also risk from litigation (e.g., in financial services, a lawsuit for losses due to poor financial advice) and from compliance violations carrying regulatory authority penalties.

Operational and strategic risks are the key levers of the six risk types where organizations can match their risk exposure to their risk appetite. This is where they can wager the big bets, both on *formulating the strategy* and subsequently on *executing the strategic objectives* that comprise that strategy.

Operational risk as defined above includes many possibilities, including quality, workforce hiring and retention, supply chain, fraud, manager succession planning, catastrophic interruptions, technological innovations, and competitor actions.

As mentioned, operational risk management includes potential benefits from risks taken and the missed opportunities of risks not taken. Should we enter a market in which we are not now participating? Should we offer an innovative product or service line while unsure of the size of the market or competitor reactions? How much should we rely on technology to automate a process? Will our suppliers dependably deliver materials or services at the right time and with the right quality? However, organizations need to first *measure* their operational risk exposure and appetite in order to manage it.

Exhibit 4.2 illustrates an aggregated quantitative risk measurement that guides balancing risk exposure with risk appetite.

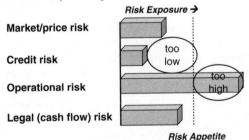

Risk appetite—The amount of risk an organization is willing to absorb for returns it expects to gain.

Risk Exposure →

Market/price risk

Credit risk   too low

Operational risk   too high

Legal (cash flow) risk

Risk Appetite

The objective is not to eliminate all risk, but rather to match risk exposure to risk appetite.

Exhibit 4.2   Balancing Risk Exposure with Risk Appetite
Source: © Gary Cokins. Used with permission.

RISK-BASED PERFORMANCE MANAGEMENT FRAMEWORK

The premise here is to link risk performance to business performance. As it is popularly described in the media, performance management, whether defined narrowly or ideally more broadly, does not currently embrace risk governance. It should; risk and uncertainty are too critical and influential to omit. For example, reputational risk caused by fraud (e.g., Tyco International), a terrifying product-related incident (e.g., Tylenol), or some other news headline–grabbing event can substantially damage a company's market value.

Exhibit 4.3 illustrates how strategy formulation and execution risk management plus performance management combine to achieve the ultimate mission of any organization: to maximize stakeholder value.

The four-step sequence includes direction setting from the executive leadership—"Where do we want to go?"—as well as the use of a compass and navigation to answer the questions "How will we get there?" and "How well are we doing in trying to get there?"

Step 1: Risk management. This involves the *strategy formulation* aspect of risk management. Here the executives stand back and assess the key value drivers of their market and environment, a process that includes the identification of their key risk indicators (KRIs). Formulating KRIs is essential to understanding the root causes of risk. KRIs include a predictive capability, so that by continuously monitoring variances between *expected* and *reforecast* KRIs, the organization can react before rather than after an event occurs.

Step 2: Strategy and value management. A key component of the portfolio of performance management methodologies is formulated here: the organization's vision, mission, and strategy map. Here the executives determine markets,

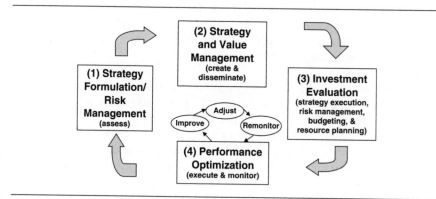

Exhibit 4.3   Risk-Based Performance Management
Source: © Gary Cokins. Used with permission.

products, and customers to target. The vision, mission, and strategy map is how the executive team both communicates with and involves its managers and employee teams. Based on the strategy map, the organization collectively identifies the vital few manageable projects and select core processes to excel at that will help it attain the multiple strategic objectives causally linked in the strategy map (see Chapter 12, "First Barrier to Performance Management: How Do We Get Started?"). This is also where research and development plus innovation projects are incubated.

Step 3: Investment evaluation. A plan is one thing, but how much to spend accomplishing the plan is another. That amount is determined in this step. This involves the *strategy execution* aspect of risk management. Resources, financial or physical, must always be considered as being scarce, so they must be wisely chosen. The capital markets now ultimately judge commercial companies on their future net positive free cash flow. This means that every next incremental expense or investment must be viewed as contributing to a project requiring an acceptable return on investment (ROI), including recovering the cost of capital. Spending constraints exist everywhere. That is, customer value and shareholder value are not equivalent and positively correlated, but rather they have trade-offs with an optimum balance that companies strive to attain. This is why the annual budget and the inevitable rolling spending forecasts, typically disconnected from the executive team's strategy, must be linked to the strategy.

Step 4: Performance optimization. In this final step, all of the execution components of the performance management portfolio of methodologies kick into gear. These include but are not limited to customer relation management, enterprise resource planning, supply chain management, activity-based costing, and Six Sigma/lean management initiatives. Since the mission-critical projects and select core processes an enterprise must do well on will have already been selected in step 3, the balanced scorecard and dashboards, with their predefined key performance indicators (KPIs) and performance indicators, at this stage become the mechanism to steer the organization (see Chapter 10, "How Do Business Intelligence and Performance Management Fit Together?"). The balanced scorecard includes target-versus-actual KPI variance dashboard measures with drill-down analysis and color-coded alert signals. Scorecards and dashboards provide strategic and operational performance feedback so that every employee, who is now equipped with a line of sight to how he or she helps to achieve the executives' strategy, can daily answer the fundamental question, "How am I doing on what is important?" The clockwise internal steps— "improve, adjust, remonitor"—are how employees collaborate to continuously realign their work efforts, priorities, and resources to attain the strategic objectives defined in step 2.

The four steps are a continuous cycle where risk is dynamically reassessed and strategy subsequently adjusted.

STRATEGY EXECUTION RISK MANAGEMENT BEGINS WITH STRATEGIC OBJECTIVES

Measuring and managing the operational risks identified in step 3 is now transitioning from an intuitive art to more of a craft and science. To introduce quantification to an area that involves quality and subjectivity, at some stage each identified risk requires some form of ranking, such as by level of importance—high, medium, and low. Since the importance of a risk event includes not just its impact but also its probability of occurrence, developing a *risk assessment map* can be a superior method to quantify the risks and then collectively associate and rationalize all of them with a reasoned level of spending for risk mitigation. A risk map helps an organization visualize all risks on a single page.

Exhibit 4.4 displays a risk assessment map with the vertical axis reflecting the magnitude of impact of the risk event and the horizontal axis reflecting the probability of occurrence. Individual risk events located on the map are inherent risks and not yet selected for mitigation actions; that evaluation comes next. The risks located in the lower-left area require periodic glances to monitor whether the risk is growing—nominal to no risk mitigation spending. At the other extreme, risk events in the upper-right area deserve risk mitigation spending with frequent monitoring.

The risks in the risk map are evaluated for mitigation action. This risk map reveals that risks #2, #3, and #8 are in a critical zone. Management must decide whether they can accept these three risks, considering their potential impact and likelihood. If not, management might choose to avoid whatever is creating the risk—for example, entering a new market. Some mitigation action might be considered that would drive the risks to a more acceptable level in terms of impact and

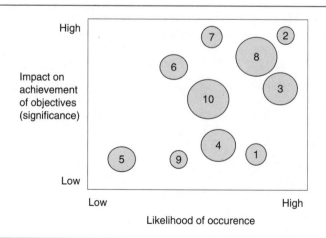

Exhibit 4.4 Risk Assessment Map

Source: © Gary Cokins. Used with permission.

likelihood. As examples, an action might result in transferring some of the risk through a joint venture, or it might involve incurring additional expense through hedging.

Management must decide on the costs versus benefits of the mitigation actions. Will the mitigation action, if pursued, move a risk event to within the predefined risk appetite guidelines? Is the residual risk remaining after mitigation action acceptable? If not, what additional action can be taken? How much will that additional action cost, and what will be the potential benefits in terms of reducing impact and likelihood? After these decisions are made, then, similar to the projects and initiatives derived from the strategy map, risk mitigation actions can be budgeted.

INVULNERABLE TODAY BUT AIMLESS TOMORROW

I continue to be intrigued by the fact that almost half of the roughly 25 companies that passed rigorous tests in order to be listed in the once-famous book by Tom Peters and Robert Waterman, *In Search of Excellence*, today no longer exist, are in bankruptcy, or have performed poorly. What happened in the 25 years since the book was published? My theory is that once an organization becomes quite successful, it becomes averse to risk taking. Taking risks, albeit calculated risks, is essential for organizations to change and be innovative.

Classic managerial methods of past decades, such as total quality management, are now giving way to a trend of management by data. However, I would caution that extensively analyzing historical data is not sufficient without complementing descriptive data with predictive information. The absence of reliable foresight explains why companies seem invulnerable one minute and aimless the next. An important competency that will be key to an organization's performance is a combination of forecasting and risk management.

Part Two

Performance Management Overview

Nothing else in the world . . . not all the armies . . . is so powerful as an idea whose time has come.

—Victor Hugo,
The Future of Man (1861)

Change in people's behavior results from the presence in great abundance of two items: dissatisfaction with their current condition and a vision of what a better condition looks like. This book is about the latter, but I suspect many readers are experiencing some of the former. This book describes a vision of an integrated suite of enterprise-wide managerial methodologies and tools that comprehensively link strategy objectives with planning, budgeting, customers, stakeholders, processes, costing, performance measures, and, most important, people. Organizations that can make this vision their reality will create economic value for their stakeholders at accelerated rates and have the opportunity to achieve a sustainable competitive advantage, presuming their competitors do not get there before them.

The first chapter of this part of the text explains why there is growing high interest in performance management. I next describe workforce planning and human capital management as being important to achieving the full vision of the performance management framework.

Executive management is also a critical factor in achieving performance management; the remaining chapters of Part Two describe the importance of leadership and distinguish between the relative improvement impacts of formulating a good strategy (doing the *right* things) as compared with improving processes (doing the right things *well*).

Chapter 5

Why the High Interest in Performance Management Now?

There is no consensus as to what performance management is. Different information technology research firms define it differently. Different consulting firms and software vendors describe it to fit their unique competencies rather than what their customers may require. Because my impression is that most of these organizations view performance management far too narrowly—as merely a bunch of dashboard dials and better financial reporting—my feeling is that it is better to discuss what performance management *does* rather than have arcane debates about defining what it *is*.

I argue that organizations have been doing performance management for decades—well before it received its recent popular references in the media. Organizations were doing performance management before there were computers! So, why is it emerging as a popular buzzphrase now?

DEBUT OF PERFORMANCE MANAGEMENT AT THE ENTERPRISE LEVEL

If you had done a Google search a few years ago on the term *performance management*, the results would have predominantly referred to the human resources and personnel departments' attention to monitoring and improving individual employees. Do that Google search today, however, and the shift is toward the performance of the organization or enterprise in its entirety.

Some would argue that this shift to where performance management now regularly appears in the media was due to the information technology (IT) research firms. Around 2000, IT research firms observed that business intelligence software vendors—vendors that had data-mining query-and-reporting functionality rather than producing the raw transactional data—were integrating analytical information across multiple departments and systems. They called it *performance management*. For example, a computer manufacturer's purchasing system detects a temporary vendor part shortage, which in turn is directly signaled to its customer order entry agents to influence its customers to select alternative product variations, perhaps with a discount or deal as inducement, until the part shortage is resolved. The risk of a missed sales opportunity is eliminated. Thus, *demand shaping* can be more powerful than *demand management*. This type of communication from the purchasing function deep in the bowels of the production function to a call center agent deep in the sales function would have rarely existed a few years ago.

Others might argue that the increasing appearance of performance management at the organizational level arose from the same IT research firms observing those same BI software vendors providing strong combination suites of at-a-glance visual dashboards and scoreboards. Further, these reporting tools are now linked to strategic planning, managerial accounting, and forecasting tools—and they are extremely scalable to handle millions of records for products and customers.

These are certainly factors, but I believe the emergence of performance management in the media and marketplace has deeper root causes.

DEEP AND EVEN DEEPER ROOT-CAUSE FORCES AS TO WHY PERFORMANCE MANAGEMENT NOW

Earlier I wrote that a better way to understand what performance management is about is to understand what problems it solves—the immense forces on management—such as:

- Failure by executives to execute their well-formulated strategy. Chief executive officer (CEO) firings are at record levels due to this frustration.
- Lack of trust among managers to achieve results is an increasing concern. Consequently, there is an escalation in accountability of managers and employee teams for results *with* consequences.
- Change is constant. Increasingly rapid decisions by employees (without time for higher management input), leveraging trade-offs and predictive analytics, and their need to understand the executive team's strategy.
- Mistrust of the managerial accounting system and its flawed, inaccurate, and/or incomplete product, channel, and customer profitability reporting.
- Poor customer value management. Surveys report customer retention as the CEO's number-one concern.[1]
- Contentious budgeting. The annual budget process is typically performed by accountants and is disconnected from the executives' strategy and driver-based volumes.
- Dysfunctional supply chain management. There is lack of trust within the traditional adversarial relationships between buyers and sellers along the chain. Ideally they should be collaborating.
- Balancing risk appetite with risk exposure to optimize financial results with anticipatory risk mitigation actions.
- Unfulfilled return on investment promises from large transactional systems (e.g., enterprise resource planning).

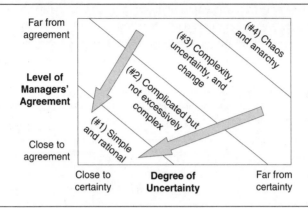

Exhibit 5.1 Performance Management Drives Improvement
Source: © Gary Cokins. Used with permission. Adapted from Ralph D. Stacey.

The effective performance management technology goes well beyond query and reporting—it addresses and resolves all of the issues listed here. The result is that rather than just *monitoring* the dials of their performance dashboards, organizations *move* those dials. The purpose of performance management is not just managing but *improving* performance.

However, there is a more deep-seated root cause than the ones just described. It involves a growing gulf between managers' ability to agree with one another and the uncertainty of future external influences on their organization.

Exhibit 5.1 is a modified and simplified framework developed by Ralph D. Stacey, a scholar in organizational management.[2] The framework proposes that different managerial approaches are required based on where a problem resides in the two-dimensional matrix with the axes "level of managers' agreement" and "degree of uncertainty."

The lower-left and upper-right zones are easiest to understand:

- *Bottom-left zone (#1): Simple and rational.* MBA programs typically focus here. Past data is gathered and used to predict the future, and spiced with modifiers (often intuition). Managers reach consensus and the expected outcomes are confidently predictable. Actions are selected and monitored with variance analysis of plans used for midcourse control.

- *Upper-right zone (#4): Chaos, anarchy, and decision avoidance.* Breakdown occurs here because traditional methods of planning, debating, negotiating, and committing do not work. Organizations become balkanized and either make strategic mistakes breaking from the past or take no action due to lack of confidence. Innovation and creativity should prevail in this zone, but often come up short. Some automobile manufacturers are currently trapped in this zone. The combination of high uncertainty and unachievable consensus is radioactive.

WIDENING ZONE (#3) OF COMPLEXITY, UNCERTAINTY, AND CHANGE

The near-bottom-left zone neighboring the "simple and rational" zone #1 is referred to as "complicated but not excessively complex" and is labeled zone #2. In this zone, farther to the upper left, is where politics and coalition building occur because there are broad differences about "how to get there" rather than the expected outcome. To the bottom right in zone #2, cause-and-effect linkages are not known or reliable, so this is where shared vision and mission of a future state beats preset project planning. The executive teams' ability to inspire employees and have continual sense-and-respond reactions are key.

I believe that the reason why there is an accelerating interest in performance management is found in the expanding mire of zone #3, the zone of "complexity, uncertainty, and change." This is the gathering-storm location threatening all organizations. It borders near the "chaos and anarchy" zone. In zone #3's upper-left region, unsubstantiated agenda building overrides fact-based decision making. In the lower-right region, blind muddling by the group overrides visioning, inspiration, and good risk management. As markets become more intensely competitive, managers are faced with more and more high-stakes decisions that are increasingly populating zone #3. As a result, success in managing zone #3 requires both making the right decision in the first place and then executing on that chosen path.

The collective suite of integrated methodologies that comprise performance management (e.g., strategy mapping, scorecards, customer value management, risk management, etc.) provides solutions for zone #3. Performance management shifts the problems and decision making in zone #3 toward the direction of zone #1—thus simplifying them. Here is how:

- A shift in emphasis toward applying analytics of all flavors, including predictive analytics with what-if and economic trade-off scenarios, bolsters proactive decision making.

- Gathering all information onto an enterprise-wide and common information platform with scalable real-time information replaces having disparate and disconnected data sources.

- Cross-functional communication and collaboration among employees and automated rule-based decisions replace self-serving silo and bunker mentalities.

- The work processes, priorities, initiatives, and target setting of managers and employee teams are aligned with the strategic intent of the executive team. These replace pet projects, minimal (or nonexistent) accountability, and internally competing performance metrics that are suboptimal and degrade attempts at maximizing stakeholder needs—such as those of shareholders or customers.

- Economic measures of customer profitability and potential customer value are made visible to support differentiated service levels, offers, or deals to achieve maximum profit yield from the sales and marketing budget.

- The vital few measures that matter (key performance indicators [KPIs]) are focused on, rather than the trivial many (performance indicators [PIs]), to distinguish the signals from the noise.

- Exception reporting, alert messaging, and at-a-glance visual reporting improves traction and accelerates speed in the strategic direction set (and constantly and necessarily reset) by the executive team.

Organizations need top-down guidance with bottom-up execution. Truly effective performance management, not simply the narrow financial view of better budgeting and control, shifts decisions that are currently wallowing in zone #3 into zones #2 and #1—and away from the dreaded zone #4 of chaos and anarchy. Zone #3 (complexity) is expanding due to the forces described earlier, and effective performance management brings rational thinking to convert problems once perceived as complicated (i.e., zone #2) into simple ones (zone #1).

Understanding what performance management *does* is more important than trying to define what it is.

WHAT? SO WHAT? THEN WHAT?. . .WHY NOT?

One of the problems with business intelligence (BI) information is that it does not always complete the task of solving a problem or moving to the next step of creating and realizing value. I refer to this as the syndrome of "What? So what? Then what?" My concern is that many organizations use BI to answer only the first question; then they are stymied when it comes to answering the next two questions.

The power of converting raw data into information, which BI does so well, is progressing to answering the next two questions to increasingly add value for decision making with each subsequent answer. The "What?" information is useful for managers and employees to more clearly observe and understand outcomes that they may have never seen before. It reports the reality of what has happened. When they use predictive analytics, it reports the possibility of what will happen.

However, an obvious follow-up question should be "So what?" What do I mean by this? Answering the "So what?" question means that based on any bothersome or exciting observations from now knowing the "what?" is there merit to making changes and interventions? How relevant to improving performance is the outcome we are seeing? But this leads to the more critical, and relatively higher value-added need to propose actions—to make decisions. This is the "Then what?" That is, what change can be made or action taken, and ultimately what then is the impact? For reasons that I do not fully understand, many organizations fall short of being creative or innovative in determining options.

There is a more thorny concern. Even when a change or solution is proposed, often the organization freezes. There is hesitancy. In the performance management framework, an example is the reluctance to construct strategy maps or a balanced scorecard, or apply activity-based costing principles to calculate and report customer profitability. I refer to this as the "Why not?" One needs to be a sociologist and psychologist to implement performance methodologies. Just for starters, it is human nature to prefer the status quo and resist change.

Until an organization gains mastery over validly answering all four questions, it will plod along and muddle through improving its performance rather than accelerate value creation.

NOTES

1. Gartner Inc. "Bank CEOs Rate Business & Technology Concerns," 2004, www.gartner .com.
2. Ralph D. Stacey, *Complexity and Creativity in Organizations* (San Francisco: Berrett-Koehler, 1996).

Chapter 6

Human Capital and Workforce Management: Art or Science?

There are two diametrically opposed managerial styles: Newtonian and Darwinian. The Newtonians like to manage quantitative-oriented things such as operations management and finance. Their mechanical thinking relies on an MBA run-by-the-numbers management approach. They see the world and everything in it as a big machine, and they seek the levers, pulleys, and dials. This managerial approach speaks in terms of production, power, efficiency, and control, where employees are hired to be used and periodically replaced as if they were disposable robots.

In contrast, Darwinians like the soft behavioral areas such as change management, ethics, and leadership. They recognize that people and human behavior matter most to improving performance. They view an organization as a living organism that is ever-changing with sense-and-respond reactions to its environment. This Darwinian way of thinking speaks in terms of evolution, continuous learning, natural response, and adaptation to changing conditions.[1]

I sense that Newtonians are relatively more numerous as managers of organizations. There is an irony to this. An organization's people represent a significant component of its total value—and an equally significant component of its expenses. Yet few organizations manage this enormous and essential asset in a truly strategic way. Human resources (HR) and personnel departments have traditionally been mired in daily administrative activities and viewed solely as a tactical support function. Should not HR look for ways to perform more strategically as part of the executive team and as a critical partner with business managers?

WHAT PREVENTS THE HR DEPARTMENT FROM BEING MORE STRATEGIC?

Some HR teams reinforce the perception that they are tactical rather than strategic by focusing on recruiting and benefits administration rather than on *optimizing* human capital to align with the executive team's strategic objectives. Even with this administrative emphasis, there are problems. In my opinion, HR departments are not reacting quickly enough to the imminent retirement of an aging workforce. These workers are being replaced by a considerably less organization-loyal younger generation who are more focused on their personal careers. A skills gap for organizations is inevitable. Most organizations have not quantified the effect of this gap, which could explain why they are slow to respond. Inevitably, traditional HR recruitment and training options will need to be revamped to attract the younger "millennial" workforce.

Admittedly, data and information about an organization's workforce can be a problem. Most organizations do not have all their relevant and specific human capital information in one place. It is scattered about and often resides in disconnected spreadsheets. It is tough to think strategically about matching future workforce skills with the organization's needs. In some cases, HR may not even know how many full-time employees are on the payroll, or they may have different headcount numbers than the finance department.

At some point, HR needs to demonstrate its value in training and developing its existing and future workforce.

ADVANCING FROM HR TO STRATEGIC HUMAN CAPITAL MANAGEMENT

Similar to other Newtonian-style managers who are being equipped with technologies that support their enterprise performance management methodologies, HR teams also need decision-support methods to help their organizations achieve constantly changing strategic objectives (and gain for themselves a seat at the executive table). Fortunately, there is hope. Current information technology can help HR teams see new insights and value from the data they already have, from systems that are already in place throughout their organization and from third-party data. This is *strategic human capital management* (HCM), often referred to as *workforce analytics*. HCM aids in aligning the behavior, priorities, and work of managers and employee teams with executives' strategic objectives derived from their strategy formulation.

One area where HR can use help is in determining what an organization has in the way of skills and abilities and what it needs. With a robust *HCM workforce planning system*, an organization can project the number and types of employees needed to execute its executives' strategy. It would no longer have to muddle its way through periodic layoffs and tardy recruiting of new employees. It would better anticipate workforce needs, and in many cases retrain employees for approaching needs.

A good HCM system can provide a talent scorecard and dashboard viewing of key performance indicator (KPI) metrics similar to those that many executive teams monitor for their enterprise performance—but these measures are customized for the HCM function. Some of the aggregate KPIs of the talent scorecard should appear in the executives' scorecard reporting. Examples of talent KPIs might include return on employee, predicted turnover of critical workers, employee absenteeism, or skills gaps segmented by various employee types or groups. By including predictive information, managers can test which planned workforce changes might have the greatest effect on performance and strategy execution.

REDUCING EMPLOYEE TURNOVER AND IMPROVING EMPLOYEE RETENTION

Imagine tapping a few computer keys and pulling up a list of who in your organization is most likely to quit next and why—rank ordered from the most to least likely employee. This is now feasible.

Human capital analytical software analyzes data such as historical wage raise amounts, frequency between raises, ages, time employed, and other data over the last five to ten years, along with who has left the organization and why. It then applies and layers those statistics onto the *current* workforce, ranking the employees most likely to quit. This listing allows an employer to intervene—if she wants to—by taking actions for those employees before they resign or are tempted to take jobs elsewhere. These actions mitigate risks and minimize adverse impacts of losing employees.

In short, more sophisticated technology and a growing acceptance of the value of business intelligence software are making predictive analytics a necessary management tool, from HR or the chief financial officer's (CFO's) office to frontline marketing and sales functions. Predictive analytics uncover relationships and patterns within large volumes of data that can be used to predict behavior and events. Predictive analytics are forward-looking, using past events to anticipate the future.

BUSINESS INTELLIGENCE AND PREDICTIVE ANALYTICS

With improvements in these tools, a manager no longer needs to be a statistician or mathematician to understand how the models work. Today's analytical HCM software displays graphical and visual information so that it feels less like programming, and makes it easier for the casual user to work with.

In the recent past, the term *analysis* (or *analytics*) was a catchall for *business intelligence reporting*, and *predictive analytics* was a relatively unknown concept. Today, predictive analytics generally has two flavors: data mining and business optimization. Data mining largely focuses on a specific problem such as credit scoring or actuary tables. Business optimization is broader, encompassing areas of quality control, continuous process improvement, inventory control, price optimization, forecasting, and statistical correlations.

Some organizations have transactional information about employees, customers, and suppliers going back 20 years; however, these organizations typically complain that they are drowning in data but starving for information. Predictive analytics combines statistics and advanced mathematics with a heavy amount of data management to create solutions to manage change. The use of analytics is not an ivory-tower science experiment run wild, as some still perceive.

There are some prerequisites when applying analytics. The data ideally should be accurate and complete and represent a large enough population or span of time that any trends or patterns in the data are reliable for projecting the future. From an organizational perspective, people involved should also agree that the data being used is the appropriate data and that the model being used is an accurate representation of the relationship of the factors to the expected outcome. This is, simply put, the human element. People have deep understanding of the organization and know where to point the tools, how to prepare the data, and how to interpret the results to provide meaningful value.

HUMAN CAPITAL AS A COMPONENT OF THE PERFORMANCE MANAGEMENT FRAMEWORK

An HCM (workforce planning) system works best by integrating data that currently resides in a multitude of silo systems and purchased databases, such as personnel systems, enterprise resource planning applications, Microsoft Access databases, learning management systems, applicant tracking systems, and payroll. An HCM system can also be integrated with third-party data, such as university recruitment lists, insurance data, or salary surveys. This information ideally can be loaded into a single repository—a human capital database—where it is continually updated, validated, reconciled, cleansed, and managed for integrity. This can provide accurate and credible answers to fundamental questions about the workforce and talent mix to acquire, grow, and retain the right types of employees for the organization's future requirements.

It would be myopic to omit human capital management from the performance management portfolio of methodologies. People are key. People matter.

NOTE

1. Stephan H. Haeckel, *Adaptive Enterprise: Creating and Leading Sense and Respond Organizations* (Boston: Harvard Business School Press, 1999).

Chapter 7

Tipping Point for Performance Management

How does an organization decide to integrate the various methodologies that comprise an enterprise-wide performance management framework? To answer this, we can turn to Malcolm Gladwell, social scientist and author of *The Tipping Point*,[1] who describes how changes in mind-set and perception can attain a critical mass and then quickly create an entirely different position of opinion. We apply Gladwell's thinking to the questions of whether the widespread adoption of performance management is near its tipping point and whether we will know this only in retrospect after it has happened.

Gladwell observed that when something is approaching the verge of its tipping point, such as an event or catalyst, it causes people to reframe an issue. For example, just-in-time production control reframed manufacturing operations from classical batch-and-queue economic order quantity thinking to the method based on customer demand-pull product throughput acceleration. So, is performance management reframing issues and nearing its tipping point? To answer this, we should first acknowledge that performance management is not a *new* methodology that everyone has to learn; rather it is the assemblage and integration of *existing* methodologies with which most managers are already familiar. Collectively, these methodologies manage the execution of an organization's strategy.

MULTIPLE TIPPING POINTS OF PERFORMANCE MANAGEMENT COMPONENTS

Because performance management is comprised of multiple methodologies, all interdependent and interacting, it is profound that we are now experiencing multiple and *concurrent* sub–tipping points. Ultimately, the collective weight of four tipping points is resulting in an overall tipping point for organizations to adopt performance management. These tipping points are:

1. *Balanced scorecard (BSC)*. Thanks to successes in properly implementing the combined strategy map and balanced scorecard framework (and there are plenty of improper implementations), executives are now viewing BSC differently. Rather than seeing BSC as a rush to put the massive number of collected measures (key performance indicators) on a diet to distill them down to the relevant few, executives now understand the strategy map and BSC framework

as a mechanism to better execute their strategy by communicating it to employee teams in a way they can understand it, and then aligning the employees' work behavior, priorities, accountability, and resources with the strategy.

2. *Decision-based managerial accounting.* Reforms to managerial accounting, led by activity-based costing (ABC), might once have been viewed as just a more rational way to trace and assign the increasing indirect and shared overhead expenses to products and standard service lines (in contrast to misleading and flawed cost allocations based on cost-distorting broad averages). Today, reforms such as ABC are now being reframed as essential managerial information for understanding which products, services, types of channels, and types of customers are most profitable—and why. There is a shift away from cost control to cost planning and shaping because most spending cannot be quickly changed. This means better capacity and resource planning and less historical cost variance analysis. Executives recognize that cost management is an oxymoron, like "jumbo shrimp" in the supermarket. You do not directly manage your costs; rather you manage the quantity, frequency, and intensity of what drives your process workloads. ABC places focus on activity cost drivers with optical fiber–like visibility and transparency to view all the currently hidden costs with their causes.

3. *Customer value management.* Customer relationship management (CRM) systems have been narrowly viewed as a way to communicate one to one with customers. However, executives have learned that it is more expensive to acquire new customers than to retain existing ones and that their products and service lines have become commodities from which there is little competitive advantage. As a result, organizations are reframing CRM more broadly as a way to analyze and identify characteristics of existing customers that are more profitable today and potentially more valuable in the future. They then apply these traits to formulate differentiated and tiered treatments (such as marketing campaigns, deals, offers, and service levels) for existing customers, as well as to attract new customers who will possess relatively higher future potential value (which, incidentally, requires ABC data to calculate customer lifetime value scores to differentiate prospects). This reframing places much more emphasis on microsegmenting customers and postsale value-adding services with cross-selling and upselling. Mass selling that snares unprofitable customers is out; it is being replaced by the new recognition that one must not merely grow sales, but rather grow sales profitably.

4. *Shareholder and business owner wealth creation and destruction.* The strong force of the financial capital markets in assigning financial value to organizations has caused the executive teams and governing boards to realize that traditional methods of placing value on a company are obsolete. The balance sheet assets now account for only a small fraction of a company's market-share price capitalization. A company's future value is linked to its intangible assets, such as its employee skills and innovation. As a result, executives are reframing their understanding of how to increase positive "free cash flow," the financial

capital markets' metric of choice, to convert potential value (ideas and innovation) into realized value (financial return on investment [ROI]). They have reframed the path to continuous shareholder wealth creation as governed by customer value management.

SYNERGY FROM THE LINKS AMONG PERFORMANCE MANAGEMENT COMPONENTS

It is not a coincidence that each of the four tipping points mentioned interdependencies among them. Transaction-based information systems, like enterprise resource planning systems, although good for their designed purposes, do not display the relevant information required for decision analysis and ultimately for decision making. Transactional systems may provide some of the raw data, but it is only through transforming that raw data into decision-based information that the potential ROI trapped in that raw data can be unleashed and realized financially. This in part explains the growing demand for the performance management framework as a value multiplier.

NOTE

1. Malcolm Gladwell, *The Tipping Point: How Little Things Can Make a Big Difference* (New York: Little, Brown and Company, 2000).

Chapter 8

An Interview with a CEO You Might Want to Work For

Have you ever worked for an organization where you doubted the leadership capability of your chief executive officer (CEO), managing director, division president, or the head of your government agency? Have you ever been disturbed that your organization is not living up to its full potential in terms of its enterprise-wide performance management? Imagine that I am a media journalist. How would you enjoy working for an organization whose leader answered my interview questions as follows?

A CEO YOU CAN DREAM ABOUT

Cokins: What is your position regarding how your organization views quality and waste?

CEO: The quality community often provides lists of the five or so quality-related problems, such as nonconformance to product design specifications or insufficient focus on customer service. My observation is that these lists always omit a much more critical deficiency: the inability to enable employees to achieve their full potential to contribute toward the organization's strategic goals. This is a huge waste—and an opportunity. My position is that our managers' main function is to unleash the power and intellect of our employees.

Cokins: How have you created a work environment that makes this possible?

CEO: I set the tone at the top as a role model by placing a high priority on three character traits: trust, a high tolerance for dissent, and innovation. Their combination is potent in a positive way. Without trust, employees do not feel they are adequately involved in decision making. Failing to allow a time period for dissent will cause employees to feel there was not enough opportunity for their opinions to be considered. Without innovation, others will catch us and leave us chasing them.

Cokins: This sounds like you are big advocate of employee empowerment, but can't this lead to chaos from employee teams exhibiting departmental self-interests rather than a unified interest in your organization as a whole?

CEO: Conflict and tension is natural in all organizations. There are always trade-offs, and from my view at the top I struggle to properly balance multiple dimensions, such as how to improve customer service levels and cost-saving process efficiencies while restricted to financial budget constraints and profit targets. I constantly assess our risk management compared to our risk appetite. My belief is that the primary role of my executive team is to set direction, and secondarily to hire, grow, and retain excellent employees. With empowerment and involvement, then, our employees are tasked to determine how we get there—to follow our strategic direction. An autocratic command-and-control style of management no longer works. My managers and employee teams decide on which initiatives are required and which processes we must excel at. I then assure protected financial funding of their projects and process improvements—regardless of any temporary dips in our short-term financial results. We must put our money where our strategy is.

Cokins: You sidestepped my question. How do you unify your organization?

CEO: It's basic. My executive team communicates our strategy with a strategy map, and then afterward our workforce constructs and continuously modifies our balanced scorecard of initiatives, key processes, and associated performance measures derived from our strategy map. This aligns our employees' priorities, plans, and actions with our strategy. With the cascading cause-and-effect linkage of strategic objectives from our strategy map, the tension and conflict I mentioned becomes self-balancing. Our performance measurements are critical. You get what you measure.

Cokins: How do you motivate employees?

CEO: Leaders like myself must motivate through communicating vision and providing inspiration. Not all executives do this well—many do it poorly. But to get true organizational traction, we link financial bonuses for all employees in a large part to the performance indicators against targets from their cascaded scorecards. The employees were involved in selecting the appropriate metrics, so they accept the accountability that is associated with them. Their financial bonuses are also augmented by traditional soft and subjective assessments, such as their personal growth and attitude toward working together cohesively.

Cokins: How are you compensated? Are you the typical CEO, rewarded handsomely sometimes despite a waning enterprise financial performance and associated shareholder wealth destruction?

CEO: The controversial and inflationary run-up of CEO financial rewards is disheartening to employees everywhere, and some blame goes to the guilt-creating executive compensation consultants who circulate the same Power-Point presentation to boards of directors that concludes with "Do you want your CEO to be paid in the bottom half of CEOs in your industry?" There must always be a bottom half. My personal compensation formula is radically different by being directly based on the performance of my direct reports in marketing, sales, production, service delivery, and administration. It's straight-forward. My reward entirely depends on their performance. My executive team's bonuses are tied to their balanced scorecard key performance indicators (KPIs), and my bonus is a weighted formula based on their bonuses. That moti-vates me to remove obstacles that prevent them from achieving their objectives and to facilitate the conflicts among them. It is a closed loop.

Cokins: Okay. So, monitoring the KPI dials of your balanced scorecard is obvi-ously important, but how do you *move* the financial and nonfinancial dials to achieve or surpass your organizational targets that in turn ideally realize your strategy, vision, and mission?

CEO: That is where business intelligence and performance management fit in. More than a decade ago, we implemented compulsory transaction-based systems such as enterprise resource planning and customer relationship management software. But we realized that this type of software does not fulfill its promise of performance lift and return on investment. Those operational systems merely kept us at parity with our competitors. We rocketed beyond by implementing and integrating our decision support methodologies with modeling techniques and their supporting technologies. We view employee competency with analytics of all flavors—particularly predictive analytics—as our means to a sustainable competitive advantage. We have shifted from focusing on control to anticipatory planning so that we can be proactive instead of reactive.

Cokins: One final question: Are you winning?

CEO: Organizational performance improvement is a marathon where there is no finish line. It's a matter of being and staying ahead, rather than of winning. Where we are winning is with the hearts, minds, and loyalty of our customers, our employ-ees, our suppliers, and our governance boards. And there is a bigger stakeholder. Where we all need to win—and that includes all organizations collectively—is with our planet. My organization takes corporate social responsibility very seri-ously. All organizations need to embrace the green and sustainability movements.

What would such an interview be like with members of your executive team? How would their answers be different? Are there next steps that your organization can progress to as it strives to realize the full vision of the performance manage-ment framework?

LACK OF LEADERSHIP?

One wonders why companies that were once very successful, such as Digital Equipment and Wang Laboratories, no longer exist or went bankrupt. One could make a case that their great success led them to be averse to taking risks—a case of reduced risk appetite. Are organizations today overmanaged but underled? *Management* and *leadership* are not the same thing. Management copes with *complexity*, relying on budgets, plans, targets, and organizational charts. Managers tend to follow rules and are risk averse. In contrast, leaders cope with *change*—change that is accelerating. Leadership requires vision, direction-setting, inspiring employees, and intelligent risk management.

Is it a problem that, where they should be exhibiting leadership, managers who are promoted into higher and more executive positions revert to just managing more intensively? Effective managing is the skill that helps managers get promoted to executive levels, but leadership is what is required for them to improve their organization's overall performance.

Risk-based performance management will inevitably be the overarching integration of methodologies. Advances in information technologies, business intelligence, and analytical software will enable this vision.

Chapter 9

Does "A Word to the Wise" Mean Ignore the Dummies?

Getting people to understand what performance management is (at least my interpretation of it) is fraught with challenges. This is due in part to the lack of consensus and the confusion in the marketplace regarding performance management that is caused by diverse definitions and descriptions by management consultants, business journalists, information technology research firms, business intelligence and enterprise resource planning software vendors, and systems integrators.

The position that I have consistently taken is that rather than debate these definitions, one's time and energy are better spent coming to agreement on *what performance management does*—and, more important, agreement on what forces and pressures have caused interest in performance management. Performance management has been around for decades (albeit managed poorly), so why all the buzz and emphasis on it now?

When I created the title for this chapter, "A Word to the Wise," I was sort of referring to you, the reader. My blog, books, articles, and seminars are "words" for you. I am presuming that you are in a position to in some way drive positive change for your organization. However, my reference in the title to "dummies" was intended to grab attention, not to be insulting or derogatory. (I apologize if it was to you.) What I mean is that a word to the wise does not mean ignore everyone who might not have a complete understanding of performance management concepts. It means that a hint is likely enough for people already familiar with performance management methods (e.g., balanced scorecards, customer relationship management); those who are less familiar with it will need a clearer delineation of performance management.

Let us get back to the dilemma: How do we get people to understand performance management? Here are a few performance management–related questions and answers:

Question: Why does an organization need to understand performance management?
Answer: Because if your organization is not pursuing the full vision of the performance management framework, then it will never be able to embrace the concept of *enterprise optimization,* which is a likely to be the next big thing for business and government.

Question: Who in the organization needs to understand performance management?
Answer: Ultimately, everyone; initially, some more than others.

Question: Who needs to understand it initially?

Answer: I am hoping it is you! Otherwise, you would not have read up to this point. The day-to-day worker involved in repeatable processes, like sales order entry, will eventually be involved with performance management (e.g., monitoring and responding to performance indicators in their dashboard); but it is the executive leaders, managers, and key performance management methods implementation folks who must initially grasp the full vision of performance management.

Performance Management Supports Business Intelligence and Decision Making

There are three classes of people: Those who see. Those who see when they are shown. Those who do not see.

—Leonardo da Vinci,
Florentine painter and inventor,
Note Books, c. 1500

Part Three begins by explaining the difference between business intelligence and performance management with the emphasis that decision support is the primary purpose for the performance management framework. It ends with a chapter that warns of executive teams that state lofty goals but do not have the underlying capability to achieve those goals.

Chapter 10

How Do Business Intelligence and Performance Management Fit Together?

The late Nobel Prize–winning nuclear physicist Richard Feynman learned a valuable lesson as a child. His father showed him a picture of a species of bird and told Feynman its name in several languages—all uniquely different. Then his father noted that regardless of the bird's various names, they did not in any way affect the reality of the bird's existence or its physical features. The lesson for Feynman was that no matter what name people use for something, it does not alter the thing itself. We can apply that lesson to the confusion today about the difference between mainstream business intelligence (BI)[1] and performance management.

Are BI and performance management different words for the same species of bird or two different birds (or animals)? Is BI a part of performance management? Or is performance management a part of BI?

There is ambiguity since the underlying inputs, processes, outputs, and outcomes of an organization—whether a public sector government agency or a commercial business—may arguably have some parts that belong to BI and others that belong to performance management. The key word in that sentence was *arguably*. This argument arises because information technology (IT)–centric people often see an enterprise as a ravenous consumer of billions of bytes of data intended to manage the business (a BI view). In contrast, leaders, managers, and employee teams typically view the same enterprise as an organism with a purpose and mission (a performance management view); they desire solutions and applications that achieve results. How can BI and performance management be reconciled? *The enterprise is like the single species of bird*—and nothing can change the reality of its existence.

HOW DO BUSINESS INTELLIGENCE AND PERFORMANCE MANAGEMENT RELATE TO EACH OTHER?

There are two things that most folks can agree on about business intelligence and performance management: (1) BI involves raw data that must first be cleansed and *integrated* from disparate source systems and then *transformed* into information; and (2) performance management *leverages* that information. In this context, information is much more valuable than data points, because integrating and transforming data using calculations and pattern discovery results in potentially meaningful information that can be used for decisions. For example, an automobile manufacturer's warranty claims can be globally analyzed to detect a design problem. In another instance, the history of an individual's credit card purchase transaction data can be converted into information that in turn can be used for decisions by retailers to better serve the customer or provide customized offers.

A survey by the global technology consulting firm Accenture reported that senior U.S. executives are increasingly disenchanted with their analytical and BI capabilities.[2] Although they acknowledged that their BI (regardless of how they personally define it) provides a display of data in terms of reporting, querying, searching, and visual dashboards, they felt their mainstream BI still fell short. An organization's interest is not just to *monitor* the dials; it is, more important, to *move* the dials. That is, merely reporting information does equate to managing for better results; but what is needed are actions and decisions to improve the organization's performance. Having mainstream BI capability is definitely important; however, it has often come about as the result of departments needing advances that their IT function could not provide. Extending BI across the organization so that mini-BI applications can talk to each other is a mission-critical differentiator for organizational success and competitiveness.

Managing and improving are not the same thing. Many people manage like the coach of a sports team, and they get by. *Improving*, however, is how an organization wins. To differentiate BI from performance management, performance management can be viewed as *deploying* the power of BI, but the two are inseparable. Think of performance management as an *application* of BI. Performance management adds context and direction for BI. BI provides a platform of transactional data and its partial conversion to useful information. Then the integrated performance management applications, built on top of the BI platform, provide its various methodologies as solutions, each infused with analytical capabilities, to turbocharge the potential in the BI platform.

As in physics, BI is like potential energy, while performance management is the conversion of potential energy into kinetic energy. Coal, when heated, provides power to move things. Using a track-and-field analogy, BI is like the muscle of a pole vaulter, and performance management is that same athlete clearing greater heights. BI is an enterprise information platform for querying, reporting, and much more, making it the foundation for effective performance management. Performance management drives the strategy and leverages all of the processes, methodologies, metrics, and systems that monitor, manage, and, most important, *improve* enterprise performance. Together, BI and performance management form the bridge that connects data to decisions.

With performance management, the organization's strategy spurs the application of technology, methodologies, and software. As methodologies—which are typically implemented sequentially or operated in isolation of each other—are integrated, the strength and power of performance management grows. Technologies, such as software, support the methodologies. Software is an essential enabler, but the critical part is in the thinking. That is, one must understand the assumptions used in configuring commercial software and, more important, have a vision of the emerging possibilities to apply the new knowledge that BI and performance management produces. When it comes to performance management software, I jokingly say, "A fool with tool is still a fool!" Unlike transactional software (e.g., enterprise resource planning software) that is configured, performance management software typically involves *modeling*.

Recalling the bird that Feynman's father described, we should not waste valuable energy debating BI versus performance management—we might get caught up in semantics. Rather, we should progress to where performance management deploys the power in BI with its enterprise information platform so that organizations can advance from managing to improving.

NOTES

1. The information technology community distinguishes between *little* business intelligence, for query and reporting, and *big* business intelligence, for the platform where information is stored and managed. The emphasis in this chapter is on the latter.
2. Accenture.com, 2005 News Release, "Companies Need to Improve Business Intelligence Capabilities to Drive Growth, Accenture Study Finds."

Chapter 11

CEO's Targeted Financial Return: A Goal or a Wish?

How often have you heard executives proclaim that next year the target for financial results will be at a substantial lift from the current year? For example, "Next year, we expect to improve from a 10.3% to 15.4% rate of return on shareholder equity." Is this leadership or wasted words? Where did the 15.4% come from? Is this expectation a goal or a wish?

Such a high-level, aggregate target, typically stated in financial terms, is *not* a goal—it is a result. That is, aggregate targets are a consequence of collectively accomplishing many other outcomes. Similar to a track-and-field pole vaulter, who must have so many things come together to clear the bar—speed, knee lift, arm pushoff, and body form—an organization must collectively get it right to optimize the use and strategic alignment of its spending and resources.

Even if an organization can get it collectively right, how does the chief executive officer come up with such a precise financial target—or any target number? The financial return is a *dependent* variable, not an independent one. That means there can be dozens, even hundreds, of interrelated factors—the inherent variables—that can collectively contribute to the financial results. However, there is a way to optimize an organization's performance.

The heralded solution to obtaining maximum financial results is to use strategy maps with a balanced scorecard. Together they work like a GPS navigation instrument in a car. If, after reading the previous sentence, your mood has switched to skepticism or ridicule, that is understandable. To begin with, there is little consensus about what a balanced scorecard is. To complicate matters, many organizations claim they have a scorecard full of performance measures, but they have no strategy map (or they did not derive their key performance indicators from it). To clarify this, see Chapter 17, "The Promise and Perils of the Balanced Scorecard."

A strategy map and scorecard do not provide the power to optimize financial results. They set direction and determine which projects and core processes to improve. The underlying power comes from all the other business methodologies that, when integrated and infused with reliable analytics—particularly predictive analytics—constitute the portfolio of methodologies of the performance management framework. This is a major reason why performance management will be so important going forward. No organization has yet achieved its full vision, but many are well along the way.

Is the target a goal or a wish? Summary/aggregate enterprise measures are not goals, but rather results. True target setting must shift to project selection and core process improvements—the independent variables.

Implementing Performance Management

Failing to prepare is preparing to fail.

—Vince Lombardi,
former coach of the Green Bay Packers,
U.S. National Football League

This part of the book tackles the thorny questions of how to successfully implement and integrate the various methodologies of performance management. The initial chapters describe the challenges of the barriers that slow the adoption rate of performance management's methodologies, how to get started, and where to get started.

The remaining chapters of Part Four explain the executive team's role in making performance management work. This involves their setting the tone by communicating their vision and inspiration of what their organization's performance management framework could look like. One chapter discusses motivation of employees by using financial compensation incentives linked to the strategy.

Chapter 12

First Barrier to Performance Management: How Do We Get Started?

Throughout my career, I have had the good fortune to travel extensively around the globe. As a result, I continuously learn about the issues and concerns facing executives, midlevel managers, and those in the project team trenches. One question has repeatedly emerged: How do we get started? At my gray-haired age, I am not sure why I have overlooked this fundamental issue, but it is becoming clearer to me now that a key barrier preventing organizations from pursuing their vision of performance management—regardless of their vision of it—is that they do not know how to get started. There are other barriers, too, such as the false perception of some senior executives that the benefits from performance management do not exceed the administrative effort and expense; but the behavior of senior executives is a topic for another day. We need to talk about the barrier that prevents organizations from getting started and how it has slowed the adoption rate of performance management.

PERFORMANCE MANAGEMENT: AN ENIGMA OR SIMPLY AMBIGUOUS?

There will continue to be confusion as to the precise definition of *performance management*. The good news is this: Performance management is not a *brand-new* methodology that everyone now has to learn; rather it is the assemblage and integration of *existing* improvement methodologies with which most managers are already familiar, spiced with all flavors of analytics—particularly predictive analytics. Collectively, these methodologies are interdependent, working together to manage the execution of an organization's strategy. Most organizations have already begun to implement some of the methodologies of the performance management portfolio, such as the balanced scorecard, but not enough of them have reached that flashpoint where substantial synergy kicks in.

Some executives and many midlevel managers have misconceptions about the components of the performance management suite. For example, many believe that high accuracy in calculating product and service-line costs requires employee timesheets recorded at 15-minute intervals, when in truth the major and dominant determinant of cost accuracy is far more influenced by better mapping of how work activities are uniquely consumed by outputs. Regardless of these misconceptions (and there are many, as most managers have yet to see or experience an organization that is nearing the complete vision of performance management), the problem is that they prevent an organization from making progress—from moving ahead!

One proven way to break through this barrier and get the ball rolling for good is to implement *rapid prototyping* coupled with *iterative redesign* and *remodeling*. Rapid prototyping works because within two or three days you have successfully accomplished it. The getting-started part is over before you really knew it had begun.

RAPID PROTOTYPING OF ACTIVITY-BASED COST MANAGEMENT AND THE BALANCED SCORECARD

Those who remember the miscues of the early 1990s in implementing activity-based costing systems now with hindsight realize that those activity-based cost management (ABC/M) implementations that fell short of expectations were way overdesigned and overbuilt. The diminishing returns in additional accuracy were not worth the exponentially burdensome level of administrative effort required to collect and calculate the cost data. Worse yet, it took forever to create that gargantuan cost model. These implementations collapsed under their own weight long before the employee teams and managers could effectively use the cost data originally promised.

Whereas ABC/M answers the eternal organizational questions—"Where do we make or lose money?" "What does something cost now?" and "What will something cost if something else changes?"—what has rescued this initiative is the application of rapid prototyping. Calculating costs is not bookkeeping, but rather a modeling exercise to transform spending expenses on resources (e.g., salaries, travel, power, supplies) into the calculated costs of the consuming outputs and outcomes (ultimately, the costs of products, channels, and customers); so, the first model can be scaled at a high level. The prudent approach is to build the first complete-scope ABC model in two days, using estimates from only four or five cross-functional employees who are familiar with their areas. On the third day, these folks brief a peer group—and maybe, cautiously, an executive or two—so more people can get a vision of what an ABC/M system might eventually look like in their organization.

Of course, the cost data in this initial model is not accurate, but the next iteration becomes more accurate and granular by taking a few more days, going deeper, and replacing estimates with fact-based data in a few crucial areas. You benefit from making your design and assumption mistakes early, and not later, when it will be much more difficult. Better yet, during the coworker briefing that follows each iteration, people internalize the data they are seeing and can immediately relate it to their problems. Project teams need two parallel plans: (1) an implementation plan and (2) a communication plan.

The second is much more important than the first! Resistance to change is what stops progress, and this can be overcome when the buy-in process starts out in a positive way.

Can a strategy map and its associated balanced scorecard be completed as quickly as this? You bet—but only if the executives are willing. Some balanced scorecard consultant facilitators are mastering *rapid brainstorming* methods. Some are as simple as taking four short hours to have each executive on the team individually fill out 30 to 40 SWOTs (an organizational *s*trengths, *w*eaknesses, *o*pportunities, and *t*hreats assessment) on sticky notes and paste all of them on panels divided into focus areas using frameworks like the Malcolm Baldrige Award, the European Foundation for Quality Management, or Norton-Kaplan. The next step is to manually cluster the sticky SWOTs into common groups with similar characteristics, and then finally describe each cluster on a larger sticky note in words reflecting a goal or objective. *That's it!* These larger notes now can be pasted on a wall-size posterboard, and the executives can return to their offices.

At this point, the core process managers from the next managerial level take over. Over the next day or two, they identify the few manageable projects or initiatives that can be accomplished (or the area of their process that they must excel at) for each strategic objective; then they define those vital few key performance indicators—three at most—for each project or process specified. *Voila!* The initial strategy map, key initiatives, and vital few (rather than trivial many) relevant measures are then done. As a bonus, many of those middle managers will for the first time have learned the senior executives' strategy in a way that they can understand it.

Exhibit 12.1 illustrates the rapid prototyping approach with iterative remodeling to accelerate learning. Its permits you to make your mistakes early and often, and not later, when it becomes more difficult and costly to make design changes.

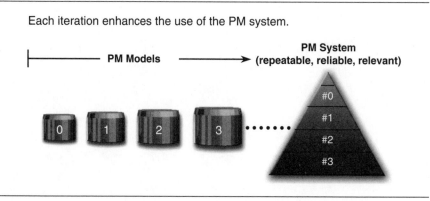

Each iteration enhances the use of the PM system.

PM Models ⟶ **PM System** *(repeatable, reliable, relevant)*

0   1   2   3   ....   #0 #1 #2 #3

Exhibit 12.1   Performance Management: Rapid Prototyping with Iterative Remodeling
Source: © Gary Cokins. Used with permission.

IS A *READY-FIRE-AIM* APPROACH ALL THAT BAD?

Rapid prototyping achieves the benefits advocated by W. Edwards Deming, the popular quality management guru, with his *plan-do-check-act* iterative cycle. This is all about accelerating organizational learning rates. Typically, people do not like taking responsibility for decisions, so they fail to make any. However, it is the courage to make decisions that differentiates leaders from mere managers. Managers are risk averse and prone to overplanning and underexecuting, whereas leaders take calculated risks, knowing that they can always adjust. Leaders exhibit vision and inspiration. They do not wait for the stars to align to get started.

There is no single jewel-in-the-crown methodology around which there are less important methodologies. What matters is the crown itself—how all the methodologies fit together. Performance suffers when managers and employees must react repeatedly to unexpected changes. To realize maximum benefits, all of the methodologies—such as strategy mapping, balanced scorecard feedback, customer relationship management, Six Sigma, lean management, and anticipatory capacity resource planning—must be robust, seamlessly integrated, and in sync. Determining where to start on integrating a performance management framework depends on the organization's weaker links.

Chapter 13

Where Do You Begin Implementing Performance Management?

As organizations embrace the full vision of the performance management framework—not just the narrow financial definition of dashboards and better financial reporting—they frequently ask, "Where should we start?" Some may be eager to begin with a balanced scorecard, and others by measuring channel and customer profitability. Still others want to take it to the limit by redesigning their core business processes.

In fact, there is no one-size-fits-all answer. The starting point depends on which of the performance management methodologies provides the fastest significant return and gets the ball rolling on employee buy-in.

ONE PERFORMANCE MANAGEMENT FRAMEWORK, BUT MANY RECIPES

Self-help writers and journalists often simplify a topic by describing the "X" number of steps to succeed. Examples include weight reduction diets or the pursuit of wealth. Business writers often do the same. Some people believe it is not advisable to implement all the changes of the performance management framework in one big bang. These people believe the most successful route as a series of sequential steps. My belief has consistently been that implementing the performance management framework does not lend itself to a series of predefined steps.

Is the performance management framework a recipe or a stew? I believe it is the latter. What I mean by this is that the *full vision* of performance management is a majestic end state that can be arrived at through many routes, not just one. And like a stew, it will contain many ingredients where the mix of flavors provides the synergy of the whole being greater than the sum of the parts.

There are many variations on how to apply the performance management framework. Just as our grandmothers each had their own recipe for a holiday fruitcake, organizations are concocting their own customized versions of the performance management framework. Performance management is not a process; rather it is the integration of multiple methodologies, such as customer relationship management, strategy maps, balanced scorecards, and lean/Six Sigma quality management. These methodologies are spiced with all flavors of analytics, and particularly predictive analytics. All of these components are to be synchronized—better, faster, cheaper, and *smarter*. How are organizations mixing these ingredients and baking them into their performance management framework?

As organizations realize that performance management is much more about improving performance than just controlling and managing it, they start asking, "Where do we begin in order to take what we already do to a much higher level?"

PERFORMANCE MANAGEMENT IS ABOUT INTEGRATION AND SPEED

An organization attains the full vision of the performance management framework when executive leaders have communicated their strategy to their managers and employees in a timely manner and are committed to providing continuous updates to their plans. This allows everyone to act in sync and without wasted effort. Speed is vital in communications. Performance suffers when managers and employees must react repeatedly to unexpected changes. To realize maximum benefits, all of the methodologies—such as strategy mapping, customer relationship management, Six Sigma/lean management, and anticipatory capacity resource planning—must be robust, seamlessly integrated, supported with embedded analytics, and in sync with each other. Because some organizations already have several of these methodologies in place (although not necessarily interconnected), the "where to get started" question depends on key factors related to the organization's current situation.

For example, if a reasonably sound activity-based accounting system already provides information on which specific combinations of products, services, channels, and customers earn or lose profit, executives may want to focus next on successful execution of their strategy by applying a strategy map and its associated balanced scorecard. Failure to execute a well-formulated strategy is a major frustration that frequently prompts executives to pursue performance management. However, if the executive team is receiving cost information that is inaccurate because it distorts indirect cost allocations or is incomplete (e.g., the team is receiving only product or service-line profit reporting but not full-channel and customer-segment reporting), executives may want to upgrade their management accounting system by applying activity-based principles. Alternatively, some organizations with competitive cost pressures might start by integrating their process management and cost measurement system.

Again, determining where to start on integrating the performance management framework depends on the organization's weaker links. The sequence of integration depends on which components will provide the highest value-creating lift, and it is admirable to see executive teams who select a good integration sequence. Just as it was with Grandma's holiday fruitcake, eventually all of the essential ingredients must be included.

RAPID PROTOTYPING TO ACCELERATE LEARNING

Organizations will not make speedy progress by focusing exclusively on one methodology, such as better forecasting, and taking a year or longer to implement those improvements in a sequential way. Competitors will beat them, or customers' expectations will outpace them. Multiple methodology improvements should take place simultaneously. An increasingly accepted best practice for such improvements is to apply the *plan, do, check, act* cycle. Start with rapid prototyping, followed by iterative remodeling for all of the relevant methodologies. Naysayers will argue that the organization can handle only a few projects at a time, but naysayers underestimate the ability of people to work together when they are being guided by leaders, and not just by managers.

With rapid prototyping techniques, an organization makes mistakes early and often, instead of later, when it is more costly to make corrective changes. This do-it-quick approach accelerates learning and brings fast results that gain buy-in from employees who are naturally resistant to change. Resistance to change is human nature. Iterative remodeling continues to scale and expand each of the prototyped methodologies into repeatable and reliable production systems.

Performance management is like the gears in a machine: The more closely linked and better meshed the methodologies are during implementation, the quicker the organization moves forward, because it is working better, faster, cheaper, and smarter. Performance management helps organizations gain better traction and faster speed—in the right direction. Software technologies are very relevant, but their purpose is to *support* all of the methodologies. They are *enablers*, not solutions.

My belief is that by using a rapid prototyping approach, managers and employee teams will ultimately see performance management as an integrated framework. Some will debate that employees can tolerate only small phases of change. My belief is that underestimates how capable employees can be if they simply are provided strong leadership.

EMBRACE UNCERTAINTY WITH PREDICTIVE ANALYTICS

Gradually, managers and employee teams will see and understand the big picture, including how all of the methodologies fit together. Those in commercial organizations will realize that creating higher profits and increasing shareholder wealth is not a goal but a result. The true independent variable here is finely managing the innovation-based research and development and marketing spending in order to focus on and target the types of customers to retain, grow, acquire, and win back—as well as the types of customers to avoid wasting money on. Leaders in public sector government organizations tend to view funding as a scarce commodity; therefore, they need to maximize outcomes by increasing output or improving service delivery without additional resources.

Executives are constantly on a quest for the next breakthrough in managerial innovation. My suggestion is to start by integrating and enhancing existing methodologies that have already proved their worth—but can provide even further lift. It is likely that the organization is implementing most of these at some level of competence. However, integration deficiencies may exist in some areas, leading to time lags that cause excessive and costly reactions.

Successful organizations adapt by performing much deeper analysis, such as better and more granular customer segmentation, helping to provide insight into all of the elements being managed. This is called *leveraging business intelligence.* Leaders in these organizations integrate their methodologies and supporting systems for better decision making. Their next major task is to get in front of the wave, using predictive analytics to mitigate risk by making changes before problems occur or escalate. Predictive analytics may well be the next major competitive differentiator, separating successful from mediocre or failing organizations. The uncertainty of future demands or events should not be viewed as a curse, but rather embraced as something organizations can tame with the powerful and proven probabilistic tools and techniques that already exist.

PRIORITIZE OR MAXIMIZE?

The truly exceptional organizations are those that can quickly implement, sequence, and integrate improvement initiatives. Many improvement initiatives are well intentioned and can add value. Because many improvement initiatives have been recognized as central to strengthening a company's competitiveness, today's more complicated debates arise over such issues as whether to implement several initiatives at once for a long-term benefit, or whether it is better to prioritize projects and seek to maximize short-term results.

A strong case can be made that superior companies excel in almost all areas where improvement initiatives are promoted. They plan and manage time, quality, cost, and service levels in anticipation of different customer demands and expectations. With strong leadership that exhibits vision and creates a healthy culture that is less rules based (to maintain status quo) and more principles based (to empower behavior), many programs and methodologies can be implemented in parallel. These superior organizations are the ones that will achieve the full vision of the performance management framework—managing, improving, and strengthening their enterprise-wide performance and competitiveness on a continual and sustained basis.

Start now—everywhere. Most organizations overplan and underexecute. For organizations that have experienced recent upheaval, now is the time to regain some order. With a nurturing attitude from executive leaders who act more like coaches than bosses, and with accelerated learning by managers and employee teams, organizations can move forward to complete the full vision of the performance management framework.

Chapter 14

The Many Rooms of the Organization Mansion

The organization mansion has many rooms.

Business schools tend to divide their curriculum between hard quantitative-oriented courses, such as operations management and finance, and soft behavioral courses, such as change management, ethics, and leadership. The former relies on a run-by-the-numbers management approach. The latter recognizes that people and human behavior matter most. This dividing of the curriculum is like chambers in a mansion.

In one set of chambers are managers who apply the *quantitative* approach of Newtonian mechanical thinking. They see the world and everything in it as a big machine. This approach speaks in terms of production, power, efficiency, and control, where employees are hired to be used and periodically replaced, as if they were disposable robots.

In another set of chambers are managers who apply the *behavioral* approach. They view an organization as a living organism that is ever-changing and responding to its environment. This Darwinian way of thinking speaks in terms of evolution, continuous learning, natural responding, and adapting to changing conditions.[1]

DIFFERENT ROOMS FOR DIFFERENT FUNCTIONS

No matter which managerial style is used, Newtonian or Darwinian, specific rooms in the mansion are dedicated to functions such as developing new products, marketing to acquire new customers, or fulfilling customer orders by delivering products and services. We often refer to these functional rooms as *silos*. Suboptimization typically exists among the rooms. Managers operate their rooms to their own liking. In the old days, each room had its own fireplace, so the room's comfort level was individually controlled. When the mansion was refitted with central heating and air conditioning, managers were increasingly forced to compromise and agree. Most managers were not happy with the new arrangement.

In today's organization mansion, there is an increasing need to understand how one room affects another. For example, managers in the production room have grown to like a minimalist décor with low inventory clutter so that they can quickly assemble parts in reaction to widely varying tastes of customers. In a neighboring room, sales managers like tall stacks of products so that they never miss a sales opportunity due to a shortage. A growing problem in the mansion is that these managers' methods increasingly affect one another.

The ideal way to live in the organization mansion is with teamwork and collaboration. Despite all of the encouragement from scholars and media, good teamwork is tricky to attain. Success comes only to those teams whose members place their own self-serving interests below the more important needs of their organization. The mansion is more important than its rooms.

As Patrick Lencioni describes in his book, *The Five Dysfunctions of a Team*,[2] one problem in team behavior cascades into another, and collectively they escalate to degrade any organization's performance. For example, when different managers secretly tamper with the mansion's central thermostat, they are exhibiting lack of trust in each other. Rather than confront one another, managers typically avoid conflict. Instead of debating what will work best for all, they resort to secret discussions with a few other room managers. Once someone assumes authority and resets the thermostat, the adverse consequence is others' lack of commitment to it because no one listened to their opinions.

The breakdown in teamwork becomes more serious. Because of the lack of commitment and buy-in to choices made by others, room managers avoid accepting accountability for the conditions (i.e., performance) of their own rooms. They begin locally adjusting things to offset whatever they do not like, and pay less attention to the mansion as a whole. They revert to putting their individual needs above the collective goals of the team. Overall performance does not improve and may possibly decline.

PROCESS EFFECTIVENESS OR STRATEGY?

There are two areas of the organization mansion that potentially are in conflict. The sign on the doors to some rooms says A GOOD STRATEGY. The sign on the doors to other rooms says EFFECTIVE AND EFFICIENT OPERATIONAL BUSINESS PROCESSES. Which door would you choose as more important? You cannot walk through both doors. There is no more information provided (in part so that management consultants cannot reply with their universal answer to all questions— "It depends").

I have posed this scenario to corporate leaders during the executive workshops that I frequently facilitate. Which door do you think they most frequently select? Before I answer, the more valuable learning to me is the executives' *reasoning* regardless of their door choice. There seems to be a pattern of agreement.

"A good strategy" has been the more popular choice, but not by an overwhelming margin—approximately by 60% to 40%. Support for the strategy choice is typically explained in this way: Regardless of how good organizational effectiveness and operational process designs are, a poor strategy cannot be overcome. One chief executive officer (CEO) summed it up: "A good strategy will always trump good organizational execution."

But there is a segment of CEOs that select the operational process door. In some cases, I think these CEOs are so confident they already have a good strategy in mind that they do not feel they need a better one. (I probably should add AND A BAD STRATEGY to the process door sign.) However, some CEOs are fervent process types. Executives and managers who highly regard the importance of good processes believe that without them, the organization is in trouble. It cannot provide reliable and timely service to customers. It also cannot perform profitably due to excess costs.

What is the overall answer? Leaders need to spend time in *both* types of rooms—pursuing good strategy and effective processes.

PERFORMANCE MANAGEMENT CHAMBERS

My belief is that there are in some rooms (perhaps just closets) managers who see usefulness in *blending* the characteristics of the Newtonian and Darwinian styles. They believe in teamwork and collaboration. The trick to general management is integrating and balancing the quantitative and behavioral approaches, with all the managers behaving as a team. These managers are the ones who understand the full vision of enterprise-wide performance management as the seamless integration of multiple managerial methodologies, such as customer relationship management and Six Sigma quality techniques.

Command-and-control-style managers, who prefer to leverage their workers' muscles but not their brains, run into trouble. Ultimately, things get done by *people*, and not by the computers or machines that are simply the tools used to arrive at results. Most employees are not thrilled with being micromanaged. The good performers are people and teams who manage themselves and positively collaborate with others, as long as they are given some direction and timely feedback. Management creates value by communicating strategic direction and produces results by leveraging people who focus on how to get there. The capability of people is arguably the most wasted asset of an organization.

In the *performance management mansion*, each chamber is furnished with strategy maps that set the direction from the executive team. Each room is further provided with information and analysis tools, heavy with predictive analysis, so people can determine ways to achieve the strategy. Balanced scorecard dashboards are in each room for feedback so that everyone knows how they are doing on what is important. The mansion has a single enterprise-wide information platform, rather than many disparate, out-of-sync data sources. People are empowered to make quick decisions because there is less and less time to seek answers from higher-level executives. By behaving as an effective team and collaborating together, managers in this mansion do not merely manage performance—they *improve* it.

The performance management mansion might have many rooms, but its managers are all on the same team.

NOTES

1. Stephan H. Haeckel, *Adaptive Enterprise: Creating and Leading Sense and Respond Organization* (Boston: Harvard Business School Press, 1999).

2. Patrick Lencioni, *The Five Dysfunctions of a Team* (San Francisco: Jossey-Bass, 2002).

Chapter 15

Accountability and Incentives for Rewards: How Disconnected Are They?

Over the past few years, I have made it a practice to ask friends, college classmates, and business contacts the question "During your career, what changes in management have you observed, particularly in the past five years?"

I expected to hear about trends like the need to be more customer-centric or the move toward outsourcing. Instead, many people told me about seeing a sharp escalation in the tendency of businesses to hold managers and employees accountable for results. They said there is now no place to hide in an organization if you are not a value-adding producer. If you are not delivering expected outcomes, your job security or your job position is at risk.

It is a fact that competitive pressures in the commercial sector and increasingly activist board-level governance have led to the demand for greater accountability. Underperformers are increasingly being detected and their career paths adversely affected. In higher education, the tradition of faculty tenure is gradually being abandoned. I am not trying to characterize organizations as cruel and insensitive entities that treat employees as disposable parts, but merely pointing out that economic forces are bringing pressure on organizations for higher yields with the same or fewer resources.

How fair and equitable is the process of evaluating individuals? Do performance measures cause the desired behavior that management seeks? Can adopting the full vision of enterprise-wide performance management remedy these problems by deploying effective incentive, reward, and recognition systems?

REWARD PERFORMANCE YOU WANT TO ENCOURAGE: BUCKS FOR BEHAVIOR

Many organizations have implemented balanced scorecards and use the results to determine bonuses in pay. Regardless of how fancy and eye-appealing the visual meters and dashboards, at the core of a balanced scorecard is the selection of appropriate measures and how many to use. (See Chapter 18, "How Are Balanced Scorecards and Dashboards Different?") If the wrong key performance indicators (KPIs) are chosen, then the behavior, priorities, and decisions of employees and their organization as a whole will not be well aligned with the direction of the executive team. And if the KPIs are appropriate but too many KPIs are assigned to an individual, then the employee's ability to focus is diluted. I advocate no more than three KPIs per employee. With hierarchical cascading and linked KPIs, which are traits of a good balanced scorecard, that individual's supervisors will have higher-level KPIs that can be included in the weighted-mix formula of the individual's cash bonus.

To complicate matters, if performance incentives are not strong enough or not adequately linked to employees, then there will not be sufficient traction. For example, receiving a tiny cash bonus or one that results mainly from high-level companywide measures (such as the company's year-end profit) may not motivate individuals. And if the KPIs are simply the traditional measures of the past, then do they measure what can be measured? What *should* they measure to realize the executive team's strategy?

For decades, compensation consultants have proposed elixirs, such as profit-sharing pool bonuses or gain-sharing, but are they enough? If working harder to earn a higher cash bonus motivates an employee, how focused will that person be if the contribution she makes has minimal influence on the overall results of the enterprise? Will the distribution of cash bonuses be equitable? The term *pay for performance* (i.e., a bonus contingent on varying results) has been around for years, but the "performance" measured is typically not directly under the employee's control.

HOW EFFECTIVE ARE PERFORMANCE MEASURES WITHOUT CONSEQUENCES?

I asked a specialist in a leading compensation consulting firm how sophisticated the year-end cash bonus formula can be for individuals. He replied that it must be kept simple and should not link the incentive pay equation to KPIs, which this person believed to be too complicated. I was surprised. If the reward basis is too simple, how can you differentiate one individual's performance from that of another—particularly if the determination is based on high-level enterprise financial results, such as year-end profits? A key factor in motivating people is their sense that over-performers in the organization are differentiated from underperformers and that they are accordingly (and materially) recognized. Otherwise, free riders gain inequitably awarded rewards, which can provoke resentment.

To clarify, the incentives I am referring to are merit-based annual bonuses—variable-at-risk payments—not salary increases. Linking salary increases to performance is ineffective, but many organizations continue to do it. The common wisdom of human resource experts is to link salary increases to market increases of a job skill, such as regional salary level for a financial controller, except perhaps for underperformers. Numerous salary surveys exist, but the key point here is to link performance to a *variable* annual bonus.

Incentive compensation is a sensitive topic with many thorny issues. These include group-based versus individual-based incentives; short-term immediate bonuses versus longer-term deferred ones; payment frequency (e.g., annually, quarterly); and allowances for wide swings in the bonus pools, which are affected by business cycles or poor decisions by senior management. Ultimately, we can talk all we want about increasing accountability, but performance measures *without consequences* simply have no teeth.

HOW DOES PERFORMANCE MANAGEMENT SOLVE THIS PROBLEM?

Historically, economists have wrestled with determining the appropriate organizational structure for implementing business strategy. In the 1970s, Professor Alfred D. Chandler of the Harvard Business School led the field with research and published articles that explored three *S*s of management: strategy, structure, and systems. Businesses have constantly shifted organizational (i.e., human) structures to attempt to achieve better performance. But advocates of the balanced scorecard with KPIs that are determined by linked organizational objectives in strategy maps believe that there may never be a perfect organizational structure. The essence of the balanced scorecard is to focus less on the organizational structure and more on designing a managerial system that aligns an individual's behavior directly with the executive team's strategic objectives through cascading and linked KPIs.

In an article published in the *World of Work* journal,[1] two compensation specialists with Sibson Consulting compared successful implementation of a broad-based compensation incentive system to building a bonfire on a beach for an all-night gathering. It takes a powerful spark to ignite the fire, a carefully constructed foundation, and stamina to keep it burning throughout the evening. The article confirmed my belief that the *foundation* of an incentive system is critical. Three components of the foundation are relevant:

1. Seeking involvement from employees in selecting the KPIs, thus gaining their buy-in and commitment
2. Setting objective, quantifiable, and agreed-on measures
3. Recognizing employees with a carefully weighted bonus formula that differentiates overperformers from underperformers[2]

Of course, any performance review that affects an individual's compensation should contain elements of work behavior (e.g., their personal skill and behavior growth) as well as the enterprise's financial results. The case I am making here is that additional elements should be included to show how the individual is contributing to results that align with the executive team's strategic objectives.

The full vision of performance management is not only to integrate all methodologies and systems, but to position all of them on a common information platform where the data is cleansed, integrated, and reliable. This eliminates the excuse that the administrative effort to operate a complex contingent pay-for-performance system exceeds the benefit.

A WAY FORWARD

Can employees handle several weighted factors in their bonus equation to determine their compensation incentive? The compensation consultant I referenced earlier said no. However, Bob Paladino, the balanced scorecard project leader for Crown Castle who received the top honor in 2005 from the Balanced Scorecard Collaborative,[3] argues the opposite in his presentations at conferences about his company's scorecard implementation journey. His ideas are captured in his book, *Five Key Principles of Corporate Performance Management*.[4] Paladino describes the husband of an employee who approached a high-level executive in the aisle of a supermarket to ask, "How will the company end up at year-end with our safety index?"—a reference to a KPI affecting his wife's bonus. The startled executive initially asked the spouse, "Why would you want to know?" to which the spouse replied that his family was considering purchasing a new lawnmower and he was wondering if they would have the extra money to afford it.

The message here is that if a spouse can track KPIs and equate them in cash to an expected bonus, then maybe employees can handle multifactor weighted incentive formulas where some of the factors reflect the individual's performance regardless of how well or poorly the organization performed.

Organizations should not get it backward. Those that say "The bonus plan does not work, and that is why we were unsuccessful" are confusing the roles of *manager* and *executive*. It is more likely that the strategy was unsuccessful, and the employees were striving to meet poorly chosen objectives.

Ultimately, leaders must be able to communicate their vision of what success looks like if everything goes as planned. Leaders must inspire and empower others, combining their aspirations with delegated accountability. This is a cornerstone of performance management. Strategic vision has to be cascaded through the organization so everyone aligns. In communicating the vision, the rewards system is important, but there are other factors. The executive team should also consider nonfinancial incentives and motivations for employees to perform. It is important to create and develop effective employee teams with favorable group dynamics and the right interpersonal behavior.

Performance management is a powerful way of linking employee behavior to the strategic intent of the executive team. And it provides business intelligence supported by predictive analytics, giving managers and employee teams the information they need to make better decisions and perform trade-off analysis. This is not just about monitoring the dials—it is about *moving* the dials.

NOTES

1. Christian M. Ellis and Cynthia L. Paluse, "Blazing a Trail to Broad-Based Incentives," *World of Work* (Fourth Quarter, 2000): 33–41.

2. Rosabeth Moss Kanter, "The Attack on Pay," *Harvard Business Review* (March–April, 1987): 61.

3. www.bcsol.org.

4. Bob Paladino, *Five Key Principles of Corporate Performance Management* (Hoboken, NJ: John Wiley & Sons, 2007).

Chapter 16

Why Do You Have to Be a Sociologist to Implement Performance Management?

In my book *Activity-Based Cost Management: An Executive Guide,*[1] I mentioned that most organizations make the mistake of believing that implementing this modestly advanced costing methodology is 90% math and 10% organizational change management with employee behavior alteration. In reality, it is the other way around. As another example, successfully implementing a balanced scorecard (see Chapter 17, "The Promise and Perils of the Balanced Scorecard") performance measurement system implies an impact on employee teams and managers that is even more extreme—probably 5% math and 95% about people.

One problem all organizations suffer from is the imbalance in how much emphasis they place on being *smart* as opposed to being *healthy*. Most organizations overemphasize trying to be smart by hiring MBAs and management consultants in their quest to achieve a run-it-by-the-numbers management style. These types of organizations miss the relevance of how important it is *also* to be healthy—assuring that employee morale is high, that employee turnover is low, and that managers and employees are deeply involved in understanding the leadership team's strategic intent and direction setting. Healthy behavior improves the likelihood of employee buy-in and commitment. (For more about how organizations can be *both* smart and healthy, refer to Patrick Lencione's book, *The Five Dysfunctions of a Team: A Leadership Fable.*[2])

What is needed to correct this imbalance between being smart and being healthy? Right from the start, you have to think like a sociologist, and arguably you need to be a psychologist, too, because people matter a lot. Never underestimate the magnitude of resistance to change. It is natural for people to love the status quo.

PLANNING VERSUS COMMUNICATING

When organizations embark on applying one of the many methodologies that constitute the performance management portfolio, they need two plans: (1) an implementation plan and (2) a communication plan. The second plan is arguably far more important than the first. There are always advocates for a new project, but there are also naysayers. Knowing in advance who the naysayers are is critical to either winning them over or avoiding them.

A command-and-control style of management that tries to mandate change through force went out the window years ago with the Iron Curtain's Berlin Wall. Today's employee is a knowledge worker. When the executive team proclaims, "We are now going to shift direction and go this new way," most managers still fold their arms in resistance and silently say to themselves, "Convince me."

The trick to general management is integrating and balancing the quantitative and behavioral managerial approaches and styles. Today, command-and-control-style executives who prefer to leverage their workers' muscles but not their brains run into trouble. Things get done by people, not by the computers or machines that are simply tools for arriving at results. Most employees do not like being micromanaged. The good performers are people and teams who manage themselves, given some direction and timely feedback. Management creates value and produces results by leveraging people. Performance management is much more than dials and levers. It is about people.

NOTES

1. Gary Cokins, *Activity-Based Cost Management: An Executive Guide* (Hoboken, NJ: John Wiley & Sons, 2001).
2. Patrick Lencione, *The Five Dysfunctions of a Team: A Leadership Table* (Hoboken, NJ: John Wiley & Sons, 2002).

Part Five

Strategy Maps, the Balanced Scorecard, and Dashboards

A new scientific truth does not triumph by convincing its opponents and making them see the light, but rather because its opponents eventually die out, and a new generation grows up that is familiar with it.

—Max Planck,
physicist and originator of the quantum theory,
in *The Philosophy of Physics* (1936)

This part of the text (Strategy) and the next three parts (Managerial Accounting, Customers, Shareholders) describe four key interrelated components of the performance management framework.

An important component of the performance management framework is formulating strategy and then executing it by aligning resources and their focused behavior on that execution. This part covers the strategy map, the balanced scorecard, dashboard measures, and how to effectively use the results from them.

These chapters describe how to make a strategy operational—without excessive reliance on quarterly financial measures as the primary evidence that demonstrates whether a strategy is successful. One chapter removes the confusion between a balanced scorecard (with its key performance indicators) and dashboards (where the non–key performance indicators reside).

Chapter 17

The Promise and Perils of the Balanced Scorecard

The balanced scorecard, the methodology developed by Drs. Robert S. Kaplan and David Norton,[1] recognizes the shortcoming of executive management's excessive emphasis on after-the-fact, short-term financial results. It resolves this myopia and improves organizational performance by shifting attention from financial measures to managing nonfinancial operational measures related to customers, internal processes, and employee innovation, learning, and growth. These influencing measures are reported *during* the period so that quick action can be taken. This in turn leads to better financial results.

The balanced scorecard is one of the underpinnings needed to complete the full vision of the performance management framework. Will the adoption of the balanced scorecard meet with the same difficulties encountered by activity-based costing (ABC) systems in the 1990s? It took many failures in ABC system implementations before organizations learned what ABC is and how to shape, size, and level the detail of ABC systems and begin to get them ready for use. Are balanced scorecard implementations going to travel down the same bumpy road?

LACK OF CONSENSUS

An early indication of trouble is the confusion about what a balanced scorecard is, and what its purpose is. There is little consensus. If you ask executives whether they are using a balanced scorecard, many say they are. But if you ask them to describe it, you will get widely different descriptions. There is no standard—yet. Some executives have successfully transferred their old columnar management reports into visual dashboards with flashing red and green lights and directional arrows. Some realize a scorecard is more than that, and have put their old measures on a diet, compressing them into smaller, more manageable and relevant measures. However, neither of these methods may be the correct one.

How does anyone know whether those measures—the *key performance indicators* (KPIs)—support the strategic intent of the executive team? Are the selected measures the *right* measures? Or are they what you *can* measure rather than what you *should* measure? Is the purpose of the scorecard merely to better *monitor* the dials, or is it to facilitate the employee actions needed to *move* the dials?

Talk about balanced scorecards and dashboards seems to be appearing in business magazines, Web site discussion groups, and conferences. Today's technology makes it relatively simple to convert reported data into a dashboard dial. But what are the consequences? What actions are suggested from just monitoring the dials?

In the performance management framework, results and outcome information should answer three questions: What? So what? and Then what? Sadly, most scorecards and dashboards answer only the first question. Worse yet, answering the *what* might not even focus on a relevant issue. Organizations struggle with determining what to measure.

Organizations need to think more deeply about which measures drive value and reflect the accomplishment of the direction-setting strategic objectives of their executive team. Once they have the correct measures, organizations should strive toward optimizing them and ideally be continuously forecasting their expected results.

IMPLEMENTING TOO QUICKLY AND SKIPPING KEY STEPS

Why is it that so many people are familiar with the term *balanced scorecard* but are unfamiliar with the term *strategy maps*? I believe the strategy map is orders of magnitude more important than the scorecard, which is merely a feedback mechanism. Why do executives want a balanced scorecard without a strategy map? One possible explanation is the mistaken belief that those vital few KPI measures (as opposed to the trivial many) can be derived without first requiring employee teams and managers to understand the answer to the key question: "Where does the executive team want the organization to go?" This question is best answered by the executive team's *vision and mission*—they must point out the direction in which they want the organization to go. That is the executive team's primary job—setting direction. The strategy map and its companion scorecard are important, too, but their combination answers a different question: "How will we get there?"

Exhibit 17.1 illustrates a generic strategy map with its four stacked popular perspectives. Each rectangle represents a strategic objective and its associated projects or competencies to excel at, plus their appropriate measures and targets.

Note that there are dependency linkages in a strategy map with an upward direction of cumulating effects of contributions. The derived KPIs are not in isolation, but rather have context in the mission and vision. To summarize, a strategy maps linkages from the bottom perspective upward:

- Accomplishing the employee innovation, learning, and growth objectives contributes to the internal process improvement objectives.
- Accomplishing the internal process objectives contributes to the customer satisfaction objectives.
- Accomplishing the customer-related objectives results in the achievement of the financial objectives, typically a combination of revenue growth and cost management objectives.

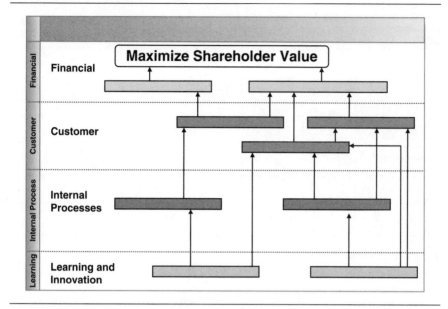

Exhibit 17.1 Generic Strategy Map
Source: © Gary Cokins. Used with permission.

The strategy map is like a force field in physics, as with magnetism, where the energy, priorities, and actions of people are mobilized, aligned, and focused. One can say, at the top of the map, that maximizing shareholder value (or, for public sector organizations, maximizing community and citizen value) is *not* really a goal—it is a result. It is the result of accomplishing all of the linked strategic objectives with cause-and-effect relationships.

The peril that threatens the success of this methodology is executive teams that are anxious to assign measures with targets to employees and hold them accountable. Executives typically skip two critical steps: involving the employees to gain their buy-in (and commitment to the measures) to ensure that they understand the executive team's strategy, and the more critical, prior step of identifying the mission-essential projects and initiatives that will achieve the strategic objectives. The presence of enabling projects and initiatives is what distinguishes a strategic objective from just getting better at what you have already been doing.

Exhibit 17.2 illustrates ideally who should be responsible for each of the five elements of a strategic objective: the executive team or the managers and employees. Sadly, many organizations neglect the first two elements identified in a strategy map. They begin with the third column to select KPIs without constructing a strategy map. The performance management intelligence resides in the strategy map.

Measurement Period	1st Quarter					
	Strategic Objective	Identify Projects, Initiatives, or Processes	KPI Measure	KPI Target	KPI Actual	Comments/ Explanation
Executive Team	X	↑↓	↑↓	X		
Managers and Employees		X	X		*their score*	*X*
					<----- *period results* ------->	

A scorecard is more of a *social* tool than a technical tool.

Exhibit 17.2 Who Is Responsible for What?
Source: © Gary Cokins. Used with permission.

Strategy maps and their derived scorecard are navigational tools that guide the organization to *execute* the strategy, not necessarily to formulate the strategy. Executive teams are pretty good at defining strategy, but a high involuntary chief executive officer (CEO) turnover rate and the increasingly shorter tenure of CEOs are evidence of their failure to implement their strategy.

MEASUREMENTS ARE MORE OF A SOCIAL TOOL THAN A TECHNICAL TOOL

Please do not misunderstand me; selecting and measuring KPIs are critical. You get what you measure, and strategy maps and scorecards serve more of a social purpose than a technical one (although information technology and software are essential enablers). Performance measures motivate people and focus them on what matters most.

Imagine if every day, every employee in an organization, from the janitor at the bottom of an organization to the CEO or managing director at the top, could answer this single question: "How am I doing on what is important?" The first half of the question can be easily displayed on a dial with a target; it is reported in a scorecard or dashboard. But it is the second half of the question that is key—"on what is important"—and that is defined from the strategy map.

The risk and peril of the balanced scorecard involve the process of identifying and integrating appropriate cause-and-effect linkages of strategic objectives that are each supported by the vital few measures, and then cascading the KPIs down through the organization. KPIs ultimately extend into performance indicators (PIs)—operational performance indicators—that employees can relate to and directly affect.

The primary task of a strategy map and its companion balanced scorecard is to align people's work and priorities with multiple strategic objectives that, if accomplished, will achieve the strategy and consequently realize the end game of maximizing shareholder wealth (or maximizing citizen value). The strategic objectives are located in the strategy map, not in the scorecard. The KPIs in the scorecard reflect the strategic objectives in the strategy map.

Debate will continue about how to arrive at the vital few KPIs for workgroups. Here are two contrasting approaches:

1. *Newtonian-style managers*, who believe the world is a big machine with dials, pulleys, and levers to push and pull, find appeal in looking at benchmark data to identify which relevant and unfavorably large performance gaps should be areas for their focus. They want to know "What must we get better at?" The KPIs are then derived. Strategies are then deduced from recognizing deficiencies.

2. *Darwinian-style managers*, who believe the organization is a sense-and-respond organism, find appeal in having the executive team design the strategy map by applying a SWOT (*s*trengths, *w*eaknesses, *o*pportunities, and *t*hreats) analysis approach. This approach begins with the executive team freely brainstorming and recording an organization's SWOTs. They then cluster similar individual SWOTs into strategic objectives with causal linkages in the strategy map. Following this initial step, the middle managers and core process owners are then tasked with identifying the few manageable projects and core processes to improve that will attain the executive team's strategic objectives in the strategy map. After that step, those same middle managers can identify the KPIs that will indicate progress toward achieving the projects and improving critical core processes. This latter approach not only ensures that middle managers and employee teams will understand the executive's strategy (about which most middle managers and employees are typically clueless), but it further encourages their buy-in and ownership of the scorecard and KPIs since these have not been mandated to them from the executives. (Of course, the executive team can subsequently challenge and revise their lower managers' selected projects and KPIs—debate is always healthy—but only after the buy-in and learning has occurred.)

SCORECARD OR REPORT CARD? THE IMPACT OF SENIOR MANAGEMENT'S ATTITUDE

Regardless of which method is used to identify the KPIs, the KPIs ideally should reflect the executive team's strategic intent and not be reported in isolation—disconnected—as typically the annual financial budget is disconnected from the strategy (see Chapter 23, "Put Your Money Where Your Strategy Is"). This is the peril of the balanced scorecard. Its main purpose is to communicate the executive team's strategy to employees in a way they can understand it, and to report the impact of their contribution to attaining it. But starting with KPI definition without the context of the executive's mission and vision precludes this important step.

Research from Professor Raef Lawson when he was at the State University of New York, Albany, suggests that a major differentiator of success from failure in a balanced scorecard implementation is senior management's attitude. Is it a scorecard or report card? Will it be used for punishment or remedy? Do we work for bosses we must obey as if we were dogs—"roll over"? Or do we work for coaches and mentors who guide and counsel us?

For example, is senior management anxiously awaiting those dashboards so they can follow the cascading score meters downward in order to micromanage the workers under their middle managers, acting like Darth Vader to see which of their minions may need to be cut off from their air supply? Or will the executives appropriately restrict their primary role and responsibility to defining and continuously adjusting strategy (which is dynamic, not static, always reacting to new insights) and then allow empowered employee teams to select KPIs from which employees can actively determine the corrective interventions to align with the strategy?

The superior strategy map and scorecard systems embrace employee teams communicating among themselves to take actions, rather than a supervisory command-and-control, in-your-face style from senior managers. An executive team micromanaging the KPI score performance of employees can be corrosive. If the strategy map and cascading KPI and PI selection exercise is well done and subsequently maintained, then higher-level managers need only view their own score performance, share their results with the employee teams below them, and coach the teams to improve their KPI and PI scores and/or reconsider adding or deleting KPIs or PIs. More mature scorecard users using commercial software can readjust the KPI and PI weighting coefficients to steer toward better alignment with the strategic objectives.

WHY NOT AN AUTOMOBILE GPS NAVIGATOR FOR AN ORGANIZATION?

The latest rage is to have a global positioning system (GPS) route navigator in our automobiles. As with most new technologies, such as the handheld calculators that replaced slide rules, or laptop computers, the GPS is evolving into a must-have. It gets you to your destination without a hassle and with a comforting voice to guide you along the way. Why not have a similar device for an organization?

My belief is that with their refinement in usage, the strategy map and its companion balanced scorecard are becoming the GPS route navigator for organizations. The destination input to the GPS is the executive team's strategy. As described earlier, the executive team's primary job is to set strategic direction, and the "top" of their strategy map is their destination. A GPS has knowledge of roads and algorithms to determine the best route; managers and employee teams must map which projects, initiatives, and business process improvements are the best ones to get to the destination of realizing the strategy. In addition, when you are driving a car with a GPS instrument and you make a wrong turn, the GPS's voice chimes in to tell you that you are off track—and it then provides you with a corrective action instruction. However, with most organizations' calendar-based and long-cycle-time reporting, there is delayed reaction. The performance management framework includes a GPS.

Next, the organization, as with the automobile itself, needs to be included. The motor and driveshaft are the employees with their various methodologies, such as customer value management and service delivery, that propel the organization toward its target. Collectively, the many methodologies, including lean management and activity-based costing, constitute performance management as the organization's intermeshed gears.

To some people, the rearview mirrors of an auto implies that events have already happened, so they are already behind you and cannot be affected. These people promote only looking through the front windshield. I personally like having rearview mirrors, and when driving I glance at them often. I want to see what types of vehicles are behind me and what rate they may be speeding up on me. With performance management there is much to be gained from analyzing trends and drawing inferences from the past. A trend starts back in time, but it ends with last moment you checked. Collectively that information is near real time. An inference is a conjecture that allows you to deduce what is going on, and in many cases our wonderful human brain can instantly draw conclusions about what it all means to respond with a next action. If I am driving in the fast lane, the passing lane, of the German autobahn, and I see a BMW approaching me, then I should shift to the slow lane. In some cases your inference and subsequent alternative actions need to be validated. This is where the symbolism of the windshield comes in. The ability to project what-if scenarios is powerful because then you can select the best alternative—strive for optimization.

There is an important aspect of this automobile analogy that is missing—fuel efficiency. Performance management as a framework has arguably been around for decades (although information technology research firms, like the Gartner Group and IDC, have only recently tagged this new name in the late 1990s). However, just as a poorly performing car that has some broken gears, tires out of alignment, and gunky lubrication will yield poor mileage, poorly integrated methodologies, impure raw data, and lack of digitization and analytics result in a poor rate of shareholder wealth creation. The full vision of performance management removes the friction and vibration and weak torque to optimize the consumption of the organization's resources—its employees and spending—and gets the organization to its strategy destination faster, cheaper, and smarter. The result is a higher shareholder wealth creation yield.

Finally, as mentioned, a strategy is never static; it is constantly adjusted. This means that the destination input to the GPS navigator is constantly changing. This places increasing importance on predictive analytics to determine what is the best destination for stakeholders. How much longer do you want to drive your existing automobile when a performance management car with a GPS is now available to lift wealth creation efficiency and yield?

HOW IS YOUR ORGANIZATION DIFFERENT FROM TIGER WOODS?

If you play golf, you know how frustrating it is to try to improve your score. Similarly organizations striving to improve results know that raising performance can be frustrating. But Tiger Woods, the greatest golfer today, rarely seems to be frustrated. How is your organization different from Tiger Woods? The answer is about one foot. Tiger Woods may be just over six feet tall, but where he excels and differs from everyone is in his upper five feet!

In golf, the immediate result of your golf stroke is in where the club head strikes the ball. But how far and where the ball goes is all about what happens above. It is Tiger Woods' arms and body movement that control his swing. The club head simply carries out the action.

How is this comparison similar to performance management? The problem with most organizations is their performance management systems put too much emphasis on their financial and aggregate outcome results. These are after-the-fact lagging indicators. They are the golf-club head. These companies need to shift their emphasis to the influencing leading indicators. They need to work on the upper-body golf-club swing.

An organization's balanced scorecard and supporting dashboards are intended to improve an organization's performance. But there is little consensus as to how scorecards differ from dashboards. Worse yet, organizations typically have far too many key performance indicators (KPIs) reported in their scorecard, many financial measures, that arguably should be reported as operational performance indicators in their dashboards. In any golf shot the bottom 12 inches is what you did. Everything above that is what you need to do next—to improve results.

ARE FAILURES DUE TO ARROGANCE, IGNORANCE, OR INEXPERIENCE?

Some proposed management improvement methodologies, such as the lights-out manufacturing factory touted in the 1980s as a manufacturing facility totally automated with machines and parts conveyers that do not require workers, are fads that come and go. But the strategy map and its companion balanced scorecard for feedback are certain to be a *sustained* methodology in the long term—perhaps forever. It is logical. The executive's role is to set direction by formulating strategic objectives, and then the managers and employee teams should be involved in determining how to accomplish each objective. Are the early-twenty-first-century missteps and misunderstandings in implementing the balanced scorecard due to arrogance, ignorance, or inexperience? I suggest they are due to inexperience.

Conflict and tension are natural in all organizations. Therefore, it takes time for managers and employees to stabilize a behavioral measurement mechanism of cause-and-effect KPIs, to distinguish between KPIs and PIs, and then to get mastery in how to use both of these types of measures to navigate, power, and steer as an integrated enterprise. As stated by the author Peter Senge,[2] who was a thought leader in the field of organizational change management, the differentiator between successful and failing organizations will be the *rate*, and not just the amount, of organizational learning. Intangible assets—employees as knowledge workers and the information provided to them—are what truly power the performance management framework.

NOTES

1. Robert S. Kaplan and David P. Norton, *The Balanced Scorecard: Translating Strategy into Action* (Boston: Harvard Business School Press, 1996).

2. Peter M. Senge, *The Fifth Discipline: The Art and Practice of the Learning Organization* (New York: Doubleday, 1990).

Chapter 18

How Are Balanced Scorecards and Dashboards Different?

There is confusion regarding the difference between a balanced scorecard and a dashboard. There is similar confusion differentiating key performance indicators (KPIs) from the normal and routine measures that we refer to merely as performance indicators (PIs). The adjective *key* of a KPI is the operative term. An organization has only so many resources and so much energy to focus. To use a radio analogy, KPIs are what distinguish the signals from the noise—the measures of progress toward strategy execution. As a negative result of this confusion, organizations are including an excessive number of PIs in a scorecard system that should be restricted to KPIs.

One misconception about the balanced scorecard is that its primary purpose is to monitor results. That is secondary. Its primary purposes are to report the carefully selected measures that reflect the strategic intent of the executive team, and then enable ongoing understanding as to what should be done to align the organization's work and priorities to attain the executive team's strategic objectives. The strategic objectives ideally should be articulated in a strategy map, which serves as the visual vehicle from which to identify the projects and initiatives needed to accomplish each objective, or the specific core processes that the organization needs to excel at. After this step is completed, then KPIs are selected and their performance targets are set. With this understanding, it becomes apparent that the strategy map's companion scorecard, on its surface, serves more as a feedback mechanism to allow everyone in the organization, from frontline workers up to the executive team, to answer the question: "How are we doing on what is important?" The scorecard should also facilitate analysis to know *why*. The idea is not to just *monitor* the dials but to *move* the dials.

THE VITAL FEW VERSUS THE TRIVIAL MANY

Michael Hammer, the author who introduced the concept of business process re-engineering, described the sad situation of measurement abuse in his book, *The Agenda: What Every Business Must Do to Dominate the Decade*:

> In the real world . . . a company's measurement systems typically deliver a blizzard of nearly meaningless data that quantifies practically everything in sight, no matter how

unimportant; that is devoid of any particular rhyme or reason; that is so voluminous as to be unusable; that is delivered so late as to be virtually useless; and that then languishes in printouts and briefing books without being put to any significant purpose. . . . In short, measurement is a mess. . . . We measure far too much and get far too little for what we measure because we never articulated what we need to get better at, and our measures aren't tied together to support higher-level decision making.[1]

Hammer is clearly not hiding his feelings. But has the cure been worse than the ailment? Simply reducing the number of measures can still result in an organization measuring what it *can* measure as opposed to what it *should* measure. But to determine what you *should* measure requires deeper understanding of the underlying purposes of a balanced scorecard relative to a dashboard.

SCORECARDS AND DASHBOARDS SERVE DIFFERENT PURPOSES

The terms *scorecard* and *dashboard* have a tendency to be used interchangeably, but each brings a different set of capabilities. The sources of the confusion are:

- Both represent a way to track results.
- Both make use of traffic lights, dials, sliders, and other visual aids.
- Both can have targets, thresholds, and alert messages.
- Both can provide drill-down to other metrics and reports.

The difference comes from the context in which they are applied. Historically, as busy executives and managers have struggled to keep up with the amount of information being thrust at them, the device of traffic lighting has been applied to virtually any and all types of reporting. As technology has improved, more bells and whistles have been added; an example is the ability to link to other reports and to drill down to finer levels of detail. The common denominator is speed in focusing on something that requires action or further investigation. The terminology evolved to reflect how technology vendors described what provided this capability. As a consequence, *dashboard* and *scorecard* are being used interchangeably.

Exhibit 18.1 illustrates the difference between scorecards and dashboards using a taxonomy starting with all measurements in general. Scorecards and dashboards are not contradictory; they are used for different purposes.

At the top of the exhibit is the realm of scorecards. *Scorecards* are intended to be *strategic*. They align the behavior of employees and partners with the strategic objectives formulated by the executive team. In contrast, *dashboards,* at the bottom of the exhibit, are intended to be *operational*.

Some refer to dashboards as "dumb" reporting and scorecards as "intelligent" reporting. The reason is that dashboards are primarily for data visualization; they display what is happening during a given time period. Most organizations begin with

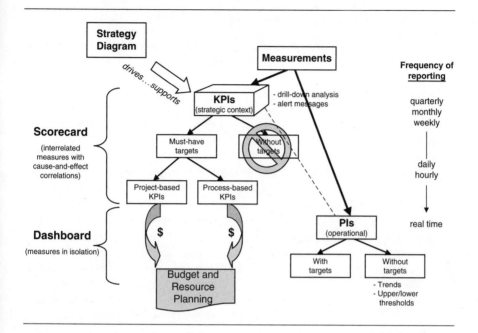

Exhibit 18.1 Scorecard versus Dashboard
Source: © Gary Cokins. Used with permission.

identifying what they are already measuring and construct a dashboard dial from there. However, dashboards do not communicate why something matters, why someone should care about the reported measure, or what the impact would be if an undesirable declining measure continues. In short, dashboards report what you *can* measure.

In contrast, a scorecard provides the information lacking in dashboards. A scorecard additionally answers questions by providing deeper analysis, drill-down capabilities, traffic-light alert messaging, and forecasting for inferences of performance potential to determine motivational targets. Scorecards do not start with the existing data; rather they begin with identifying which strategic projects to complete and core processes to improve and excel in.

The selection and validation of the correct or best KPIs is a constant debate. Statistical correlation interaction analysis among KPIs can determine the degree of influence and "lift" that various cascaded KPIs have on the higher-level enterprise-wide KPIs—hence correlation analysis validates or improves the KPI selection. In addition, this type of analysis can automatically uncover previously unknown statistical relationships that may suggest cause and effect and can be used for predictive power. You want to make changes based on anticipated targets and constantly refocused outcomes so that employees can proactively make changes *before* unexpected events occur, instead of allowing for the much more expensive after-the-fact reaction. In short, scorecards report what you *should* measure.

Here are some guidelines for understanding the differences:[2]

- *Scorecards chart progress toward strategic objectives.* A scorecard displays periodic snapshots of performance associated with an organization's strategic objectives and plans. It measures organizational activity at a summary level against predefined targets to see whether performance is within acceptable ranges. Its selection of KPIs helps executives communicate strategy to employees and focuses users on the highest-priority projects, initiatives, actions, and tasks required to execute plans. The adjective *key* differentiates KPIs from the PIs reported in dashboards.

  Scorecard KPIs ideally should be derived from a strategy map rather than being just a list of important measures that the executives have requested to be reported. Regardless of whether the Kaplan and Norton[3]–suggested four stacked perspectives are used, or some variant of them, scorecard KPIs should have cause-and-effect linkages (e.g., statistical correlations). Directionally upward from the employee-centric innovation, learning, and growth perspectives, the KPIs should reveal the cumulative build of potential-to-realized economic value.

  There are two key distinctions of scorecards: (1) Each KPI *must* require a predefined target measure; and (2) KPIs should be comprised of both project-based KPIs (e.g., milestones, progress percentage of completion, degree of planned versus accomplished outcome) and process-based KPIs (e.g., percent on-time delivery versus customer promise dates). A scorecard comprised mainly or exclusively of process-based KPIs is not an efficient engine of change; it merely monitors whether progress from the traditional drivers of improvement, such as quality or cycle-time improvement, is occurring. Process improvement is important, but innovation and change are even more so.

- *Dashboards monitor and measure processes.* A dashboard, however, is operational, and reports information typically more frequently than scorecards and usually with measures. Each dashboard measure is reported with little regard to its relationship to other dashboard measures. Dashboard measures do not directly reflect the context of strategic objectives.

  This information can be more real time in nature, like an automobile dashboard that lets drivers check their current speed, fuel level, and engine temperature at a glance. It follows that a dashboard ideally should be linked directly to systems that capture events as they happen, and it should warn users through alerts or exception notifications when performance against any number of metrics deviates from the norm or what is expected.

The caution I have for organizations that are paying more attention to their performance measurements involves (1) the linkage of scorecard KPIs to the strategy diagram (often referred to as a *strategy map*) and also to the fiscal budget (as well as rolling financial forecasts); and (2) the linkage of dashboard PIs selected to influence behavior that will ultimately result in achieving or exceeding the KPI targets. Strategy diagrams and the budget are located in Exhibit 18.1 and are described below.

SCORECARDS LINK EXECUTIVES' STRATEGY TO OPERATIONS AND TO THE BUDGET

A *strategy diagram* is located in the upper left of Exhibit 18.1. The exhibit denotes that KPIs should be *derived from* the executives' strategic objectives and plans. If KPIs are selected independently of the strategy, then they will likely report only what *can* be measured as opposed to what *should* be measured. Failure to execute a strategy is one of a chief executive officer's major concerns; therefore KPIs should reflect either mission-critical projects and initiatives or core business processes that must be excelled at. (Hence there is need for both project-based and process-based KPIs.)

The budget (and, increasingly, rolling financial forecasts) should be derived from the required funding of the projects (i.e., the nonrecurring strategy expenses and capital investments) and of the operational processes (i.e., the recurring operational capacity-related expenses that vary with driver volumes, such as customer demand).

A strategy is dynamic, never static, as executives appropriately shift directions based on their new insights and observations. Reliably accurate forecasting is critical for both strategy formulation and future resource capacity management. Hence, both the KPIs and the necessary funding to realize the strategic plans will continuously be derived from the "living" strategy diagram.

DASHBOARDS MOVE THE SCORECARD'S DIALS

The organization's traction and torque is reflected in the dashboard's PI measures—the more frequently reported operational measures. Although some PIs may have predefined targets, PIs serve more to monitor trends across time or results against upper or lower threshold limits. As PIs are monitored and responded to, the corrective actions will contribute to achieving the KPI target levels with actual results.

Cause-and-effect relationships between and among measures underlie the entire approach to integrating strategy diagrams (formulation), scorecards (appraisal), dashboards (execution), and fiscal budgets (the fuel).

STRATEGY IS MORE THAN PERFORMING BETTER: IT INVOLVES DOING DIFFERENT THINGS

A key to organizational survival involves differentiation from competitors. An important role of the executive team is to exhibit vision and constantly determine innovation to differentiate their organization from others. This explains the misunderstanding about strategic objectives. Some mistakenly believe the purpose of strategic objectives is to keep an organization bound to a single, unbroken path. This is certainly not the case. As mentioned earlier, strategy is dynamic, not static. The purpose of strategic objectives in a strategy map is to redirect the organization from the tyranny of maintaining the status quo. Strategy is about constant change. If an organization does not constantly change, then it is exposed to competitors constantly converging to similar products, services, and processes. Differentiation is key to maintaining a competitive edge. Strategic objectives are about the changes an organization should make to maintain a competitive edge.

Dashboards and scorecards are not mutually exclusive. In fact, the best dashboards and scorecards merge elements from one another.

A simple rule is to use the term *dashboard* when you merely want to keep score, as in a sports event, and use the term *scorecard* when you want to understand the context of key scores in terms of how they influence achievement of strategic outcomes. A scorecard's measures will be fewer in number—they are strategic and carry more weight and influence. In contrast, dashboard measures could number in the hundreds or thousands—you still need a way to quickly focus on the unfavorable-to-target ones for tactical action. However, action with respect to a single metric in a dashboard is less likely to change strategic outcomes as dramatically as compared to action on metrics reported in a scorecard.

In general, scorecard KPIs are associated with the domain of the performance management framework. In contrast, dashboard PIs are associated with business intelligence (see Chapter 10, "How Do Business Intelligence and Performance Management Fit Together?").

GETTING PAST THE SPEED BUMPS

I believe that the scorecard and dashboard components of commercial performance management software should have predefined KPIs. However, for the integrated software component that reports measurements, the vendor's software should deliberately come with a limited rather than a comprehensive selection of KPIs that are commonly used by each type of industry. The purpose of providing standard KPIs should be merely to jump-start an organization's construction and implementation of its scorecard/dashboard system.

The reason for *not* providing a comprehensive and exhaustive list of industry-specific measures is that caution is needed whenever an organization is identifying its measures. Measures drive employee behavior. Caution is needed for two major reasons:

1. Measures should be tailored to an organization's unique needs.
2. Organizations should understand the basic concepts that differentiate scorecards from dashboards and KPIs from PIs.

I would like to see organizations successfully implement and sustain an integrated strategic scorecard and operational dashboard system. Organizations should understand the distinctions described here. This is why I caution against simply using an out-of-the-box list of various industries' common KPIs and PIs regardless of their source.

As with any improvement methodology, experience through use refines the methodology's effectiveness and impact. The plan-do-check-act cycle is a great practice for learning organizations. With improvement methodologies, it can be difficult to "get it perfectly right" the first time. There will always be a learning curve. Many organizations overplan and underexecute. With regard to KPI and PI selection, first learn the principles, and then apply them through selecting, monitoring, and refining the KPIs. Strategy maps and balanced scorecards are a craft, not a science.

NOTES

1. Michael Hammer, *The Agenda: What Every Business Must Do to Dominate the Decade* (New York: Crown Business, 2001), p. 101.

2. Wayne W. Eckerson, *Performance Dashboards: Measuring, Monitoring, and Managing Your Business* (Hoboken, NJ: John Wiley & Sons, 2006), p. 8.

3. Robert S. Kaplan and David P. Norton, *The Balanced Socrecard: Translating Strategy into Action* (Boston: Harvard Business School Press, 1996).

Chapter 19

When Performance Management Becomes Surgery

Change is now a given. Most of us accept that we have little control of forces and pressures that impact our organizations, our executive leaders, the managers we report to, and ultimately ourselves. Fighting or resisting change can be a fool's errand in many situations—often you have to go with the flow. What are the conditions when the magnitude of the change is tsunami-like rather than just a big wave? How does an organization survive unusually large pressures? What role can the performance management framework play in engineering the change so that the result will be a stronger organization?

One example of a large force might be an aggressive competitor, such as when Netflix's mailbox approach to renting movie DVDs horned in on Blockbuster's drive-to-store business. Another example might be a substantial technology shift, such as when compact discs replaced tapes. Regardless of the change stimulant, today the required reaction by executives, managers, and employees is often extraordinary, compared to what they had to cope with earlier in their careers.

THE LARGER THE CHANGE, THE GREATER THE RISK OF FAILURE

According to a 2006 survey by McKinsey & Company cited in the Winter 2007 *McKinsey Quarterly*, only 38% of the global executives who responded claimed that the largest organizational transformation that they experienced was "mostly successful." Around 10% said it was "mostly unsuccessful."[1]

The article's authors referenced this study to determine what makes the difference between big changes that work and those that do not. The two most critical success factors for executives from their findings are: (1) to describe their vision of the new direction in which the organization should go, and inspire their workforce to go there; and (2) to generate the ideas and motivation—as I would say, the *traction*—to gain speed for the journey.

How can we place these prerequisites into the context and language of performance management? Competence in using strategy maps and balanced scorecards helps prepare an organization to quickly shift, turn the organizational steering wheel, and step on the fuel pedal. But the executives cannot do it alone. Many hands are needed—namely, the managers and workforce. Executives who are reluctant to communicate their vision and the strategic objectives needed to achieve it will likely fail or fall short. As evidence, a March 2006 survey by the Balanced Scorecard Collaborative[2] asked the respondents whether they had a formal strategy execution process in place. Seventy percent of the "yes" respondents described their organization's current performance as "breakthrough results or better than our peers." In stark contrast, 73% of the "no" respondents described their performance as "same as or below our peers." This provides proof that formally managing the strategy is superior to a laissez-faire approach.

Producing and monitoring a balanced scorecard is not enough. Far more important is for the executives to *clearly* communicate their strategy in a way that managers and employee teams can understand it—with the strategy map. My conversations with external consultants and internal scorecard project champions has unscientifically led me to conclude that despite executives' relatively high interest in developing and reporting scorecard key performance indicators (KPIs), relatively few bother to invest energy in first creating the strategy map from which to derive their KPIs.

ARROGANCE, IGNORANCE, DELUSION, OR SOMETHING ELSE?

The strategy map has progressed from an art form to a *craft*. It may never be a science. But its becoming a craft, like carpentry, is a good thing. Executives who practice the craft of strategy mapping can move well past the stick-and-rudder approach to navigating their organizations toward higher economic value. For example, the traditional design of strategy maps, with their displays of connected strategic objectives as bubbles and traditional four-layer perspectives, is evolving into occasionally five or more layers, such as an "improve safety" perspective layer for chemical companies. More notably, the vertically connected strategic objectives in the map are naturally appearing in the linked form of streams representing *strategic themes*, such as "customer revenue growth" or "cost productivity."

It is not the intent of this chapter to describe the wonderful progress being made in strategy map design. You can research that on the Internet. It is to discuss the reasons why so few organizations deploy a strategy map at the onset of their journey to more formally manage the execution of their executives' strategy. The larger the change, the more important it is to take a formal approach. Strategy maps support the McKinsey & Company critical success factors of executives describing their vision and stimulating ideas and initiatives to realize the vision. Organizational surgery is needed, and not just an examination.

Some companies have said that one reason for not applying the strategy map is that they tried it, and it did not work. To me, that is an excuse. My take on this explanation is that the consultant or designer did not have sufficient experience to develop an effective strategy map from which the identified projects, core processes to excel at, and associated KPIs can all be derived.

Another reason I have heard is that the executives simply do not believe the strategy they have in their heads can be drawn on paper. I say *rubbish*—that is another excuse. Beethoven had the notes of his symphonies in his head, and not only did they get onto paper (i.e., sheet music), but generations of people continue to marvel at the results of collective sounds executed by the string, wind, brass, and percussion instruments for which Beethoven wrote those notes.

I did challenge a chief executive officer's (CEO's) rationale for not using the strategy map from which to derive the scorecard and its KPIs. He scolded me for being insubordinate. (*Note to self:* Be more careful asking CEOs strategy map questions.) I do not know whether executives' reluctance formally to map their strategy is due to arrogance, ignorance, or the delusion that they have a better way (such as the *management by objectives* approach, where the objectives are typically not linked!).

URGENCY MEANS *NOW*

If your organization is drifting sideways or not living up to what you believe is its full potential, then maybe your executive team's seat-of-the-pants, planning-spreadsheets-on-steroids, and death-by-PowerPoint approaches to strategy management are insufficient. Those approaches do not have enough discipline or rigor. Urgency means *now*, where I come from. Delaying the adoption of performance management methodologies may lead to a worsening condition.

Research conducted by myself and my colleague Bob Paladino shows that the companies with the best performance management practices are the ones with a corporate performance management office and officer.[3] Strategy execution is too important to be a part-time job of the chief operating officer, chief financial officer, or strategic planning vice president. It needs a formally dedicated manager with strategy execution competence. When that tsunami-like radical change requirement eventually comes, one should want its managers to guide the transformation in an organized, not chaotic, manner.

NOTES

1. Andreas Beroutsos, Andrew Freeman, and Conor F. Kehoe, "What public companies can learn from private equity," *The Mckinsey Quarterly,* Winter 2007.

2. www.bscol.com.

3. Gary Cokins and Bob Paladino, "Performance Promotion: Why CPM Needs Its Own Office," *Business Performance Management* (http://www.bpm.com), August 2007, pp. 18–22.

Part Six

Financial Performance Management

It is a common criticism of cost accountants that they spend too much time in working out elaborate distributions of expenses which are unimportant in themselves and which do not permit of an accurate distribution. Undoubtedly some of that criticism is deserved, but it should also be remembered that once the basis for distribution has been worked out, it can generally continue in use for some time.

—H. G. Crockett,
"Some Problems in the Actual Installation of Cost Systems"

Several times in this book I mention that maximizing shareholder wealth creation is not a goal—it is a result. It is a result of improving performance by integrating and synchronizing the components of the performance management framework and embedding it with analytics of all flavors. However, aggregate, after-the-fact financial reporting typically done for external use (e.g., by investors or government regulators) is much different from the application of internal managerial accounting used to support decision making. The purpose of managerial accounting information is to support decisions to create value.

Part Six begins with a chapter that has a somewhat sarcastic view of accountants and their traditional practices. The chapters that follow in this part of the text describe basic principles that accountants can apply for more accurate costing with greater transparency and visibility, and how these same practices can be applied to improve budgeting, resource capacity planning, and rolling financial projections that link the organization's strategy to operational spending.

The concluding chapter differentiates managerial accounting from financial accounting. This is important to understand, because accounting practices for external purposes, which comply with rules and laws defined by governments, can be misleading when used in making internal decisions.

Chapter 20

Do Accountants Lead or Mislead?

Over the past few years, I have discussed a paradox with Doug Hicks, president of D.T. Hicks & Co., a performance-improvement consulting firm in Farmington Hills, MI. The paradox, which continues to puzzle me, is how chief financial officers (CFOs) and controllers can be aware that their managerial accounting data is flawed and misleading, yet not take action to do anything about it.

I am not referring to the financial accounting data used for external reporting; that information passes strict audits. I am referring to the managerial accounting used internally for analysis and decisions. For this data, there is no governmental regulatory agency enforcing rules, so the CFO can apply any accounting practice he or she likes. For example, the CFO may choose to allocate substantial indirect expenses for product and standard service-line costs based on broadly averaged allocation factors, such as number of employees or sales dollars. The vast differences among products mean each product is unique in its consumption of expenses throughout various business processes and departments, with no relation to the arbitrary cost factor chosen by the CFO. By not tracing those indirect costs to outputs based on true cause-and-effect relationships—called *drivers*—some product costs become undervalued and others overvalued. It is a zero-sum-error situation.

PERILS OF POOR NAVIGATION EQUIPMENT

I speculated to Doug that I think some CFOs and controllers are simply lazy. They do not want to do any extra work. Doug explained this counterintuitive phenomenon using a fable:

> Imagine that several centuries ago there was a navigator who served on a wooden sailing ship that regularly sailed through dangerous waters. It was the navigator's job to make sure the captain always knew where the ship had been, where it was, and how to safely and efficiently move the ship from one point to another. In the performance of his duties, the navigator relied on a set of sophisticated instruments. Without the effective functioning of these instruments, it would be impossible for him to chart the safest and most efficient course for the ship to follow.

> One day the navigator realized that one of his most important instruments was calibrated incorrectly. As a result, he provided the captain inaccurate navigational

information to use in making the decisions necessary to safely and efficiently direct the ship. No one but the navigator knew of this calibration problem, and the navigator decided not to inform the captain. He was afraid that the captain would blame him for not detecting the problem sooner and then require him to find a way to report the measurements more accurately. That would require a lot of work.

As a result, the navigator always made sure he slept near a lifeboat, so that if the erroneous navigational information led to a disaster, he would not go down with the ship. Eventually, the ship hit a reef that the captain believed to be miles away. The ship was lost, the cargo was lost, and many sailors lost their lives. The navigator, always in close proximity to the lifeboats, survived the sinking and later became the navigator on another ship.

PERILS OF POOR MANAGERIAL ACCOUNTING

Doug continued on with his story:

Centuries later, there was a management accountant who worked for a company in which a great deal of money was invested. It was the job of this management accountant to provide information on how the company had performed, its current financial position, and the likely consequences of decisions being considered by the company's president and managers. In the performance of his duties, the management accountant relied on a managerial cost accounting system that was believed to represent the economics of the company. Without the effective functioning of the costing practices reported from this system, it would be impossible for the accountant to provide the president with the accurate and relevant cost information he needed to make economically sound decisions.

One day the management accountant realized that the calculations and practices on which the cost system was based were incorrect. It did not reflect the economic realities of the company. The input data was correct, but the reported information was flawed. As a result, the current and forward-looking information he provided to support the president's decision making was incorrect. No one but the management accountant knew this problem existed. He decided not to inform the president. He was afraid that the president would blame him for not detecting the problem sooner and then require him to go through the agonizing effort of developing and implementing a new, more accurate and relevant cost system. That would require a lot of work.

Meanwhile, the management accountant always made sure he kept his network with other professionals intact in case he had to find another position. Not surprisingly, the president's poorly informed pricing, investment, and other decisions led the company into bankruptcy. The company went out of business, the owners lost their investment, creditors incurred financial losses, and many hardworking employees lost their jobs. However, the management accountant easily found a job at another company.

THE ACCOUNTANT AS A BAD NAVIGATOR

What is the moral of the story? The *2003 Survey of Best Accounting Practices*, conducted by Ernst & Young and the Institute of Management Accountants, showed that 98% of the top financial executives surveyed believed that the cost information they supplied management to support their decisions was inaccurate. It further revealed that 80% of those financial executives did not plan on doing anything about it.

The widely accepted solution is to apply activity-based cost (ABC) principles—not just to product and standard service-line costs but to various types of distribution channels and types of customers. The goal is to apply direct costs to whatever consumes resources. For resources that are shared, these costs are to be traced using measurable drivers that reflect the consumption rate—not arbitrary cost allocations.

When one compares the properly calculated costs and profit margins using ABC principles to costing methods that violate the key accounting principle of cause and effect, the differences are surprising huge: The company makes and loses money in opposite areas from what the numbers show. This creates false beliefs throughout the organization.

Why do so many accountants behave so irresponsibly? The list of answers is long. Some believe the error is not that big. Some think that extra administrative effort required to collect and calculate the new information will not offset the benefits of better decision making. Some think costs do not matter, because the focus should be on sales growth. Whatever reasons are cited, accountants' resistance to change is based less on ignorance and more on misconceptions about accurate costing.

Doug Hicks observed to me: "Today commercial ABC software and their associated analytics have dramatically reduced the effort to report good managerial accounting information, and the benefits are widely heralded." Furthermore, the preferred ABC implementation method is rapid prototyping with iteratively scaled modeling, which has destroyed myths about ABC being too complicated. By leveraging only a few key employees and lots of estimates, usable ABC results as a repeatable reporting system are produced in weeks, not years. A survey by www.bettermanagement.com reported that the number-one challenge in implementing ABC is designing and building the model, which is what the rapid prototyping method solves—make your mistakes early and often.

Reasonably accurate cost and profit information is one of the pillars of performance management's portfolio of integrated methodologies. Accountants unwilling to adopt logical costing methods, and managers who tolerate the perpetuation of flawed reporting, should change their ways. Stay on the ship or get off before real damage is done.

Chapter 21

Confusion with Managerial Accounting

An organization's managerial accounting system design can help or hinder its journey toward completing the full vision of performance management as I have been defining it. It is understandable that people without financial background and training have difficulty understanding accounting—for many, accounting is outside their comfort zone. But there is a gathering storm in the community of management accountants where the need for *advanced* accounting techniques (e.g., activity-based costing [ABC], resource consumption accounting, lean accounting, time-driven activity-based accounting) is confusing even the trained accountants and the seasoned practitioners. What is the problem?

The fields of law and medicine advance each decade because their body of knowledge is codified. Attorneys and physicians stand on the shoulders of their predecessors' captured learning. In a sense, the generally accepted accounting principles (GAAP) published by the Financial Accounting Standards Board and the International Financial Reporting Standards (IFRS) organization have also codified rules and principles (though with lots of loopholes). Accounting standards support external reporting for government regulatory agencies and bankers. Unfortunately, unlike financial accounting, with its codification, managerial accounting has no such framework or set of universal standards. Accountants are left to their own devices, which are typically the methods and treatments at their organization that they inherit from their predecessors. Accountants burn the midnight oil with lots of daily problems to solve, so getting around to improving (or reforming) their organization's management accounting information to benefit their managers and employees is not a frequent routine. The escalation of global compliance reporting, such as with Sarbanes-Oxley, is a major distraction from investing time to evaluate improvements to the organization's managerial accounting system.

But in managerial accounting, although rules are many, principles are few. Sadly, many accountants were apparently absent from school the day the teacher defined the purpose of managerial accounting as *to provide data that influences people's behavior and supports good planning, control, and decision making.* Of course, how to apply cost information for decision support can lead to heated debates. For example, what is the incremental cost of taking and delivering one additional customer order? For starters, the answer depends on several assumptions; but if the debaters agree on them, then the robustness of the costing system and the resulting accuracy requirement to make the correct decision to answer that question might justify an advanced costing methodology.

Another accounting principle is "precision is a myth"—there is no such thing as a *correct* cost because the cost of a thing is determined (i.e., calculated) based on assumptions that an organization has latitude to make. For example, should we include or exclude a *sunk* cost like equipment depreciation in a product's cost? The answer depends on the type of decision being made. It is this latitude that is causing increasing confusion among accountants. If we step back for a better view, we can see that an organization can refine its managerial accounting system over time through various stages of maturity. Changes to managerial accounting methods and treatments are typically not continuous, but occur as infrequent and sizably punctuated reforms.

Let me be clear that the topic we are discussing is managerial accounting. Under the big umbrella of accounting there is also bookkeeping, financial accounting for external reporting, and tax accounting. Those are peripheral to performance management. Management accounting information should be viewed as having two broad purposes:

1. *Cost autopsy (historical, descriptive).* This information uses cost accounting information for analysis of what already happened in past time periods. Types of analysis include actual versus budgeted spending for cost variance analysis, activity cost analysis, benchmarking, and performance measure monitoring.
2. *Decision support (future, predictive).* This planning and control information serves for economic analysis to support decisions to drive improvement. It involves numerous assumptions such as what-if volume and mix based on projections, and draws on prior economic cost behavior for its calculations. Types of analysis include price and profit margin analysis, capital expenditures, outsourcing and make-or-buy decisions, project evaluation, incremental (or marginal) cost analysis, and rationalization of products, channels, and customers.

To be clear, the relatively higher value-add for performance improvement comes from decision support as compared to cost autopsy reporting. The good news is that the administrative effort for decision support is relatively less because the source information is typically used as needed and for infrequent decisions, such as when setting catalog or list prices, rather than for daily operations. However, some organizations must daily quote prices for custom orders to a wide variety of customers, so it is important their cost modeling supports profit margins—whether they are on an incremental or fully absorbed cost basis.

HISTORICAL EVOLUTION OF MANAGERIAL ACCOUNTING

If we travel back through time and revisit the weeks in which an organization's *managerial* accounting system was initially architected, we first realize that it is a spinoff or variant of the ongoing *financial* accounting system already in place. The nature of the organization's purpose and economic conditions it faces governed the initial financial accounting system design. So, for example, if the organization's output is nonrecurring with a relatively short life cycle, like constructing a building or executing a consulting engagement, then project accounting is the more appropriate method—a very high form of direct costing. Similarly, if the organization is a manufacturer of unique one-time engineer-to-order products, then they will likely begin with a job-order cost accounting scheme.

In contrast, if the products made or standard service lines delivered (e.g., a bank loan) are continuously recurring, as consequently will be the associated employee work activities, then the initial financial accounting method would likely take on a standard costing approach (of which ABC is simply a variant), where the repeating material requirements and labor time/effort of work tasks is first measured and then the equivalent costs for both direct material and labor are assumed as a constant average and applied in total based on the quantity and volume of output—products made or services delivered. Of course, the actual expenses paid each accounting period to third parties and employees will always differ slightly from these averaged costs that were calculated "at standard," so there are various methods of cost variance analysis (e.g., volume variance, labor rate or price variance, etc.) to report what actually happened relative to what was planned and expected.

The overarching point here is that an organization's initial condition—the types of products and services it makes and delivers as well as its expense structure—governs its initial costing methodology.

SHARED AND INDIRECT EXPENSES

An organization that was founded with recurring products and work, typically with longer product life cycles, cannot last long as a one-trick pony. Inevitably, proliferation of different types of products (e.g., more colors, sizes, and ranges) occurs, or standard service lines evolve, in order for it to remain a viable organization. Innovation is key to any organization's survival. Increases in the diversity and variation (i.e., heterogeneity) of outputs quickly result in complexity, which in turn causes the need to add support people and system resources to manage the increasing complexity. Gradually, these support-related expenses are no longer insignificant or immaterial. Exhibit 21.1 illustrates how over the decades, indirect expenses have been displacing direct expenses for this reason.

As a result of this accelerating relative growth of indirect to direct costs, organizational managers begin requesting visibility of these costs, too, not only as part of the organization's monthly expenses (i.e., inputs) but also as they are associated with each product or standard service line—the *calculated* costs of outputs.

This need by managers to view output costs consumed, not just input expenses incurred and money spent, ultimately leads an organization to experience one of those punctuated reform changes along the accounting system's stages of maturity—full absorption costing with *overhead* cost allocations of the indirect and shared expenses.

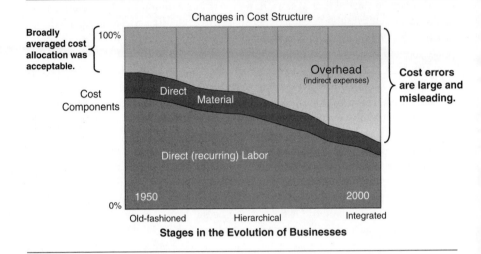

Changes in Cost Structure

Exhibit 21.1 Need for Tracing, Not Allocating, Costs
Source: © Gary Cokins. Used with permission.

This stage of maturity is where concepts such as support department–to–support department stepdown overhead expense allocation evolved, and in the 1980s, its more granular allocation method—ABC. Many organizations now realize that their predecessor accountants' past method of choice was a single convenient cost allocation factor that simplistically relies on broad-based averages (such as number of output units produced or labor input hours) as the factor or basis for the overhead cost allocation to products or service lines. Hence, using that method, the true cost of each product or standard service line does not reflect the true consumption of the portion of the indirect resources that each product or service is uniquely consuming.

What are the consequences of misallocating costs? First, we must acknowledge that the descriptive view of expenses incurred (i.e., money spent in a historical past period) is a permanent irreversible event; any error in allocating that spending into calculated costs is a zero-sum-error game. As a result, some products will be over-cost and, therefore, all of the other products *must* be under-cost. Hence, the cost data being used by managers and employee teams for decisions or profit margin–validated pricing is somewhat (in many cases, grotesquely) flawed and misleading. ABC resolves this problem with its rational cause-and-effect cost tracing logic. It complies with accounting's causality principle. Exhibit 21.2 illustrates the basic concept of ABC transforming a department's expenses as captured in the general ledger accounting system into its calculated costs of work activities (that belong to business processes) and ultimately into its products, service lines, channels, and customers.

Exhibit 21.3 illustrates an organization's enterprise-wide expense structure flowing into the ultimate final costs of its end customers and its organizational

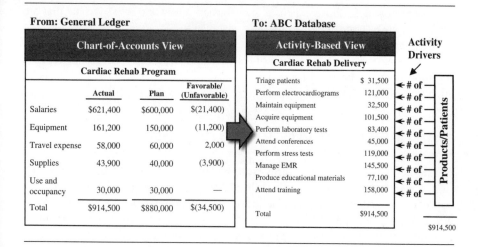

Exhibit 21.2 Each Activity Has Its Activity Cost Driver
Source: © Gary Cokins. Used with permission.

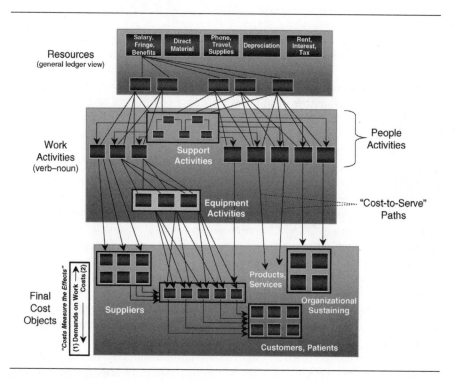

Exhibit 21.3 Activity-Based Cost/Management Cost Assignment Network
Source: © Gary Cokins. Used with permission.

sustaining cost (i.e., those expenses transformed into work activity costs that are not caused by or traceable to products or customers).

Equipped with a costing methodology that correctly models the consumption of resources based on accounting's causality principle, one can depend on its information to be valid for reliable analysis, control, planning, and decision support.

TIME-DRIVEN ACTIVITY-BASED COSTING

Before describing what one learns from better managerial accounting information, I want to briefly discuss time-driven activity-based costing (TDABC) because it has recently received attention as yet another advanced managerial accounting technique. When the condition exists that a substantial amount of resource expenses are in a highly repeatable process, such as for a credit card processing facility, the ABC model may replace the activity driver quantities with an average (i.e., standard) time required for each activity event. This method is referred to as *time-driven activity-based costing*.[1] As in what an atom is to an element, like carbon, in chemistry, time is the ultimate decomposed measurement for any activity driver. For example, an activity driver might be the number of automobile driver licenses processed daily for license bureau staff, say 200 per day. But 15 minutes per each processing event would be the time duration. A new license registration might take 25 minutes. A different number of atoms combine to make up the fundamental elements in chemistry. In costing, a different number of minutes are consumed for a single activity driver quantity of one.

One difference between TDABC and ABC as earlier described is that TDABC is capacity-sensitive and computes a standard activity cost using standard rates. That is, activity driver rates remain constant. In contrast, ABC is capacity-insensitive (but can be capacity-aware if known unused capacity in the resource is isolated and assigned to a business-sustaining final cost object). ABC computes the activity cost each period as "actual," and therefore the final cost object's unit cost fluctuates each period. TDABC requires an up-front investment to measure event times and to continuously maintain them. ABC simply requires activity quantities typically imported from operational systems.

Some argue that the magnitude of any organization's unused capacity rarely becomes substantial because of management by sight—managers can detect when employees have run out of work or have slowed down. Hence, quantifying unused capacity as a cost may not be a burning platform concern. If the extra incremental administrative effort to collect and maintain the detailed time data for TDABC does not exceed the incrementally more useful information (e.g., measuring unused capacity cost), then TDABC may not be justified. Applying activity driver quantities may be adequate.

WHAT DO PROPERLY TRACED COSTS REVEAL?

With valid cost modeling, Exhibit 21.4 displays a graph line at the top—referred to as the "profit cliff" of the true cumulative buildup of each product's profit, rank ordered from the most profitable to the least (often products at a financial loss where their costs exceed their revenues). The graph illustrates how *unrealized profits* can be hidden due to inadequate costing methods. The accountants are not properly assigning the expenditures based on the causality principle of accounting. The graph is of each product's cost, net of sales, to reveal *each* product's and service line's profit.

The products are rank sorted left to right from the largest to the smallest profit margin rate. The very last data point equals the firm's total net profit, as reported in its profit and loss statement. For this organization, total revenues were $20 million, with total expenses of $18 million, to net a $2 million profit, but the graph reveals the distribution of the mix of that $2 million net profit. Although not empirically tested, experiences with these measures show that the total amount of the profits, excluding any losses, usually exceeds 200% of the resulting reported net profit; greater than 1000% has even been measured.

The last data point in Exhibit 21.4 exactly equals the *total* reported profit, but that single point gives no visibility to the parts. Think of the last data point as being on a vertical metal track; it can slide only up or down. Looking at the graph this way reveals that products and service lines to the left of the peak, where an item's sales exactly offset its costs, are also fair game for increasing profits. Many people focus only on the losers to the right.

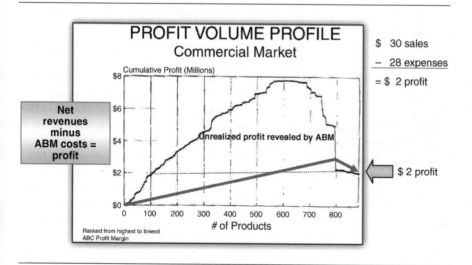

Exhibit 21.4   Cumulative Profit Distribution by Product
Source: © Gary Cokins. Used with permission.

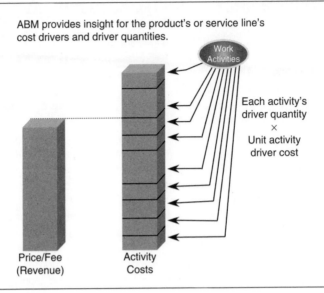

ABM provides insight for the product's or service line's cost drivers and driver quantities.

Work Activities

Each activity's driver quantity
×
Unit activity driver cost

Price/Fee (Revenue)

Activity Costs

Exhibit 21.5   Each Product's Activity Costs Pile Up
Source: © Gary Cokins. Used with permission.

ABC information is typically shocking to executives and managers since their prior belief from their traditional broadly averaged costing method is the flat graph line at the bottom with the small decline where each product's cost was distorted. This graph line has its accuracy removed by the broad-brush averaging of traditional cost allocations rather than tracing and assigning each activity cost using its proportionate activity cost driver.

Exhibit 21.5 clarifies the "profit cliff" exhibit. This exhibit provides visibility of each product's stack of consumed activity costs, which were not only hidden as a single lump-sum cost, but also distorted from the broadly averaged cost allocation method just described. It reveals the information that constitutes a single data point on the right down-sloping side of the graph. The exhibit illustrates that each product's, service line's, or customer's final cost object's activity costs have piled up in a stack.

Each product is in effect looking up and asking each work activity how much of that activity cost it consumed in the past period, and it stacks these costs like pancakes, where the thickness of the pancake reflects the quantity of the activity driver multiplied by the unit activity cost driver rate. This not only provides visibility into the indirect costs that were previously hidden and rendered inaccurate by the single broad-brushed average, but it also focuses workers on the driver of the cost. If the organization could reduce the quantity or frequency of the driver (or eliminate it altogether), then the height of the stacked cost will go down. To reduce costs, one must attack what causes them. The term *cost management* is an oxymoron. You do not really manage your costs, but rather you manage what causes your costs to occur. The assignment of activity costs to their cost objects comes from the ABM cost assignment network, where each activity driver and rate apportions the proper amount of activity costs consumed.

ACCOUNTING FOR LEAN MANAGEMENT: AN ALTERNATIVE OR COEXISTING COSTING METHOD?

Lean management can be described as a systematic approach to identifying and eliminating waste, including non–value-adding activities, through continuous improvement by flowing product or services at the pull of a customer, in pursuit of perfection. Lean management techniques increasingly are merging with Six Sigma quality initiatives to accelerate throughput via end-to-end processes. Productivity increases as throughput accelerates without adding resources or incurring errors.

Nonmonetary process data is foundational to continuous improvement projects. Employees are trained to use tools such as process flowcharts, checksheets, fishbone charts, Pareto diagrams, process control charts, histograms, and scattergrams. In addition, they measure movement of products or transactions, such as flow times and distances, as well as unplanned events such as product rework and errors.

A popular method to visualize and measure processes is *value stream mapping*. It removes the barriers of functional or departmental silos to aid improvement teams with better communications and decision making. Value stream maps support a lean management guideline to reveal visibility of the processes before moving forward with lean actions for improvement.

Exhibit 21.6 illustrates what activity costs look like as cost stacks in a value stream map. Each stack's height reflects the amount of resource expenses consumed,

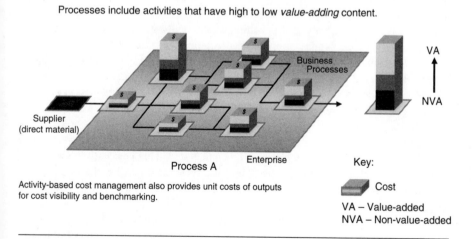

Processes include activities that have high to low *value-adding* content.

Supplier (direct material)

Business Processes

VA

NVA

Process A   Enterprise

Activity-based cost management also provides unit costs of outputs for cost visibility and benchmarking.

Key:

Cost

VA – Value-added
NVA – Non-value-added

Exhibit 21.6   Processes: Six Sigma, Lean Management, and Value Stream Mapping
Source: © Gary Cokins. Used with permission.

such as wages, supplies, or energy. Each cost stack can also be scored and tagged in monetary terms with attributes. Attributes are like the color of money; they do not change the amount of a cost but add insights into aspects or characteristics of what comprises the cost. Examples of attributes are the degrees of economic value-adding along the continuum or of cost-of-quality categories: (1) error free; (2) costs of conformance (prevention or appraisal activities); and (3) costs of nonconformance (internal failure or external failure related activities).

Each value stream may have multiple measures, such as for safety, quality, time, delivery, and cost. The last metric, cost, has spawned a method referred to as *lean accounting* or, more appropriately, *management accounting for a lean operations environment*. The management accounting community is currently wrestling with controversy, conflicts, and ambiguities caused by competing forms of accounting for lean management environments.

After providing a basic explanation of accounting for lean and its differences from commonly accepted costing principles, we can go on to discuss the issues and controversies.

For the purpose of more accurately measuring output costs, such as for products and services, plus to provide visibility and transparency into indirect or shared costs hidden by traditional broadly averaging standard costing methods, ABC has been adopted by many organizations. With the value stream mapping technique, work activities that are traced and reassigned to final cost objects with the ABC methodology are, in contrast, sequenced in time as a process flowchart. Think of this as pivoting on the activities in the ABC cost-assignment model and time-sequencing the activities in a different direction—not tracing and reassigning the costs, but rather accumulating them.

Accounting for lean is based in part on the idea that time is money. For example, a night's stay at a hotel might cost 11¢ per minute. Attending a music concert might be 63¢ per hour. An hour meeting with ten employees might be $6.50 per minute. Any value stream's cost-per-minute rate can be calculated as a ratio of its annual expenses (e.g., wages, supplies, depreciation, etc.) divided by the total minutes that resources worked, excluding holidays and a percent factor for coffee breaks, illness, and so on.

The other idea on which accounting for lean is based is to quantify *non-value-added costs*. For any value stream, first the calculated time of work to make error-free products or deliver error-free services based on that product's or service's average unit processing time (e.g., a bank teller's 4.26 minutes per customer), multiplied by the volume of units processed, is calculated. This cost is then subtracted from the total value stream expenses, and the difference can be classified as the *non-value-added (NVA) costs*. It is a total NVA cost amount with little visibility as to what it is made up of, and it assumes that no very diverse items were processed. That is, with accounting for lean, there would be no visibility of the cost stacks in Exhibit 21.6—only a single lump sum of the value stream expense and lump sum of the NVA. But at least it can calculate a financial figure that the traditional accounting spending or income statement cannot report.

My observation is that accounting for lean developed as a result of frustrations that managers and employee teams in operations had with traditional cost accounting's inability to evaluate lean projects for their cost savings potential or to measure improvements after they are completed. Additional frustrations from operations personnel involved questioning whether their daily efforts to collect transactional data were worth it, given that many operations people have found little use for actual-to-standard cost variance reporting. This frustration is understandable in light of what is now generally understood about deficiencies in traditional standard costing.

There is usefulness to line operations employees and managers in more clearly viewing and understanding the costs of their processes plus the elimination of some transactional paperwork no longer deemed useful, such as standard cost variance reporting. Accounting for lean attempts to solve some of operations' immediate financial measurement problems since as employees make improvements such as to eliminate NVA costs, reduce resources, and increase the rate of throughput in processes, they can measure productivity improvements that ultimately show up on the bottom line.

However, the previously mentioned conflict surfaces if the cost of outputs (not the resource expenses) of a value stream are calculated. This is because distortions from broad averages or the exclusion of applicable indirect expenses will be reported differently from the ABC tracing method. This conflict arises because ABC complies with a universal accounting principle—the principle of *causality*. The causality principle states that a cost should proportionately reflect the consumption of its inputs. In contrast, accounting for lean follows a flow principle as the guiding principle behind monetary management information.[2]

Accounting for lean's violation of the accounting principle of causality raises this question: Is accounting for lean a viable replacement for, complement to, and/or supplement for current and evolving management accounting approaches such as ABC? Does it have the capability to advance the main purposes of management accounting of decision support (i.e., discovery, ideas, and validation) and enterprise resource optimization?

Another way of asking this question is: Should there be two different coexisting costs for the same product—one cost for operations that is tactical and short term in nature and another cost for marketing and sales to analyze profit margins that is strategic in nature? Or should a single universal managerial accounting method prevail that complies with or knowingly violates accounting's causality principle? There will be debates, but eventually some form of consensus will prevail.

My opinion is that the criticisms that lean management advocates have of standard costing, though valid, are misplaced. Their real argument is with the inappropriate ways that many companies use information generated by the standard costing systems and the inappropriate actions that result. Cost accounting system information and cost information that should be used for decision making are not the same thing.

Key tests for accounting for lean will be: How does it handle economic projections? Does it classify resource expenses as variable, semivariable, fixed, or unavoidable versus avoidable (allows for adjustability of capacity)? Does it isolate unused/idle capacity expenses?

The good news is that organizations are questioning and challenging archaic forms of accounting, so in the end any accounting treatments that yield better decision making should prevail. The concern will be where two or more costing approaches coexist, one that complies with the causality principle and one that violates it.

COSTING STAGES OF MATURITY

An organization's executive management and employee teams need detailed output, product, channel, and customer cost information to make specific decisions regarding product pricing, mix, service levels, or dedication of resources. Exhibit 21.7 illustrates the progressive stages of maturity ranging from the primitive broad-average allocation method to the multistage cost assignment technique of activity-based management (ABM).

ABM provides the finer level of granularity and also the architecture of multistage cost assignment paths. That is, with ABM there are activity-to-activity assignments among indirect and support costs, because all indirect activity costs

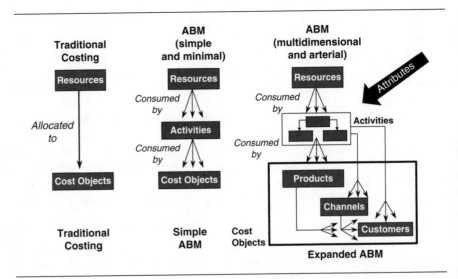

Exhibit 21.7 Stages of Maturity of Cost Accounting Methods

Source: © Gary Cokins. Used with permission.

cannot directly reflect variation caused by products or customers. There are also cost object–to–cost object assignments. An example of the latter assignment type is the cost to process a special transaction (versus a standard transaction) traced to a specific customer or a group of customers consuming a unique quantity and mix of products, services, or outputs.

EXCEL HEAVEN—OR IS IT HELL?

Spreadsheets such as Excel can be a dragging anchor that impedes progress toward adopting the full vision of the perform management framework. Disjointed spreadsheets, which I refer to as the spreadsheet-itis disease, have been nuisance that have now become a serious problem. This is not only because their use involves cumbersome and untimely reporting, but because it denies people a single, unified view of vital data—one version of the truth.

There may be good spreadsheet reports within a given department, but generally the rest of the organization is not aware of them. Additional pain results when others re-create their own version of the same report—a wasteful duplication of effort. With multiple spreadsheets, when data differs, which are the right numbers? Linked spreadsheets, some perhaps a decade old, and disjointed legacy systems are just not dynamic enough, nor are they flexible. Finally, problems with maintaining undocumented or documented spreadsheets surface when the employee who personally developed the spreadsheet transfers to elsewhere in the organization or departs it altogether. And it gets worse.

When data is stored on clients' computers (e.g., a laptop or personal computer) rather than on a server or a Web-accessible source, this means the data is not stored centrally, making dissemination and analysis difficult. Nonintegrated data means that assumptions in one person's plans will likely not include the most recent version from someone else's assumptions and plans. Most spreadsheet users have a widely held misconception that their spreadsheet application is some sort of database. It's not. It is a calculator effective at manipulating and viewing data, but it is not particularly good at storing and managing it in a reliable, secure, scalable way.

Spreadsheets are also poor at handling *sparcity* where a substantial number of cells are blank. You drag around the deadweight of a lot of "0s" with only a few cells populated with real data—not a very efficient use of computer memory or processing power.

Organizations cannot continue to spend 80% of their time collecting, copying, pasting, and reformatting data, 10% weeding out errors, and then realize in the remaining 10% that the resulting data is not structured in a way that allows it to be analyzed. They cannot rely on undocumented macros and formulas when no one remembers how to maintain them—or the business policy they were invented to support.

The hard truth is that most organizations are not equipped with managerial information that is properly structured to make prudent business decisions. A robust enterprise performance management framework integrates multiple methodologies in near real time, and it converts transactional data and its summaries (think =SUM(A1:A25)) into meaningful and relevant information for analysis and decisions. The more that spreadsheets clog the front end, the back end where the payoff is becomes obstructed.

FINANCIAL ACCOUNTING VERSUS MANAGERIAL ACCOUNTING

Let us discuss further the confusion between financial and managerial accounting. In sports, there are some legendary rivalries. For example, in baseball, one is between the New York Yankees and the Boston Red Sox. In college football, another is the University of Michigan versus Ohio State University. There is also a rivalry between financial accountants and managerial accountants. The financial accountants, who are typically CPAs employed by firms that audit financial disclosure statements of companies or who are the accountants producing those reports, would likely not be aware of any rivalry. That is because in a sort of arrogant way, the financial accountants view managerial accountants, who mainly produce internal information for decision making, as minor-league players. However, make no mistake, the managerial accountants resent their second-class status in the accounting community.

When you step back to assess a perspective of importance, financial accounting simply deals with *valuation*—for example, what would an organization be worth if you were to sell it? Managerial accounting is about *creating value*—its information contributes to management decisions that financial accounting ultimately deals with afterward in the form of reporting. Which type of accounting is more important?

It is true that rules-based compliance-related activities (such as with financial reporting standards, auditing standards, tax laws, and government legislation such as Sarbanes-Oxley) contribute to ensuring that an organization remains accountable to its investors. But management accounting is about supporting internal operations to optimize organizational performance. And management accounting, though perceived by some as focused on cost reduction and containment, has arguably shifted its role to that of enhancing revenue growth.

The animosity between the two accounting communities may even be worse in academia. Many financial accounting professors who teach or write about producing financial statements, compliance with U.S. GAAP and IFRS rules, or how to approach organizational mergers and acquisitions view their stature as well above that of faculty who teach cost accounting. As evidence, some universities have shifted managerial accounting courses from being required to being elective.

I think this pecking order is backward. The role rankings between financial and managerial accounting should be *reversed*.

First consider how well the audit profession has been doing at preventing financial scandals and "perk walks" by executives from appearing in front-page newspaper headlines or on the national evening news. Not very well; Enron is only one of many company names that people equate with financial disclosure failure. Yes, I realize it is important to the capital markets and the financial investment community to have confidence in financial reporting.[3] But I think it is even more important for managers and employee teams to have reasonably accurate and relevant managerial accounting information for organizational planning, control, and decision making. Managerial accounting supports managerial economics.

Professor Peter C. Brewer promotes the idea that effective management accounting is not confined to a narrow world of debits, credits, and cost variances, but rather embraces a broad spectrum that in addition to providing decision support information can and should include the following elements:

- Leadership to reinforce the executive team's messages
- Risk and strategy management and execution
- Operational alignment with the strategy to measure processes and motivate employees
- Facilitation of continuous organizational and individual learning and improvement, including cross-functional communication and collaboration[4]

Professor Brewer adds that a factor that creates the unsubstantiated impression of the higher importance of financial accounting relative to managerial accounting is university accounting curriculums where the initial course for first- and second-year students is excessively weighted toward financial reporting. This influences student behavior going forward with a bias toward financial accounting.

I would add that the problem gets worse. As some university accounting majors initially join auditing firms, their early-year assignments involve compliance testing. Eventually some of these professionals change jobs to become financial controllers and chief financial officers of commercial and public sector organizations. In those jobs, their time is often substantially consumed with maintaining compliance with ever-changing financial accounting rules. With whom might they interact for guidance on these?—the partners and senior managers of audit firms, who themselves are steeped in the tradition that financial accounting holds the high ground relative to managerial accounting. It is self-reinforcing cycle.

For the full vision of performance management in any organization to be fulfilled, there will need to be a shift in the balance. Financial reporting is a *result*. Managerial accounting helps *create* the result. Managerial accounting is one of the important components that constitute the various methodologies of the performance management framework. Its information can give an organization a superior and sustainable long-term economic advantage to satisfy the needs of its investors and employees. If investors in a company were given the choice of having superior strength and competence in *either* financial accounting *or* managerial accounting, astute investors would choose managerial accounting.

COMING TO GRIPS WITH REALITY

Increasingly more organizations are coming to this realization of flawed or dysfunctional cost reporting; however, they are intimidated by the perceived heights that they would need to scale to return to the levels of cost accuracy once enjoyed when output diversity was narrow and overhead expenses were small. Inevitably, they come to grips with their predicament. Should they reform their managerial accounting method using ABC principles and lean accounting techniques? Or should they take no action and remain with the status quo, hoping that the lack of transparency of indirect costs and their drivers and the degree of misleading information will not too adversely affect decision making? In either case, these are choices the accountants are making. To change or not to change—both are choices, where either option could be inappropriate.

The important point to appreciate here is that when one considers managerial accounting as having a "stages of maturity" framework, progressing to a next higher stage does not necessarily equate to being better off. Each progressive advance, which again is typically a disruptive and punctuated reform change to an organization's existing managerial accounting method, should be evaluated as to whether it is worth it. Is the climb worth the view? That is, the test for advancing is whether the incremental benefits in the form of better and more accurate information exceed the incrementally higher investment and administrative effort to collect, calculate, and deploy the information.

Sound managerial accounting practices and relevant performance measurements are foundational to completing the full vision of performance management. The accountants must assess how well they enable their organization's planning, control, and decision making. Some level of ABC will inevitably be applied. ABC information can be insightful for daily operations but arguably of greater impact in decision support to assure long-term profitable growth. An organization's managerial accounting practices should be defined and designed to provide accurate and relevant cost information. This information should be necessary to support decisions that require the understanding of a proposed action's incremental impact on the organization or its impact on the long-term sustainable economic structure of the organization.

NOTES

1. Robert S. Kaplan and Steven R. Anderson, "Time-Driven Activity-Based Costing," *Harvard Business Review* (November 2004).

2. F. Kennedy and J. Huntzinger, "Lean Accounting for Operations," *Target— Innovation at Work* (journal of the Association of Manufacturing Excellence), 21, No. 4 (2005): 8.

3. For more on this topic, read my article, "If Only Internal Financial Transparency Were as Good as the U.S. Government's SEC Laws," posted at www.dmreview.com/article_sub .cfm?articleId=1087039.

4. Peter C. Brewer, "Redefining Management Accounting: Promoting the Four Pillars of Our Profession," *Strategic Finance* (March 2008): 27–34.

Chapter 22

What Is Broken about Budgeting?

How many people in your organization love the annual budgeting process? Probably none. The mere mention of the word *budget* raises eyebrows and evokes cynicism. It should. As a simple test, in how many boxes in Exhibit 22.1 would you place a checkmark as applicable to your organization? Probably all.

What is broken about the annual budgeting process? We can more deeply discuss some of the issues related to budgeting:

- *Obsolete budgeting.* The budget data is obsolete within weeks after it is published because of ongoing changes in the environment. Customers and competitors usually change their behavior after the budget is published, and a prudent reaction to these changes often cannot be accommodated in the budget. In addition, today's budget process takes an extraordinarily long time, sometimes exceeding a year, during which time the organization often reshuffles and resizes.

- *Bean-counter budgeting.* The budget is considered a fiscal exercise produced by the accountants and is disconnected from the strategy of the executive team— and from the mission-critical spending needed to implement the strategy.

- *Political budgeting.* The loudest voice, the greatest political muscle, and the prior year's budget levels should not be valid measures to award resources for next year's spending.

- *Overscrutinized budgeting.* Often the budget is revised midyear or, more frequently, with new forecast spending. Then an excessive amount of attention focuses on analyzing the differences between the actual and projected expenses. These include budget-to-forecast, last-forecast-to-current-forecast, actual-to-budget, actual-to-forecast, and so on. This reporting provides lifetime job security for the budget analysts in the accounting department.

- *Sandbagging budgeting.* The budget numbers that roll up from lower- and midlevel managers often mislead senior executives because of sandbagging (i.e., padding) by the veteran managers who know how to play the game.

- *Wasteful budgeting.* Budgets do not identify waste. In fact, inefficiencies in the current business processes are often baked into next year's budget. Budgets do not support continuous improvement.

- *Blow-it-all budgeting.* Reckless use-it-or-lose-it spending is standard practice for managers during the last fiscal quarter. Budgets can be an invitation to managers to spend needlessly.

☐ Is invasive and time consuming, with few benefits

☐ Takes 14 months from start to end

☐ Requires two or more executive tweaks at the end

☐ Is obsolete in two months due to events and reorganizations

☐ Starves the departments with truly valid needs

☐ Caves in to the loudest voice and political muscle

☐ Rewards veteran sandbaggers who are experts at padding

☐ Incorporates last year's inefficiencies into this year's budget

☐ Is overstated from the prior year's use-it-or-lose-it spending

Exhibit 22.1   Quiz: Our Annual Budgeting Exercise
Source: © Gary Cokins. Used with permission.

The annual budget is steeped in tradition, yet the effort of producing it heavily outweighs the benefits it supposedly yields. How can budgeting be reformed? Or should the budget process be abandoned altogether because its inflexible, fixed social contract incentives to managers drives behavior counter to the organization's changing goals and its unwritten "earnings contract" with shareholders? And, if the budget is abandoned, what should replace its underlying purpose?

EVOLUTIONARY HISTORY OF BUDGETS[1]

Why were budgets invented? Organizations seem to go through an irreversible life cycle that leads them toward specialization and eventually to turf protection. When organizations are originally created, managing spending is fairly straightforward. With the passing of time, the number and variety of their products and service lines change as well as the needs of their customers. This introduces complexity and results in more indirect expenses and overhead to manage the newly created complexity.

Following an organization's initial creation, all of the workers are reasonably focused on fulfilling the needs of whatever created the organization in the first place. Despite early attempts to maintain flexibility, organizations slowly evolve into separate functions. As the functions create their own identities and staff, they seem to become fortresses. In many of them, the work becomes the jealously guarded property of the occupants. Inside each fortress, allegiances grow, and people speak their own language—an effective way to spot intruders and confuse communications.

With the passing of more time, organizations then become internally hierarchical. This structure exists even though the transactions and workflows that provide value and service to the ultimate customers pass through and across internal and artificial organizational boundaries. These now-accepted management hierarchies

are often referred to, within the organization itself as well as in management litera-
ture, as *silos*, *stovepipes*, or *smokestacks*. The structure causes managers to act in a
self-serving way, placing their functional needs above those of the cross-functional
processes to which each function contributes. In effect, the managers place their
personal needs above the needs of their coworkers and customers.

At this stage in its life, the organization becomes less sensitive to the sources of
demand placed on it from the outside and to changes in customer needs. In other
words, the organization begins to lose sight of its raison d'être. The functional silos
compete for resources and blame one another for any of the organization's in-
explicable and continuing failures to meet the needs of its customers. Arguments
emerge about the sources of the organization's inefficiencies, but they are difficult
to explain.

The accountants do not help matters. They equate the functional silos to the
responsibility cost center view that they capture expense transactions in their
general ledger accounting system. When they request each cost center manager to
submit the next year's budget, ultimately it is an "incremental or decremental"
game. That is, the managers begin with their best estimate of their current year's
expected total spending—line item by line item—and they incrementally increase
it with a percentage. Budgeting software reinforces this bad habit by making it easy
to make these calculations. At the very extreme, next year's spending for each line
is computed as shown in Exhibit 22.2. Using spreadsheet software, you multiply
the first line-item expense by the increment, in this example by 5%, and simply
copy and paste that formula for every line item below it.

By this evolutionary point in budgeting, there is poor end-to-end visibility about
what exactly drives what inside the organization. Some organizations eventually
evolve into intransigent bureaucracies. Some functions become so embedded inside
the broader organization that their work level is insensitive to changes in the number and types of external requests. Fulfilling these requests was the reason why

	a	b	c
1		Current Year	Budget Year
2	Wages	$400,000.00	Formula = ColumnB * 1.05
3	Supplies	$ 50,000.00	
4	Rent	$ 20,000.00	Copy down
5	Computer	$ 40,000.00	
6	Travel	$ 30,000.00	
7	Phone	$ 20,000.00	
8	Total	$560,000.00	

Exhibit 22.2   Spreadsheet Budgeting: Incremental
Source: © Gary Cokins. Used with permission.

these functions were created in the first place. But they have become insulated from the outside world. This is not a pleasant story, but it is pervasive.

A SEA CHANGE IN ACCOUNTING AND FINANCE

How can budgeting be reformed? We need to step back and ask broader questions. What are the impacts of the changing role of the chief financial officer (CFO)? How many times have you seen the obligatory diagram with the organization shown in a central circle and a dozen inward-pointing arrows representing the menacing forces and pressures the organization faces—such as outsourcing, globalization, governance, brand preservation, and so on? Well, it is all true and real. But if the CFO's function is evolving from that of bean-counter and reporter of history into strategic business advisor and enterprise risk and regulatory compliance manager, what are CFOs doing about the archaic budget process?

Progressive CFOs now view budgeting as consisting of three streams of spending that converge like a river:

1. *Recurring expenses.* Budgeting becomes an ongoing resource-capacity-planning exercise, similar to a 1970s factory manager projecting the operation's personnel planning and material purchasing requirements.
2. *Nonrecurring expenses.* The budget includes the one-time investments or project cash outlays to implement strategic initiatives.
3. *Discretionary expenses.* The budget includes optional spending that is nonstrategic.

Of the broad portfolio of interdependent methodologies that make up today's performance management framework, two methods deliver the capability to accurately project the recurring and nonrecurring spending streams:

1. *Activity-based planning.* In the 1990s, activity-based costing (ABC) solved the structural deficiencies of myopic general-ledger cost-center reporting for calculating accurate costs of outputs (such as products, channels, and customers). The general ledger does not recognize cross-functional business processes that deliver the results, and its broad-brush cost allocations of the now-substantial indirect expenses introduce grotesque cost distortions. ABC corrects those deficiencies. Advances to ABC's historical snapshot view transformed it into *activity-based management.* These advances project forecasts of customer-demand item volume and mix, and forecast the elusive customer cost-to-serve requirements. In effect, ABC is calculated backward, and named *activity-based planning,* based on ABC's calibrated consumption rates to determine the needed capacity and thus the needed recurring expenses. Without that spending, service levels will deteriorate.
2. *Balanced scorecard and strategy maps.* By communicating the executive strategy and involving managers and employee teams in identifying the projects and initiatives required to achieve the strategy map's objectives, nonrecurring

expenses are funded. Without that spending, managers will be unjustly flagged red as failing to achieve the key performance indicators they are responsible for in their balanced scorecards.

FINANCIAL MANAGEMENT INTEGRATED INFORMATION DELIVERY PORTAL

Today's solution to solve the budgeting conundrum and the organization's backward-looking focus is to begin with a single integrated data platform—popularly called a *business intelligence platform*—and its Web-based reporting and analysis capabilities. Speed to knowledge is now a competitive differentiator.

The emphasis for improving an organization and driving higher value must shift from hand-slap controlling toward automated forward-looking planning. With a common platform replacing disparate data sources, enhanced with input data integrity cleansing features and data-mining capabilities, an organization can create a flexible and collaborative planning environment. It can provide on-demand information access to all for what-if scenario and trade-off analysis. For the bold CFO who is not wary of radical change, continuous and valid rolling financial forecasts can replace the rigid annual budget. Organizations need to be able to answer more questions than "Are we going to hit our numbers in December?" That is not planning, but rather performance evaluation. For the traditional CFO, the integrated data platform offers a sorely needed high-speed budgeting process.

In addition, statistical forecasting can be combined with the integrated information on the platform, resulting in customer-demand forecasting that seamlessly links to operational systems, activity-based planning, and balanced scorecard initiatives for the ultimate financial view that the CFO can now offer to his or her managers. Real-time or right-time feedback to managers is part of the package.

All of this—traffic-signaling dashboards, profitability reporting and analysis, consolidation reporting, dynamic drill-down, customizable exception alert messaging to minimize surprises, Excel linkages, multiple versioning, and more—is available for decision making on a single shared solution architecture platform. Performance management resolves major problems: lack of visibility to causality, lack of timely and reliable information, poor understanding of the executive team's strategy, and wasted resources due to misaligned work processes.

Some organizations have become sufficiently frustrated with the annual budgeting process that they have abandoned creating a budget. An international research and membership collaborative, called the Beyond Budgeting Round Table (BBRT), advocates that rather than attempt to tightly control spending on a line-by-line basis, it is better to step back and question what the purposes of budgeting are. Their conclusion is that organizations would be better off moving away from long-term financial projections at a detailed level and replacing this form of monitoring by empowering managers with more freedom to make local spending decisions, including hiring employees. BBRT believes in removing second-guess approvals from higher-level managers. BBRT views fiscal year-end budget figures as if they are a fixed contract toward which managers will strive rather than reacting to changes not assumed when the budget was created. In place of budget spending variance controls, BBRT advocates a shift toward reporting emphasis on *outcomes*—performance reporting—not on the inputs. BBRT believes that secondary purposes for budgeting, such as cash flow projections for the treasury function, can be attained with modeling techniques.

Regardless of how an organization approaches its own reforms to budgeting, performance management provides confidence in the numbers, which improves trust among managers. What today will accelerate the adoption of reforms in the budgeting process and a performance management culture—senior management's attitude and willpower, or the information technology that can realize the vision described here? I would choose both.

NOTE

1. This section is drawn from Brian Plowman, "Better Budgeting," 2004, www.develin.co.uk.

Chapter 23

Put Your Money Where Your Strategy Is

Two easy ways for executive teams to attempt to raise profits are to lay off employees to cut costs or to lower prices to take away market share from their competitors. But these are merely short-term fixes. An organization cannot reduce its costs and prices to achieve long-term sustained prosperity.

Entrepreneurs know the age-old adage, "You need to spend money to make money." However, belt-tightening an organization's spending can be haphazard. Rather than evaluating where the company can cut costs, it is more prudent to switch views and ask where and how the organization should spend money to increase long-term sustained value. This involves budgeting for future expenses, but the budgeting process has deficiencies (see Chapter 22, "What Is Broken about Budgeting?)."

PROBLEMS WITH BUDGETING

Companies cannot succeed by standing still. If you are not improving, then others will soon catch up to you. This is one reason why Michael E. Porter, author of the seminal 1970 book on competitive edge strategies, *Competitive Strategy: Techniques for Analyzing Industries and Competitors*,[1] asserted that an important strategic approach is continuous differentiation of products and services to enable premium pricing. However, some organizations believed so firmly in their past successes that they went bankrupt because they had become risk-averse to changing what they perceived to be effective strategies.

Strategy execution is considered one of the major failures of executive teams. At a recent conference, Dr. David Norton, coauthor of *The Balanced Scorecard: Translating Strategy into Action*,[2] reported, "Nine out of 10 organizations fail to successfully implement their strategy. . . . The problem is not that organizations don't manage their strategy well; it is they do not formally manage their strategy."[3] Empirical evidence confirms that companies execute strategy poorly. Involuntary turnover of North American chief executive officers (CEOs) in 2006 will beat the record high set just the previous year.[4] In defense of executives, they often formulate good strategies—their problem is failure to execute them.

One of the obstacles preventing successful strategy achievement is the annual budgeting process. In the worst situations, the budgeting process is limited to a fiscal exercise administered by the accountants that is typically disconnected from

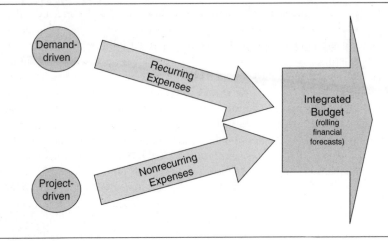

Exhibit 23.1   Resource Requirements Are Derived
Source: © Gary Cokins. Used with permission.

the executive team's strategic intentions. A less-poor situation, but still not a solution, is one in which the accountants do consider the executive team's strategic objectives, but the initiatives required to achieve the strategy are not adequately funded in the budget. Remember, you have to spend money to make money.

In addition, the budgeting process tends to be insensitive to changes in future volumes and mix of forecast products and services. The next year's budgeted spending is typically incremented or decremented for each cost center from the prior year's spending by a few percentage points.

Components of the performance management framework can be drawn on to resolve these limitations. Exhibit 23.1 illustrates in the big arrow at the right side that the correct and valid amount of spending for capacity and consumed expenses should be derived from two broad streams of workload that cause the need for spending—demand driven and project driven. Demand-driven expenses are operational and recurring from day to day. In contrast, project-driven spending is nonrecurring and can be from days to years in time duration.

VALUE IS CREATED FROM PROJECTS AND INITIATIVES, NOT THE STRATEGIC OBJECTIVES

One popular solution to failed strategy execution is the evolving methodology of a strategy map with its companion balanced scorecard. Their combined purpose is to link operations to strategy. By using these methodologies, alignment of the work and priorities of employees can be attained without any disruption from restructuring the organizational chart. The balanced scorecard directly connects to individuals regardless of their departments or matrix management arrangements.

Although many organizations claim to use dashboards and scorecards, there is little consensus on how to design or apply these tools. At best, the balanced scorecard has achieved a brand status but without prescribed rules on how to construct or use it. For example, many companies claim to have a balanced scorecard, but it may have been developed in the absence of a strategy map from executives. The strategy map is arguably many orders of magnitude more important than the balanced scorecard. Therefore, when organizations simply display their so-called scorecard of actual-versus-planned or -targeted metrics, how do the users know that those measures displayed in the dials, commonly called *key performance indicators* (KPIs), reflect the strategic intent of their executives? They might not! At a basic level, the balanced scorecard is simply a feedback mechanism to inform users as to how they are performing on preselected measures that are ideally causally linked. To improve, much more information than just reporting your performance scores is needed.

One source of confusion in the strategy management process involves misunderstandings of the role of projects and initiatives. For the minority of companies that realize the importance of first developing their strategy maps before jumping ahead to designing their balanced scorecards, there is another methodology challenge. Should organizations first select and set the targets for the scorecard KPIs and then determine the specific projects and initiatives that will help reach those targets? Or should the sequence be reversed? Should organizations first propose the projects and initiatives based on the strategy map's various theme objectives and *then* derive the KPIs with their target measures afterward?

We could debate the proper order, but what matters more is that the projects and initiatives be financially funded regardless of how they are identified. Exhibit 23.2 revisits Exhibit 17.2 described in Chapter 17 on implementing strategy maps and the balanced scorecard.

Measurement Period	1st Quarter					
	Strategic Objective	Identify Projects, Initiatives, or Processes	KPI Measure	KPI Target	KPI Actual	Comments/ Explanation
Executive Team	X			X		
Managers and Employees		X	X		*their score*	X
					<----- *period results* ------->	

Budgeting is typically disconnected from
the strategy. But this problem is solved if
management funds the managers' projects.

Exhibit 23.2 Nonrecurring Expenses/Strategic Initiatives
Source: © Gary Cokins. Used with permission.

In Exhibit 23.2, in the second column of X choices, what if the managers and employee teams that identified the projects are not granted spending approval for those initiatives by the executives? Presuming that KPIs with targets were established for those projects, these managers will score poorly and unfavorably. But worse yet, the strategic objectives the projects are intended to achieve will not be accomplished. By isolating this spending as strategy expenses, the organization protects these; otherwise it is like destroying the seeds for future success and growth. Capital budgeting is a more mature practice and not the issue that budgeting for strategic projects and initiatives is.

Value creation does not directly come from defining mission, vision, and strategy maps. It is the alignment of employees' priorities, work, projects, and initiatives with the executive team's objectives that directly creates value. Strategy is executed from the bottom to the top. Dr. Norton uses a fishing analogy to explain this: Strategy maps tell you where the fish are, but it is the projects, initiatives, and core business processes that *catch* the fish.

DRIVER-BASED RESOURCE CAPACITY AND SPENDING PLANNING

For daily operations where the normal recurring work within business processes occurs, a future period's amount of product and service-line volume and mix will never be identical to the past. In future periods, some amounts will rise and others decline. This means that unless the existing capacity and dedicated skills are adjusted, you will have too much capacity not needed and not enough capacity that is needed. The former results in unused capacity expenses, and the latter results in missed sales opportunities or customer-infuriating delays due to capacity shortages. Both drag down profits. Exhibit 23.3 illustrates an advance in applying

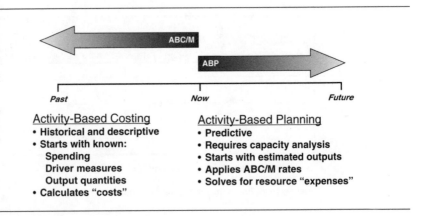

Exhibit 23.3   Recurring Expenses/Future Volumes and Mix
Source: © Gary Cokins. Used with permission.

activity-based costing (ABC) to minimize this planning problem. In this situation, ABC leverages historical consumption rates to be used for calculating *future period* levels of capacity and spending.

As an oversimplification, future spending is derived by calculating the ABC cost assignment network *backward*; this is called *activity-based planning and budgeting* (ABP/B). That is, the organization starts by forecasting its activity driver quantities (which were the actual driver quantities for past-period costing). It then uses the calibrated activity driver unit-level consumption rates from its historical costing to compute the required work activities in the operational processes. It next equates these workloads into the number and types of employees and the needed non–labor-related spending. This provides the correct and valid capacity and spending require-ments. With this knowledge, management must intervene and approve adjustments by adding or removing capacity. It is a logical way of matching supply with demand. Once the capacity interventions (e.g., employee headcount) and planned spending are approved, then a true and valid driver-based budget can be derived—not merely an incremental or decremental percent change from last year for each cost center.

THREE TYPES OF BUDGET SPENDING: OPERATIONAL, CAPITAL, AND STRATEGIC

Exhibit 23.4 decomposes Exhibit 23.1 by illustrating the two techniques for demand-driven and project-driven budgets that draw on components of the per-formance management framework:

1. *Operational budget:* activity-based planning and budgeting using calibrated consumption rates and activity driver forecasts

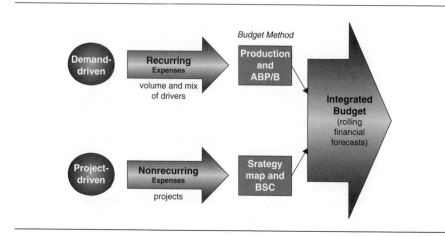

Exhibit 23.4   Match the Budget Method to Its Category
Source: © Gary Cokins. Used with permission.

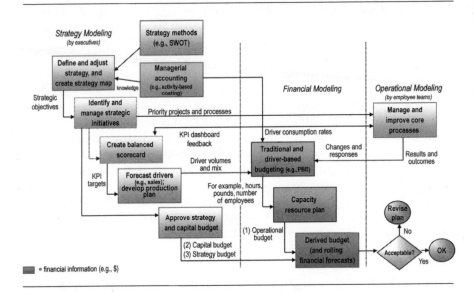

Exhibit 23.5 Link Strategy and Future Driver Volumes to the Budget
Source: © Gary Cokins. Used with permission.

2. *Strategic and capital budget:* strategy maps for identifying one-time projects and initiatives

Exhibit 23.5 continues these decompositions to a low level of detailed steps. It displays the two collective streams of spending with the operational budget in the upper arc and the strategy and capital budget in the lower arc. The exhibit begins with strategy formulation in the upper left and ends with financial budgeting and rolling forecasts in the bottom right. Some budgets and rolling financial forecasts may distinguish the *capital budget* spending (labeled 2 in the exhibit) from *operational budget* spending (1), but rarely do organizations segregate the important *strategic budget* spending (3).

Ideally, the strategy creation in the upper left uses meaningful managerial accounting information, such as understanding which products and customers are more or less profitable today and are potentially more valuable in the future. With this additional knowledge, the executives can determine which strategic objectives to focus on.

Note that the operational budget (1), those expenses required to continue with day-to-day repeatable processes, is calculated based on forecasted volume and mix of drivers of processes, such as the sales forecast, multiplied by planned consumption rates that are calibrated from past time periods (and ideally with rates reflecting planned productivity gains). This demand-driven method contrasts with the too-often primitive budgeting method of simply increasing the prior year's spending level by a few percentage points to allow for inflation. The operational budget spending level is a dependent variable based on demand, so it should be calculated that way.

Regardless of whether an organization defines the strategic initiatives before or after setting the balanced scorecard's KPI targets, it is important to set aside strategy spending (3) not much differently than budgeting for capital expenditures (2). Too often, the strategy funding is not cleanly segregated anywhere in the budget or rolling financial forecasts. It is typically buried in an accounting ledger expense account. As a result, when financial performance inevitably falls short of expectations, it is the strategy projects' "seed money" that gets deferred or eliminated. The priority must be reversed.

Note the question in the bottom-right corner of Exhibit 23.5. Since the first pass at the derived budget or rolling forecast will likely be unacceptably too high, the result is to adjust the plan; hopefully the project-based strategy budget spending will be protected. That is, organizations must protect strategy spending and allow it to go forward, as it is the key to competitive differentiation and successfully accomplishing the strategy. This leaves the only other lever to be to plan for productivity improvements in the consumption rates. It is in this way that focused cost reductions (or future cost avoidance) become part of the performance management framework.

FROM A STATIC ANNUAL BUDGET TO ROLLING FINANCIAL FORECASTS

Most executive teams request frequent updates and revisions of the financial budget. These are referred to as *rolling financial forecasts* because the projection's planning horizon is usually well beyond the fiscal year-end date, such as out 18 months to 2 years. Imagine if you as a chief financial officer or financial controller were required to reprocess the budget as a rolling forecast quarterly (or even monthly). There are not enough spreadsheets to do it! Only with computer automation that integrates several of the methodologies of the performance management framework, including good predictive analytics, can an organization produce valid derived rolling financial forecasts.

MANAGING STRATEGY IS LEARNABLE

Organizations with a formal strategy execution process dramatically outperform organizations without formal processes. Building a core competency in strategy execution creates a competitive advantage for commercial organizations and increases value for constituents of public sector organizations. Managing strategy is learnable. It is important to include and protect planned spending for strategic projects and initiatives in budgets and rolling financial forecasts. Those projects lead to long-term sustainable value creation.

NOTES

1. Michael E. Porter, *Competitive Strategy: Techniques for Analyzing Industries and Competitors* (New York: Free Press, 1998).

2. Robert S. Kaplan and David P. Norton, *The Balanced Scorecard: Translating Strategy into Action* (Boston: Harvard Business School Press, 1996).

3. Dr. David Norton, Balanced Scorecard Collaborative Summit, November 7, 2006, San Diego, California.

4. Del Jones, "Turnover for CEOs Is on Record Pace," *USA Today*, July 12, 2006, p. 2B.

Customer Value Management

Today the cost department of the average business is looked on as a right arm of first importance in management. Without the cost department today 90 percent of our businesses would be out of existence. . . . The cost department of the future is going to have more effect on the business and on the general management of business than any other single department. . . . And, gentlemen, in my opinion the major portion of the work of the cost department of the future is going to be applying recognized principles of cost analysis to sales expenses, for there is the greatest evil in present-day industry, the high cost, the extravagant, outrageous cost, of distribution.

> —James H. Rand,
> President,
> Remington Rand Company, 1921

Part Seven includes the most relevant chapters of this book. Its topic is customer-centricity. It deals with the questions "Which types of customers are valuable to acquire, to retain, to grow, and to win back? And which types are not?" It goes even further, and asks, "For customers of value, how much should be spent on each micro-segment in acquiring, retaining, growing, and winning back?"

Simply stated, "Nothing really happens unless you sell something." The initial chapters of this part of the book describe why it is no longer sufficient for a company simply to grow its sales; it must grow them *profitably*. This involves a deep understanding of which types of products, services, channels, and customers are more or less profitable—today and potentially in the future.

The concluding chapter describes the correlation that optimizing shareholder value has with optimizing differentiated service levels with different micro-segments of customers so as to maximize profits received from customers.

Chapter 24

From Working for the Boss to Working for the Customer

Our parents worked for the *boss,* and when they left the office at five o'clock, they left their job worries behind. But today's managers and employees work and worry nearly 24/7—and probably for someone other than their boss on the organizational chart. What has caused this shift, and who is this new boss? The answers to these questions are *the Internet* and *the recently empowered customer,* respectively. The Internet, with its powerful search engines and near-instant gratification, has irreversibly shifted power from sellers to buyers. And every supplier of products and services is scrambling to become more customer-focused.

Performance management, defined narrowly by most as merely better strategy, budgeting, and control, is increasingly becoming recognized as a much broader concept. Performance management runs end to end as the complete, closed-loop planning, design, marketing, selling, and customer order fulfillment cycle. One of the critical components in the portfolio of performance management methodologies is *customer relationship management* (CRM). Why is CRM now so critical to performance management?

A SHIFT OF POWER FROM SELLERS TO BUYERS

Organizations have realized that they must be increasingly focused on customers in order to stay in business today. This is due to slimmer margins, commoditization of product and service offerings, and the increased availability of information for the customer—especially through the Internet.

This does not mean that organizations should reduce their acquisition of new customers through marketing. Marketing is arguably the most critical function in an organization. But they should balance their use of financial and personnel resources between growing sales with higher-potential existing customers and acquiring new high-profit customers who share characteristics with their existing high-profit customers.

The Internet has shifted power from suppliers to buyers, because shoppers and purchasing agents can instantly view comparative pricing from a broad range of vendors while collecting more information from Web-based product and service-line resources.

Just imagine the shopping experience of a forgetful husband the evening before his tenth wedding anniversary. Once he realizes on his commuter train ride home from work that he has forgotten a gift, he types—or even speaks—these five words into a search engine on his Internet-equipped cell phone: "tenth wedding anniversary wife gift." In less than a second, his phone provides a list of gifts other husbands have purchased, ranked in order of popularity. With a click, he can view price ranges. Once he specifies his price range, he can locate nearby stores complete with driving directions and can immediately phone each of those stores to talk to a salesperson. If he had been prudent enough to remember his anniversary only a few days earlier, he could have been directed to Web sites where he could have purchased the item at a far lower than retail price and have had the gift already wrapped and shipped.

There are dozens of different purchasing experiences that you can imagine, and not just for consumers in households but also for purchasing agents in the virtual business-to-business marketplace. Buyers are no longer restricted to suppliers from the local geography; now they can order globally.

HOW CAN SUPPLIERS GAIN A COMPETITIVE EDGE?

Some suppliers overreact by becoming customer-obsessed when they attempt to transform themselves away from developing innovative new products and services and motivating their sales forces to sell them. Most eventually realize that they should work backward by first understanding the unique buyer preferences of the types of customers and prospects they want to serve. There is a difference between being customer-focused and customer-obsessed. The latter approach may cast too wide a net and capture savvy, high-maintenance, price-driven, nonloyal buyers who ultimately yield little profit margin in the long term.

As a supplier increasingly microsegments its customers and sales prospects, the company will need more accurate intelligence on the current and future potential profitability of its products, service lines, channels, and customers. The idea here is not just to know *which types* of customers to grow or acquire and which not to, but also *how much* to spend growing and acquiring the desired types. If you bribe loyal customers and prospects with unnecessary deep discounts and excessively costly differentiated services, or if you neglectfully fall short in offerings or services to nonloyal customers and prospects, thus risking their abandonment, then you destroy shareholder wealth. The spending and investment of sales and marketing is ultimately a financial optimization problem. This is why an effective managerial accounting system that helps you understand the profitability of a customer and its potential customer lifetime value is another one of the key components of the performance management portfolio of methodologies.

SINGLE VIEW OF THE CUSTOMER

Putting aside the skills and capabilities needed to measure customer value and derive a return-on-customer-value score, there are myriad other tactics available to exploit customer intelligence data. For example, sales and marketing campaigns can become continuous, closed-loop learning cycles. Based on known patterns of psychodemographic customer data (e.g., teens' TV viewing preferences) and their recency-freqency-monetary spend history (how much money was spent, how recently, and how often was it spent), offers, deals, and discounts then can be customized to microsegments and ultimately to individuals. In addition, based on the actual-versus-expected response behavior, future marketing campaigns can be fine-tuned.

To create greater shareholder wealth, a company must analyze its customer portfolio in new ways to discover new profitable revenue-growth opportunities. Many organizations have difficulty accessing, consolidating, and analyzing the necessary customer data that exists across its various business systems. This issue is exacerbated over time as the number of systems and discrete customer databases expands. Becoming customer-centric requires a view of data that involves no walls. For example, a bank should ideally consolidate its information onto a single decision-making platform, instead of keeping its credit card data in one silo, its banking account data in another, and its mortgage data in yet another. Eventually a *single view* of the customer must be created, one that consolidates relevant and accurate data related to a single customer across different organizations, databases, and operational systems. Without this single view, a customer with a variety of products may be viewed as less valuable than a customer with one product. A customer who spends a lot of money with you as well as time with technical support could be determined as highly unprofitable/undesirable in the customer service department but very valuable to sales and marketing.

As initially mentioned, CRM is one of the critical components in the portfolio of performance management methodologies for this very reason. When customer analytics is combined with the other components of the performance management portfolio, such as balanced scorecards, demand planning/forecasting, marketing automation, and predictive resource capacity management, the full vision of performance management can be realized.

Chapter 25

How Profitable to Us Is Each Customer Today—and Tomorrow?

Organizations increasingly want to better understand their revenues and costs and, in particular, the behavior of factors that drive these top and middle lines of the bottom-line profit equation. The reason for increased interest in more detail is obvious: The margin for decision error is getting slimmer. Mistakes in poor product selection, wrong channel options, or improper customer targeting can no longer be offset by good choices made elsewhere in a business.

What questions might managers and employee teams ask about their customers that can be answered with detailed profitability reporting? Here are some examples:

- Do we push for volume or for margin with a specific customer?

- Are there ways to improve profitability by altering the way we package, sell, deliver, or generally serve different types of customers?

- Does the customer's sales volume justify the discounts, rebates, or promotion structure we provide to that customer?

- Which products are relatively more profitable to cross-sell or up sell?

- Can we realize the benefits from our changing strategies by influencing our customers to alter their behavior to buy differently (and more profitably) from us?

- Can we shift work to or from some of our suppliers based on who is more capable or already has a superior cost structure compared with ours?

RISKS FROM INACCURATE COST CALCULATIONS

Companies plan and control their operations using accounting information that is assumed to accurately reflect the costs of their products and standard service lines. In fact, this is often not the case. The recorded expenses, such as salaries and supplies, may be exact in their amounts because they are externally audited and automated accounting systems capture them—but the problem is then transforming those expenses into their *calculated* costs of the business processes and the products that in turn consume those process costs.

The costing systems of many companies, with their aggregated summaries and their broad averaging allocation of indirect costs, mask reality with an illusion of precision. In fact, traditional cost systems typically provide misleading information to decision makers with minimal transparency to understand what constitutes a product's cost. Companies that apply activity-based cost management (ABC/M) principles and their supporting software systems resolve the cost-distorting error of allocating expenses using broad averages (e.g., number of units produced, sales amount, or labor input time). These cost allocations violate the accounting principle of a cause-and-effect relation to transform consumed expenses into calculated costs. ABC/M replaces broad averages with quantified activity cost drivers that trace each work activity (at a reasonable level of disaggregation) to the type of output, product, or standard service line that causes and consumes the work activity.

To further complicate matters, with the shift in attention from products to customer services, managers are also seeking granular "costs-to-serve" customer-related information. These are not all the costs related to making a product or delivering a standard service line (e.g., a bank checking account), but rather they are the costs from interactions with customers, such as a help desk call. The problem with accounting's traditional gross profit margin reporting (i.e., restricted to only product cost profit margins) is that managers cannot see the bottom half of the total picture—all the profit margin layers eroded from distribution, selling, credit, payments, and marketing costs. Exhibit 25.1 illustrates an organization's entire expenses. The product and standard service-line costs are in the shaded area. The concern here is tracing the nonshaded area costs to types of channels and customers.

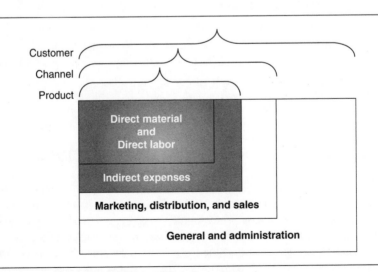

Exhibit 25.1   Costs from Sales and Marketing Are Not Product Costs
Source: © Gary Cokins. Used with permission.

The unacceptable result of not converting these types of expenses into customer-related costs is that executives, managers, and employee teams receive *incomplete* profit reporting that is not segmented by customer; and the product profitability data they do receive is flawed and misleading. They deserve fully loaded cost and profit reporting that encompasses all the traceable expenses of their end-to-end value stream costs—from supplier-related purchasing to customer service. How can recent advances in managerial accounting methods and technology deploy the vast potential that companies have from their business intelligence systems?

QUEST FOR INDIVIDUAL CUSTOMER PROFIT REPORTING

Businesses with thousands of customers want to scale up their cost and profit reporting and visibility at the individual customer level, but their costing systems cannot accomplish this. As a result, organizations lack the essential information for making much better decisions about product mix, customer mix, marketing, channel strategies, and sales programs.

To better analyze revenue, cost, and the resulting profit margin information, businesses need to be able to define segmented reports on the fly. This includes tracking profit for different time periods by individual customers, by individual products, and by specific sales channels, distribution channels, branches, service centers, or sales outlets. To enhance the identification and investigation of problems, organizations also need the flexibility of at-a-glance and drill-down views to see costs and profits with fine granularity.

ABC/M systems are designed to produce profit-and-loss income statements for customer segments and, if needed, for individual customers. With ABC/M, product- and service-line-related work activity costs are layered into each product and service line. In addition, cost-to-serve-related work activity costs are additionally layered into each channel and customer. The volume and mix of products, service lines, and channel costs that each customer consumes is also layered in.

Accountants rarely isolate and directly charge customer-related activity costs to the specific customer segments causing these costs. As a result, in financial accounting terms, the costs for selling, advertising, marketing, logistics, warehousing, and distribution are immediately charged to the *time period* in which they occur. Accountants refer to these as *period costs*. But classifying expenses that way is for *external* financial accounting for banks, investors, and regulatory agencies. What we are discussing here is *internal* managerial accounting to support the analysis and decision making of managers and employee teams. The accountants must begin applying the same costing principles for product costing, typically ABC/M principles, to types of channels and types of customers so that there is visibility to all traceable and assignable costs. Otherwise, you have no clue where you are making and losing money.

The problem is that the accountants are not tasked to trace them to channels or customer segments. But today's selling, merchandising, and distribution costs are

CUSTOMER: XYZ CORPORATION (CUSTOMER #1270)

Sales	$$$	Margin $ (Sales−ΣCosts)	Margin % of Sales	
Product-Related				
Supplier-Related costs (TCO)	$ xxx	$ xxx	98%	⎫
Direct Material	xxx	xxx	50%	⎪ Product-
Brand Sustaining	xxx	xxx	48%	⎬ related
Product Sustaining	xxx	xxx	46%	⎪ costs
Unit, Batch*	xxx	xxx	30%	⎭
Distribution-Related				
Outbound Freight Type*	xxx	xxx	28%	⎫
Order Type*	xxx	xxx	26%	Channel and
Channel Type*	xxx	xxx	24%	⎬ customer-
				related
Customer-Related				costs
Customer-Sustaining	xxx	xxx	22%	⎪
Unit-Batch*	xxx	xxx	10%	⎭
Business Sustaining	xxx	<u>xxx</u>	<u>8%</u>	
Operating Profit		**xxx**	**8%**	

* Activity Cost Driver Assignments use measurable quantity volume of Activity Output.
(Other Actvity Assignments traced based on informed (subjective) %s.)

Exhibit 25.2   Customer Profit-and-Loss Statement
Source: © Gary Cokins. Used with permission.

no longer trivial costs—they are sizable. There should be a focus on the customer contribution margin devoid of simplistic and arbitrary cost allocations. Companies with the goal of sales growth at *any* cost need to temper their plans with the goal of *profitable* sales growth.

In the end, services will be added to products, and unique services will be tailored for individual customers. Activity-based costing/management data will be essential to validate and prioritize the financial merits of *which* services to add and for *which* customers.

Exhibit 25.2 illustrates the individual customer profitability statement that is the result of these cost layers. Using ABC/M, there can now be a valid *profit-and-loss* (P&L) statement for *each* customer as well as logical segments or groupings of customers. A tremendous amount of detail lies below and within each of these reports. For example, the individual products and service lines purchased can be examined in greater detail; they comprise a mix of high and low margins based on their own unit costs and prices. In other words, in a customer-specific P&L summary, the product or service line is reported as a composite average, but details about the mix are viewable. In addition, within each product or service line, the user can further drill down to examine the content and cost of the work activities and materials for each product and standard service line.

ABC/M users refer to this data mining and navigating as *multidimensional reporting*; they use online analytical processing (OLAP) software tools for viewing the output of the ABC/M calculation engine. This is powerful information. The sum of all the customer P&L statements for this type of report will be the entire business's enterprisewide profit (or loss). That is, it can be reconciled with the company's official books: its total spending and the resulting bottom line.

Performance management systems combine activity-based management (ABM) with planning and performance measure and alignment tools; but what makes performance management so appealing is that it is work-centric. The foundation for performance management is built on what people and equipment do, how much they do it, and why.

MIGRATING CUSTOMERS TO HIGHER PROFITABILITY

What does all this information reveal? First, it quantifies what everyone may already have suspected: All customers are not the same. Some customers may be more or less profitable based strictly on how demanding their behavior is. Although customer satisfaction is important, a longer-term goal is to increase customer and corporate profitably. There must always be a balance between managing the level of customer service to earn customer satisfaction and the impact that doing that will have on shareholder wealth. The best solution is to increase customer satisfaction profitably. Because increasingly more customers will expect and demand customization rather than standard products, services, and orders, understanding this balance will be important. ABC/M data facilitate discussions about arriving at that balance. Many managers are unwilling to take any actions until presented with the facts.

In the company P&L in Exhibit 25.2, there are two major layers of contribution margin:

1. By mix of products and service lines purchased
2. By costs to serve apart from the unique mix of products and service lines

Exhibit 25.3 combines these two layers. Any single customer (or cluster) can be located as an intersection. This exhibit provides a two-axis view of customers with regard to the two layers just described, the *composite margin* of what each purchases (reflecting net prices to the customer) and its costs to serve. The exhibit debunks the myth that companies with the highest sales must also generate the highest profits.

The objective is to make all customers more profitable, represented by driving them to the upper-left corner. Although this is a partial list, making customers more profitable can be accomplished in the following ways:

- Manage each customer's *costs to serve* to a lower level.
- Improve and streamline customer-facing processes, including adding self-service models where possible.

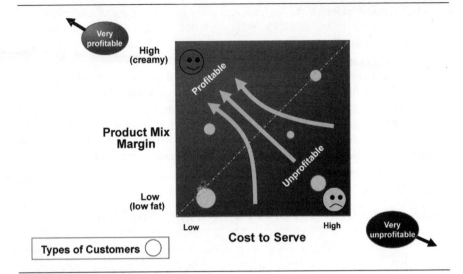

Exhibit 25.3   Migrating Customers to Higher Profitability
Source: © Gary Cokins. Used with permission.

- Establish a surcharge for or reprice expensive cost-to-serve activities.
- Reduce services; focus first on labor-intensive ones that add the least value yet cost the most.
- Introduce new products and service lines.
- Raise prices.
- Abandon products or service lines.
- Improve and streamline internal business processes.
- Offer the customer profit-positive service-level options with varying prices.
- Increase investments on activities that a customer shows a preference for.
- Up sell or cross-sell the customer's purchase mix toward richer, higher-margin products and service lines.
- Discount prices to gain more business with low-cost-to-serve customers.

Note that migrating customers to the upper-left corner is equivalent to moving individual data points in the profit profile in Exhibit 25.3 from right to left and bottom to top. Knowing where customers are located on the matrix requires ABC/M data.

Segmenting customers with ABC/M requires some different filters, which we will discuss next.

OPTIONS TO RAISE THE PROFIT CLIFF CURVE

What does a commercial organization do with the customer profit information? In other words, what actions can an organization take to increase its profits? This is all about the *M* in *ABM*, the *managing* of costs and profits. Some customers may be located so deep in the lower-right corner of the customer profitability matrix that the company will conclude that it is impractical to achieve profitability with them and that they should be terminated. After all, the goal of a business is not to improve customer satisfaction at any cost but rather to attempt to manage customer relationships in order to improve long-term corporate profitability.

Although this is a partial list, increasing profitability can be accomplished by doing the following:

- Manage each customer's *costs to serve* to a lower level.
- Establish a surcharge for or reprice expensive cost-to-serve activities.
- Reduce services.
- Introduce new products and service lines.
- Raise prices.
- Abandon products, services, or customers.
- Improve the process.
- Offer the customer profit-positive service-level options.
- Increase costs on activities that a customer shows a preference for.
- Shift the customer's purchase mix toward richer, higher-margin products and service lines.
- Discount to gain more volume with low-cost-to-serve customers.

Before doing anything or acting hastily, it is important for anyone interpreting the profit distribution diagram to understand the following key issues about it:

- This snapshot view of a time period's cost does not reflect the *life-cycle costs* of the products, service lines, or customers that have consumed the resource and activity costs for that particular time span.
- The information represented in the graph should not be prematurely or spontaneously acted on. Analysts must appreciate the large difference between what information is and what making an actionable decision is. They are not the same.

The important point is that ABM provides fact-based data from which discovery and questions can be asked. Always remember this: In the absence of facts, anyone's opinion is a good one. And usually the biggest opinion wins! This includes the opinion of your boss or of your boss's boss. So, to the degree senior managers are making decisions based on intuition, gut feel, misleading information, or politics, your organization is exposed to the risk of poor decisions.

COMPUTER TECHNOLOGY ENABLES TRANSACTION-BASED CUSTOMER PROFITABILITY REPORTING

Some companies require more real-time customer profitability reporting and have implemented transaction-based costing systems. A revolution has occurred in computer technology that allows large-scale and detailed profitability reporting. In the past, achieving ever-higher levels of cost accuracy was simply not justified given the extra work involved. But today, applying computer technology reduces that administrative effort to near zero (after the automated cost system is initially designed and configured). Further, data storage capacity is now economical. As a result, the new principle for attaining highly accurate cost and profit information is to measure price and costs consumed at the moment a consumer pays—at the instance of a transaction.

The attraction of effective transaction-based costing system is that it can economically scale to accommodate billions of transactions, access data from diverse multiple source systems, and be deployed for remote Web-enabled analysis. It reports validly calculated profits at a moment's notice rather than two weeks after a month has ended. As a bonus, with projected sales volume and mix, it enables reliable what-if scenarios for test-and-learn as well as pro forma profit-and-loss forecasts.

Profitability reporting at a detailed level gives a meaningful business context to the realm of business intelligence. In the end, managerial accounting is just data. It is to be used as a means to an end—namely decision making. The quality and accuracy of managerial accounting data are therefore critical.

With transaction-based costing at this intersection in time of any customer transaction, value is exchanged between a buyer and seller. This type of costing is a *bottoms-up* or *pull* approach. That is, the customers and products are placing demands (or pulling) on the business processes that are in turn drawing on the resource expenses. It is a *consumption* view of costs.

The accepted profit equation becomes:

$$\text{Individual customer profit} = \text{Sum of transactions}\,(\,Price - [\text{unit cost rate} \times Quantity])$$
$$- \text{Other traceable customer costs}$$

Exhibit 25.4 illustrates the information system design for transaction-based costing. The *transaction assignment modeler* is the cost calculator that serves as the central application to compute the profitability information. It is the heart of the methodology. This is where all the user-defined rules, selection criteria, data cube design, and formulas can be chosen and customized to enable flexible analysis by the casual user.

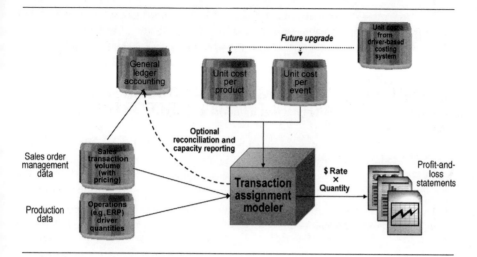

Exhibit 25.4   Transaction-Based Costing Information System
Source: © Gary Cokins. Used with permission.

The two main source data items at the left of the exhibit are (1) customer purchase history from the sales order management system for the top-line revenues and product costs (i.e., quantities purchased) and (2) operational systems, such as an enterprise resource planning (ERP) system for product and costs-to-serve events driver quantities.

Unit costs per product or per event are retrieved from the separate input files at the top of the exhibit. The challenge with these files is less about high accuracy and more about knowing what elements of expenses to include or exclude in the unit cost rates. For example, in quoting a one-time order, one could arguably exclude equipment depreciation as an irrecoverable sunk cost; but for a long-term customer contract, one would likely include that expense.

ACHIEVING EXTREME HIGH COST ACCURACY WITH TRANSACTION-BASED COSTING

With regard to cost accuracy, this bottoms-up approach quickly calculates high accuracy for measuring individual customer profitability because the two easiest elements in the profit equation to capture, each transaction's *price* and *quantity* (in italics in the profit equation), are the factors that influence the majority of the total accuracy. In contrast, a modest error in any individual unit cost rate (e.g., $25 per bank deposit +/− 5% error) will not substantially create as much total cost error as errors in price and quantity do.

Because most businesses today have automated transaction and production systems, the data that costing error is sensitive to is already accurately captured.[1] This means customer profitability information can be instantly reported at any time on demand. This provides robust information for customer profit analysis.

Future competitive differentiation will be based on the rate of speed at which organizations learn, not just the amount they learn. Having all this revenue, cost, and profit margin data is only a beginning. People have to act on and make decisions with the data.

NOTE

1. For advanced systems, there are extract, transform, and load (ETL) tools that are applied for input data cleansing to ensure higher accuracy of the calculated and reported information.

Chapter 26

Optimizing Customer Lifetime Economic Value

Estimating the return on investment (ROI) on purchasing equipment is near science. In contrast, determining the ROI on some marketing programs may be considered more of an art than a science. Thus, a large part of the marketing budget is typically based on faith that its spending will somehow grow the business. There is a very old rumored quote from a company president, stating "I am certain that half the money I am spending in advertising is wasted. The trouble is, I do not know which half." This expresses a concern—and it applies to the many marketing programs in addition to general advertising. Marketing spends money in certain areas, and the company hopes for a financial return. Was that brochure we just mailed a waste, or did it actually influence someone to purchase? Senior management has had unquestioned views that marketing and advertising are something you must spend money on—but how much money? How much is too much? And where is the highest payback on which to focus, and what should be avoided? Which customers should we target—and which not?

Business is no longer just about increasing sales. It is about increasing the *profitability* from sales. It is not enough merely to measure gross margin profitability for sales of products and standard service lines. Most products or service lines require fairly standard and predictable work activities that do not vary from month to month and are therefore not dependent on customer behavior other than volume. Companies should instead start to identify the differences in the cost to serve between different types of customers (called the *fully loaded costs of serving a customer*). This effort will help them get a full picture of where their business is making or losing money. Peter Mathias and Noel Capon of Columbia University explain the importance of measuring fully loaded costs:

> Most sales people manage for short-term revenues (regardless of profits). . . . With an increasingly sophisticated customer base that wants lower prices, greater service and more control, this strategy most often results in declining profit margins and commoditization.
>
> Increasingly buying power and market influence is being concentrated in an ever-smaller number of strategic customers. Hence, going forward, we believe that companies will have to think beyond short-term revenue and profitability of today. They will have to take the long view and manage their strategic customer relationships as assets. They will attempt to maximize the net present value (NPV) of future profit streams from these customers, thus shifting to the enhancement of long-term Customer Relationship Capital.[1]

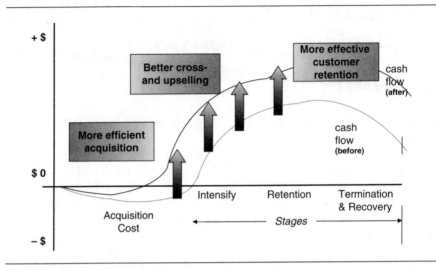

Exhibit 26.1   Customer Life Cycles Can Be Leveraged
Source: © Gary Cokins. Used with permission.

It is important to understand that customers sometimes become unprofitable as a direct result of the way the business operates in its relationship with them. For example, it may price below its true cost to deliver a product or service. As another example, a profitable customer may inadvertently be cross-sold a product or service that cannibalizes an existing source of revenue for the business. Similarly, the way the sales process is conducted and remunerated for sales staff may well encourage the acquisition of unprofitable customers.

Hence, companies should improve in several areas to develop successful strategies that focus on customer *value* but also ensure sustaining continuous shareholder wealth creation. Any customer-related initiative or interaction should differentiate customers to give insight into the value-creating potential of those customers. Customers pass through life cycles. Exhibit 26.1 illustrates some of the tactical actions that a company may take to lift the profitability and cash flow of a customer relative to the customer's current expected life cycle.

At the strategy level, many companies remain focused on pushing out products rather than drawing in customers. If a company's strategic focus is to sell as many products as possible, customers will be overwhelmed by irrelevant marketing and sales offers, and their satisfaction will be lowered. It is difficult to acquire, grow, or retain profitable customers with that approach.

Superior companies provide a differentiated customer experience to drive loyalty and gain a competitive advantage. To deliver a total customer experience, unique and value propositions are consistently offered across all the touch points with customers, regardless of varying sales channels.

Ultimately, insight into the value created by each customer relationship provides the most useful information for decision makers. Traditional *customer relationship management* (CRM) profit measures typically calculate historical revenues and costs, and therefore do not provide insights to future economic value creation.

A FINANCIAL VIEW OF CUSTOMERS MUST BE ADDED TO A BEHAVIORAL VIEW

Companies are extremely vigilant about *all* spending. They exercise draconian actions, such as layoffs, to right-size their cost structure. The budget expenditures for marketing should be subject to the same intense examination by the chief operating officer and chief financial officer (CFO) as would any other spending programs. Many marketing functions rely on imperfect metrics, anecdotes, and history that may have been a result of unusual occurrences unlikely to be repeated. How marketing spends money is critical, but it should be treated as a preciously scarce resource to be aimed at generating the highest long-term profits. This means there is a need to answer questions such as "Which types of customer are attractive to newly acquire, retain, grow, or win back? And which types are not? How much should we spend attracting, retaining, growing, or recovering the types we want?"

Although the marketing and sales functions clearly see the links between increasing customer satisfaction and generating higher revenues, the accountants have traditionally focused on encouraging cost reduction as a road to higher profits. Popular nonfinancial and intangible indicators such as brand equity, customer loyalty, and intellectual property that influence a company's future value-creation potential are admittedly difficult to measure. A way for investors, shareholders, and a management team to think about measuring a company's promise for long-term *economic value* growth performance is to measure and manage its customers and the economic value they bring to the bottom line of the financial income statement.

Although today CFOs' managerial accounting planning and control systems typically focus on operations management, CFOs are now shifting their assistance to the chief marketing officer (CMO) and sales director—and the benefits can be substantial. Typically these two functions in the organization chart rarely interact, but given the recognition that customers are arguably the source of shareholder wealth creation, companies can no longer afford to have these two functions operating in silos. There is a natural tension between their two roles, with the CFO under pressure to deliver short-term earnings expected from investors, and CMOs acquiring new customers and building brand-name recognition that influences long-term growth. There are trade-offs that involve striking a balance. If there is lack of balance, the CFO might prevail and force the cutting of advertising and customer support expenses, which can jeopardize long-term growth prospects.

THE PERFECT STORM IS CREATING TURBULENCE FOR SALES AND MARKETING MANAGEMENT

Over the past ten years, five major forces have been converging that place immense pressure on companies, particularly on *business-to-consumer* ones, to better understand their customers and what it costs to serve different types:

1. *Customer retention.* It is generally more expensive to acquire a new customer than to retain an existing one—and satisfied existing customers not only are likely to buy more but also spread the word to others like a referral service. Hence there is an increasing focus on customer satisfaction. The trend in emphasis is toward growing existing customers and making them loyal rather than focusing only on acquiring new ones. This has resulted in loyalty programs and other frequency points programs, which are growing in popularity.

2. *A shift in the source of competitive advantage.* In the past, companies focused on building products and selling them to every potential prospect. But many products or service lines are one-size-fits-all and have become commodity-like. To complicate matters, product development management methods have matured and accelerate quick me-too copying of new products or service lines by competitors. Consequently, as products and service lines become commodities, where competitors offer comparable ones, the importance of service rises. There is an unarguable shift from product-driven differentiation toward service-based differentiation. That is, as differentiation from product advantages is reduced or neutralized, the customer relationship grows in importance. This trend has given rise to many marketing organizations focusing on segment, service, and channel programs, as opposed to traditional product-focused initiatives. Business strategists all agree that differentiation is a key to competitive advantage. This was a main revelation in Michael Porter's seminal book, published in 1985, *Competitive Advantage*,[2] which launched strategic planning as an essential company function.

3. *One-to-one marketing.* Technology is being hailed as an enabler to (1) identify customer segments, and (2) tailor marketing offers and service propositions to individual customers (or segments). There is now a shift from mass marketing products a seller believes it can sell to a much better understanding of customers' unique preferences and what they can afford. You may even need to better understand your customers' customers. Traditional marketing measures like market share and sales growth are being expanded to more reflective measures of marketing performance, such as additional products and services sold to existing customers. There is frequent reference to "share of customer wallet." Customer lifetime value, to be discussed later in this chapter, is a trendy new metric used for increasing customer and shareholder economic value. In short, the message is that companies should now continuously seek ways to engage in more content-relevant communications and interactions with their customers. Each interaction is an opportunity to gain knowledge about customer preferences—and to strengthen the relationship.

4. *Expanded product diversity, variation, and customization.* As products and service lines proliferate, such as with new colors or sizes, the result is more complexity. As a result, more indirect expenses (i.e., overhead costs) are needed to manage the complexity; and therefore indirect expenses are increasing at a relatively faster rate than direct expenses. With indirect expenses growing as a component of an organization's cost structure, the managerial accounting practices typically require enhancing. (Many costing systems arbitrarily allocate indirect and shared expenses to products based on broad-brush averages, such as product sales or direct labor hours; they do not reflect each product's unique consumption of indirect expenses. Activity-based costing (ABC) is now accepted as the method that resolves this problem. ABC traces and assigns costs based on cause-and-effect relationships. This does not mean that an increase in indirect expenses is a bad thing. It simply means that a company is required to invest in and spend more on expanded product offerings and services to increase its customers' satisfaction. It therefore needs to know the resulting profit margins.

5. *Power shift to customers.* The Internet is shifting power—irreversibly—from sellers to buyers. This is a one-time event happening in our lifetime! Thanks to the Internet, consumers and purchasing agents can more efficiently explore more shopping options and quickly compare prices among dozens of suppliers. They can also more easily and quickly educate themselves. Customers have an abundance of options; and now with the Internet they can get information about products or services that interest them in a much shorter amount of time than was the case with the antiquated ways of the past. The customer is in control more than ever before. Consequently, from a supplier's perspective, customer retention becomes even more critical and treating customers as "a lifetime stream of revenues" becomes paramount. This shift in power from sellers to buyers is placing relentless pressure on suppliers. Supplier shakeouts and consolidations are constant.

The combination and convergence of these pressures and additional customer satisfaction pressures (see Chapter 25, "How Profitable to Us Is Each Customer Today—and Tomorrow?") means that suppliers must pay much more attention to their customers. The implication is clear. Profit growth for suppliers and service providers will come from building intimate relationships with customers, and from providing more products and services to their *existing* customer base as well as carefully targeting *future* customers to be acquired.

UNANSWERED BUT CRITICAL QUESTIONS

Earning, not just buying, customer loyalty is now mandatory. But how much should you spend in marketing to retain customers, and which types of customers should you spend more on? Few organizations can answer these questions. Few

organizations know how much they spend on individual customer microsegments—
or ultimately on individual customers.

When it comes to measuring the overall marketing and sales functions, many
companies miss the ROI mark. They do not have meaningful, consistent, and reliable marketing and sales performance metrics aside from just sales numbers. Worse
yet, in an attempt to build customer loyalty, they continue to deploy blanket spray-
and-pray mass-marketing strategies rather than differentiate (i.e., segment) their
customers based on cross-sell and up-sell opportunities. Good customer intelligence systems help organizations make smarter decisions faster. A workflow or
business process without the ability to measure, analyze, and improve its effectiveness simply perpetuates a problem.

How many customers does the company have? How much profit is it earning
from each customer (or at least each customer segment) today and will it earn in the
future? What kind of new customers are being added, and what is the growth rate of
additions? How and why are customers migrating through segments over time?

As a result of varying customer demands for different levels of service, the *cost-
to-serve* component of each customer's profit contribution requires measurement
and visibility. As widely varying customization and tailoring for individuals becomes widespread, how will companies distinguish their profitable customers from
their unprofitable ones? In a sense, it is the high-value customers who are partners
selected to grow the supplier's business and wealth creation. Companies now need
financial measures for how resource expenses are uniquely consumed, *below the
gross margin line*, by each *diverse* customer.

A customer-oriented strategy for improving shareholder wealth should focus on
three factors: costs, potential customer value, and customer needs. When companies miss the mark on these three areas, they end up placing customers into the
wrong value groups. This error ripples out to enable suboptimal managerial decisions, misallocation of marketing and sales resources, and, ultimately, lower profits,
slower growth, and lost competitive advantage. Companies need a complete picture
of the measurable value of each customer relationship.

"The only value your company will ever create is the value that comes from
customers—the ones you have now and the ones you will have in the future," say
Don Peppers and Martha Rogers, in *Return on Customer.* "To remain competitive,
you must figure out how to keep your customers longer, grow them into bigger customers, make them more profitable and serve them more efficiently." Over time,
enterprise value goes up because a company can maximize its return on customer.[3]

Though these measures are essential, a complete customer analysis should
address why a customer would be of value. The *why* is important to help analysts
predict the above values and extrapolate them across the customer base. The end
result of this is to enable the organization to develop marketing and sales strategies
to proactively manage customer value upward.

There is an unchallenged belief that focusing solely on increasing sales
dollars will eventually lead companies to depressed profitability. What matters is a
mind-shift from pursuing increased sales volume at any cost to pursuing *profitable*

sales volume—*smart* sales growth. If each customer's *value* is not known, then you are likely misallocating resources by underserving the more valuable customers, and vice versa.

SHOULD WE BE PURSUING THE MOST PROFITABLE OR THE MOST VALUABLE CUSTOMERS?

The goal of marketing is not only to identify potential new customers, but to reach out to *existing customers* through cross-selling (e.g., when I sell you golf clubs, I try to sell you a golf glove) and up-selling (e.g., when I sell you a shirt, I offer a second one at a lower price). Maximize the value of the relationships you already have. Metrics to evaluate customers might include retention (loyalty) rates, attrition rates, churn propensity, and the marketing standard metrics trio of a customer's purchase history: recency, frequency, and monetary spend. Indirect considerations can include a customer's referral propensity to recruit new customers. Of course, there are myriad other sociodemographic (e.g., age, income level, gender) and attitudinal variables that marketers analyze about their customers to understand their tastes and preferences. Data-mining tools are becoming essential for marketers to formulate marketing campaigns tailored to the customer segments defined by their analysis.

Exhibit 26.2 illustrates that just knowing the existing level of profitability for a customer, the vertical axis, may not always be sufficient. For some kinds of customers, such as a promising young dentist or imminent university graduate, their potential future profit as a customer is sizable. However, their current level of profitability does not reveal this. So their future potential should also be considered. This is

Segmenting existing customers by current and future potential helps determine marketing actions. There appear to be obvious customer strategies for *each* category.

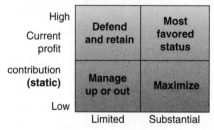

Exhibit 26.2   Current versus Long-Term Potential Customer Value
Source: © Gary Cokins. Used with permission.

measured along the horizontal axis. Each quadrant in the exhibit then suggests which general action to take toward a certain type of customer to improve profitability.

As examples, a very profitable customer with substantial future potential should be treated royally. A profitable customer without much future potential should be defended and retained, otherwise a competitor will benefit and the remaining high profit rate from the customer will be sacrificed.

In practice, the ranking of customers by their profit contribution during some past period is a continuously changing list, due to the timing and mix of customer purchases. Past-period profit measures are useful as a proxy for ranking profit-generation of customers, but the true insights that determine the level of differentiated service to various types of customers should ideally be derived by understanding the future financial rankings of the customer base.

In many industries, particularly in the service sectors, a sizable portion of revenues and costs is incurred after the initial sale of a product or service line. Post-sales activities occur in future periods, not past ones. This fact suggests the need to estimate the short-term future profit impact of past sales and reflect them on the horizontal axis of Exhibit 26.2.

DECISION SUPPORT FOR SERVICING CUSTOMERS MUST BE TAKEN TO A HIGHER LEVEL

There can be risks to automatically acting based on a customer's current quadrant location. For example, you could misjudge customers with current low profits as having low future potential and abandon them, thus missing substantial future profit opportunity. For high-future-potential customers, you could unwisely entice them with loss leaders only to not have profit followers recoup the losses or, worse yet, lose their business to a competitor. Reacting to a customer's quadrant location can also get complicated. For example, if a student, currently an unprofitable bank customer but the niece of her highly profitable aunt, requests her bank to match an auto dealer's low loan rate offer to her, thus making her more unprofitable to the bank, do you reject the niece and jeopardize the relationship with her aunt? Or do you accept her, seeing the potential to cross-sell (e.g., credit card) and generate long-term profits?

Another risk may be revealing too much about your decision process to customers and potentially appearing foolish or mean to them. Customer intelligence systems using data-mining techniques can be designed to send data into the operational CRM systems *derived from current and projected profitability information.* So, for example, a bank teller should not say to a customer, "You've got a low profit score, therefore I cannot waive your service charge," but rather say, "I'm sorry, but we already extended our one-time courtesy waiver, so I can't waive your service charge at this time."

These examples go to the heart of customer relationship management systems. Decisions should be made considering the more valuable customers, not just the currently more profitable customers. These examples involve balancing current customer satisfaction with shareholder ROI demands—and both involve trade-offs among short- and long-term decisions:

- *Achieving customer satisfaction and intimacy.* Gaining customer loyalty is more than bribes with perpetual discounts. Loyalty must be earned, not bought. So-called *loyalty programs* are typically just frequency programs lacking intimacy.

- *Increasing the company's profitability.* How do we apportion our marketing spend between customer retention and new customer acquisition or recovery (i.e., win-backs)?

The marketing function increasingly requires more financial analysis for trade-off analysis. Measuring customer lifetime value is one of those methods.

CUSTOMER LIFETIME VALUE: VIEWING CUSTOMERS AS AN INVESTMENT

To consider the future profit potential of customers as they pass through their life cycles, marketing and sales functions have begun exploring an equation called *customer lifetime value* (CLV). CLV treats each customer (or segment) as if it were an investment instrument—similar to an individual stock in a portfolio. There can be winners and losers. Since changes in customer behavior are usually not volatile, CLV may be useful to understand each customer's profit momentum. Its measures are not interrupted by "one-time charges" and other short-term but substantial financial statement surprises. CLV links customer revenues to organizational profits that result in shareholder wealth creation. Revenues and profits should never be assumed to always go in the same direction, because, as mentioned earlier, high-maintenance customers can be unprofitable regardless of their sales volume.

CLV is a forward-looking view of wealth creation. Evaluating investments in accounting and finance involves calculating future streams of revenue and their associated costs. In contrast to calculating the profit from a past time period, calculations of projected financial returns calculate the net present value of discounted cash flows. This involves time-value-of-money principles and math that considers both the timing of future cash inflows and outflows as well as the cost of capital. Most profitability measures are historical and do not consider products' and customers' prospective profit contribution.

CLV math is trickier than measuring historical customer profitability levels because you need to consider factors other than what happened in the past. CLV also considers the probability of losing some customers. By using CLV math, you can equate the future stream of net cash flow (profits) into a single cash amount (i.e., the *expected value*) of profit stated in today's money.

Exhibit 26.3 illustrates the results of calculating CLV determined by the characteristics of existing customers as well as potential new ones to be targeted. All

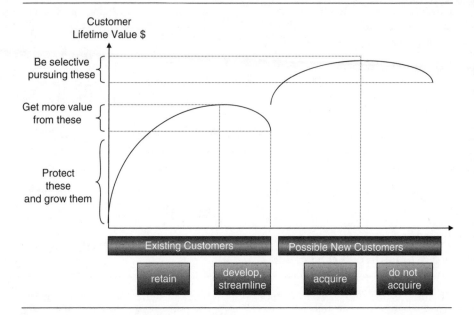

Exhibit 26.3   Value Creation via Customer Lifetime Value
Source: © Gary Cokins. Used with permission.

customer segments should be managed to generate higher economic value to share-holders, but the strategies will differ depending on the segment. The graph line is rank-ordered from highest to lowest CLV. This graph is similar to the "profit cliff" described in an earlier chapter (see Exhibit 21.4); however, it is different in that the profit cliff rank-ordered only historical past-period profits of products, services, or customers, whereas this graph reflects the future projected potential net discounted cash flow from existing and prospective customers.

The exhibit reveals that the most valuable customer segments at the left-hand side of the graph should be protected—their retention being the high priority. Earning their loyalty is critical. The less valuable customer segments should be managed for higher returns. For new sales prospects, marketing can allocate appropriate budget to acquisition programs to attract customers with similar characteristics to valuable existing customers. The marketing budget spending should focus on higher payback rather than on pursuing potentially unprofitable sales prospects.

Assumptions and forecasts with uncertainty are involved with calculating CLV. Even with customers segmented, forecasting models can be quite sensitive to assumptions. For example, how long will an active customer continue the relationship? How much and when will an active customer spend? If customers are inactive, is it temporary, or did they switch to a competitor? If so, what and how much are they purchasing from a competitor? They may spend $100 with you, but $500 with your competitor. For these last two questions you see only your data, not

$$\text{Present Value} \qquad \text{Future Value}$$

$$\mathrm{CLV}^k = \sum_{t=0}^{t=T} \frac{E_t^k - A_t^k}{(1 + i_t)^t} = \left(E_0^k - A_0^k\right) + \frac{E_1^k - A_1^k}{(1 + i_1)^1} + \frac{E_2^k - A_2^k}{(1 + i_2)^2} + \cdots + \frac{E_T^k - A_T^k}{(1 + i_T)^T}$$

CLV^k	= Customer Lifetime Value of a customer k
E_t	= revenue from a customer k
A_t	= expenses for a customer k
k	= customer k
t	= time period ($t = 0, 1, 2, ...$)
($t = 0$)	= today
T	= predicted duration of a customer's relationship
i	= interest (discount) rate

Exhibit 26.4   CLV Equation
Source: © Gary Cokins. Used with permission.

external data, forcing you to make assumptions about missing data. But that simply means you will need to gain more competency in statistical forecasting and predictive analytics. It is inevitable that to truly manage performance the shift in competencies will be from control to planning.

Customer equity (CE) is becoming a buzzword among marketers and is based on CLV math. CE is an acquisition and customer-retention management strategy geared to economic value creation for shareholders. Exhibit 26.4 displays an equation for computing CE as being the sum of the CLVs for both existing and future customers.

There are still a number of skeptics who believe this type of DCF calculation of customers is unrealistic. Even the academic world has yet to explore these interdependent relationships fully:

> Customer value management can be regarded as the key driver of Shareholder Value . . . [but] surprisingly, although being of obvious importance, literature taking a more comprehensive view of customer valuation has only recently been appearing. A composite picture of customers and investors is hardly found in business references.[4]

Assuming that the skeptics are wrong and that applying CLV to determine marketing actions and the actions' levels of intensity is sensible to do, what are the next steps? How would you use the results of a CLV ranking of existing customers and future potential ones?

TRADE-OFF BETWEEN CUSTOMER AND SHAREHOLDER VALUE

An obvious use of CLV metrics would be to identify, prioritize, and target prospective customers who are similar to your most valuable existing customers. Another option would be to migrate existing customers to higher CLV levels using crafted interactions with them. Ultimately, these possibilities are about getting a higher yield from your marketing and sales budget.

A less obvious—but possibly more important—choice would be to use CLV calculations to determine the optimal level of spending for marketing and sales, including on each customer microsegment. This type of analysis is often called *sensitivity analysis*. In essence, sensitivity analysis helps you determine what impact you will get by spending an extra dollar (or euro) on each customer.

A key point is that spending on existing customers is an optimization problem that needs to be solved to maximize shareholder wealth creation. This is because, in some cases, excess spending can lead to the destruction of shareholder wealth. With unbridled spending, you can bribe customers to retain their loyalty, but they might also become less valuable—even to the point of being unprofitable if you spend too much on differentiated services or deals with them.

In contrast, insufficient spending on a customer can also harm shareholder wealth. By neglecting customers, particularly marginally loyal ones, you risk losing them to a competitor or affecting how often they spend. Both results reduce the lifetime value of that customer.

A company affects customer loyalty constantly, through every interaction. Interactions can include actively pursuing customers with new offers or passively assigning them to segments that receive a set of dormant offers. A customer's degree of loyalty directly influences the amount of spending that may be required to retain that customer. Some advanced companies use business intelligence software to understand psychodemographic characteristics of customers and predict their future behavior. It is not unusual for the customer analytics departments in such companies to claim that their customer "survival" (i.e., retention) projections are reliably accurate. They can almost predict by name which customers are likely to defect. Still, the question remains whether it is worth the extra cost to retain them.

THE CFO SHOULD SERVE THE CMO AND THE SALES DIRECTOR

The CFO can and should work more closely with the CMO to measure and report the nonfinancial balanced scorecard key performance indicators that impact or reflect the customers' total experience and satisfaction. Progressive CFOs understand how customer experience drivers achieve strategic objectives and indirectly influence financial results.

Ultimately, managerial accounting measures, which are typically product-based and retrospective, should extend to become forward-looking, value-based measures. Evaluating customers requires calculating prospective metrics that, when acted on intelligently, truly convert to bottom-line earnings and shareholder wealth.

We began this discussion by stating that senior management has had unquestioned views that marketing and advertising are things it must spend money on—but how much money? How much is too much? Where is the highest payback to focus on, and what should be avoided? It is inevitable that the answers to these questions will require a contribution from the business analysts using managerial accounting techniques. The day is coming when the CFO function must turn its attention from operations and cost control to support the CMO and sales director to develop and monitor strategies that will assist cost planning and are customer-centric and will grow the customer base, its loyalty, its revenue, and the company's brand.

NOTES

1. Peter F. Mathias and Noel Capon, "Managing Strategic Customer Relationships as Assets," Columbia Business School, 2003, p. 2.
2. Michael E. Porter, *Competitive Advantage: Creating and Sustaining Superior Performance* (New York: Free Press, 1998).
3. Don Peppers and Martha Rogers, *Return on Customer: Creating Maximum Value from Your Scarcest Resource* (New York: Currency/Doubleday, 2005).
4. Tomas Bayon, Jens Gutsche, and Hans H. Bauer, "Customer Equity Marketing," *European Management Journal* (June 2002).

Performance Management and Shareholder Wealth Creation

The three most important things you need to measure in a business are customer satisfaction, employee morale, and cash flow. If you are growing customer satisfaction, your global market share is sure to grow. Employee satisfaction gets you productivity, quality, pride and creativity. Cash flow is the pulse—the vital sign of life in a company.

—Jack Welch,
CEO (retired),
General Electric Inc.

The first chapter of Part Eight continues with Part Seven's discussion about the correlation that optimizing shareholder wealth has with serving customers.

Part Eight's remaining chapters describe the perspective of economic value creation that conglomerates, investment companies, and private equity firms should have with respect to performance management.

Chapter 27

Can Performance Management Accomplish What Einstein Could Not?

The year 2005 was the one-hundredth anniversary of the amazing year when Albert Einstein, then only a 26-year-old patent clerk in Austria, published four profound research papers. In one paper, he arrived at his famous $E = MC^2$ equation. For another, his explanation of the photoelectric effect, he was subsequently awarded the Nobel Prize in physics. Despite these early successes, Einstein spent the rest of his life working on but ultimately failing to solve what physicists refer to as the Grand Unified Theory, which reconciles the four fundamental physical forces of nature: gravity, electromagnetism, the strong nuclear force that holds nucleons together in the atomic nucleus, and the weak nuclear force commonly seen in beta decay and the associated radioactivity.

Likewise, performance management in commercial organizations has its own huge intellectual challenge—that of reconciling customer value improvement with shareholder value creation.

QUANTUM MECHANICS AND PERFORMANCE MANAGEMENT

Einstein's contribution to knowledge was to advance the already-great work of arguably the greatest physicist who preceded him, Isaac Newton. Einstein refined Newtonian principles by theorizing that space, time, and mass are interrelated—his famous theory of relativity. His work dealt with the large-scale behavior of the universe.

Meanwhile, other physicists such as Neils Bohr and Edward Schrodinger were researching the other extreme of scale: subatomic physics. At this *micro* level, physicists examining quantum mechanics theorized and subsequently proved mind-boggling phenomena in our physical world, including the theory that mass could be simultaneously both a particle and a wave. The theoretical equations of quantum mechanics physicists were proven valid by applied physicists using powerful particle-accelerating atom smashers.

The problem, however, is that physicists have yet to reconcile the equations of quantum mechanics at the micro level with the Einsteinian equations at the *macro* level—yet the properties they both describe are part of one seamless, physical universe. Physicists are still working to make the equations converge and mesh.

What does this have to do with customer lifetime value, customer relationship management (CRM), shareholder wealth creation, and performance management? We have been describing a comparable perplexing problem in reconciling customer value with shareholder value creation. *Value* is an ambiguous, relative term. Hypothetically, companies can increase customer satisfaction (value perceived by the customer) by providing additional product features and service offerings, but if they do not raise prices, increase their market share, or grow the market, then they may have increased value to their existing customers, but they will have destroyed their shareholders' wealth. Economic value from a shareholder's perspective can be viewed in two ways: at the macro level (by the finance function) and at the micro level (by the sales and marketing functions):

- *Value according to finance.* The capital markets apply economic value equations based on free cash flow that are based on decomposition tree modeling of future revenue and expense streams. Financial analysts working for the chief financial officer attend conferences learning about economic value management with complex equations that ultimately divide projected future period net operating profit after tax in the numerator by risk-adjusted weighted average cost of capital from equity and loan financing in the denominator. Today's Einsteins of finance's macro world seek a proverbial *single* economic equation to answer this question: "What is the return on investment—the ROI?"

- *Value according to sales, marketing, and customer service.* Meanwhile, analysts in sales, marketing, and customer service examining CRM are playing around with the previously described equation that measures *customer lifetime value*—treating each customer (or more manageable customer segment grouping) as if it were an investment in a portfolio. In other words, they measure value today versus tomorrow or ten years from now to develop the appropriate customer strategy. These are the "quantum mechanics physicists" of finance's micro world.

WHICH IS THE DEPENDENT AND WHICH THE INDEPENDENT VARIABLE: CUSTOMERS OR SHAREHOLDERS?

The pressure is on to increase value to customers. The question is, which is the dependent and which the independent variable—customers or shareholders? The book *Angel Customers and Demon Customers,* by Larry Selden and Geoffrey Colvin, is subtitled "Discover Which Is Which and Turbo-Charge Your Stock (Price)."[1] As mentioned, the idea is that companies can no longer strive simply to grow sales, but rather they must grow sales *profitably.* Companies are realizing two connected factors related to customer economic value. If they could accurately measure the current profit contribution from their different types of existing customers, and also reliably predict and calculate the potential long-term stream of revenues and expenses from existing customers, then companies would view existing customers with an additional factor—a financial one. Then customers could be segmented for differentiated service-level treatment strategies (including support, self-service, and loyalty and retention programs) and targeted more appropriately for up-sell and cross-sell opportunities. Companies would also be more prudent about which *new* types of customers to acquire via their marketing.

The broader question regarding the reconciliation of customer value with shareholder value appears to start with customers, and the rate of shareholder wealth creation results as the derivative. However, the realization of shareholder value creation will be executed by the interdependent component methodologies of performance management.

THE DATA AND MATH EXIST: WHAT IS NEEDED IS THE THINKING

Einstein did not witness the completion of the Grand Unified Theory of physics, but we should expect to see the unification of customer and shareholder economic value creation in our lifetime. The data and math exist. What is needed is the thinking. The business intelligence tools, computing power, and analytical talent in companies exist today. All that is left to do is to create the modeling algorithms and to establish more collaboration between finance and customer-centric lines of business. Getting to the numbers—the overall value—is in the best interests of all involved.

In summary, it will be essential to have the analytical tools, such as for customer segmentation, forecasting, and activity-based costing for calculating customer value, reducing internal debates, and making trade-off decisions. It is inevitable that a company's executive team will navigate shareholder wealth creation based on facts, not hunches and intuition.

NOTE

1. Larry Selden and Geoffrey Colvin, *Angel Customers and Demon Customers* (New York: Penguin Group, 2003).

Chapter 28

Why Do Capital Market Organizations Underachieve Their Planned ROI?

Firms that invest in acquisitions, such as private equity firms and investment bankers, achieve their end goal only by raising the market value of their acquired companies. Acquiring organizations are called *capital market firms*. Their ultimate financial gain is realized from the buy–sell spread when they divest each investment. But research studies reveal that only a minority achieve their targeted return on investment (ROI). One study reported that less than half of all mergers achieve their goal.[1] Why do they have such poor results? Do they overplan but underexecute their economic value creation activities?

FIVE VALUE-CAPTURE CATEGORIES TO ACHIEVE RESULTS

Realizing actual economic value from mergers and acquisitions (M&A) is a "high-stakes juggling act."[2] So many things must be correctly executed to maximize the potential economic value. But problems arise, such as the disruptions from executive and employee turnover and from poor strategy execution—both the modified business strategy and the M&A integration strategy.

Exhibit 28.1 displays five value-capture categories that each contribute to lifting shareholder value from an enterprise's initial conditions. Although this exhibit describes opportunities for an M&A deal, it can be applied to any existing commercial organization.

Employees fear that the majority of the value lift will come from the third arrow, operating expense savings, which is perceived as code for employee layoffs. How can all five of the arrows generate the lift?

HOW CAN PERFORMANCE MANAGEMENT METHODOLOGIES UNLOCK POTENTIAL VALUE?

There is confusion about what performance management at the enterprise level is; and performance management is too often narrowly described as just visual dashboard measures and better financial reporting. It is much broader. Performance

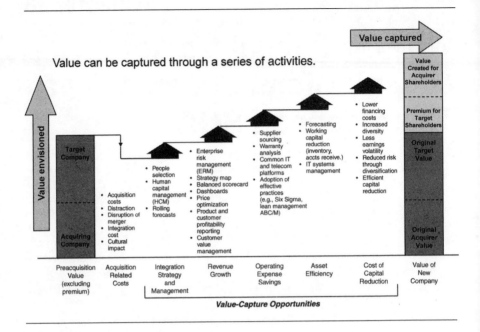

Exhibit 28.1 Value-Capture Opportunities

management is the integration of multiple managerial methodologies (e.g., customer relationship management, balanced scorecard, Six Sigma) with an emphasis on analytics of all flavors, and particularly risk management and predictive analytics. Performance management's methodologies themselves are not new; but organizations tend to independently implement each of them sequentially, often using disconnected spreadsheet tools rather than formal and proven information technologies. True performance management deploys the power of business intelligence (BI) to enable decision making.

Although there are interdependencies of performance management across all five value-capture categories, different performance management methodologies play a prominent role in each category:

1. *Integration strategy and management.* The heavy lifting is done in the next four categories to the right in Exhibit 28.1, but in this first category, the main performance management methodology is human capital management (HCM). Employees, like information, can be a powerful intangible asset to lift ROI. A robust HCM system is not just an automated personnel database, but is much more powerful in aiding employee selection and retention. For example, an analytics-powered HCM system can quantify historical employee turnover and apply statistical correlations from that history to the existing workforce to rank-order predict

the most-to-least likely next employee to resign and therefore enable management interventions. Both the employer and employee benefit. With an aging workforce approaching retirement at many companies, an HCM system becomes essential.

2. *Revenue growth.* Several performance management methodologies are engaged here:

- *Enterprise risk management (ERM).* ERM goes beyond just monitoring the traditional three pillars of market risk, credit risk, and operational risk. ERM also formally manages an organization's risk appetite with its risk exposure.

- *Business strategy management and execution.* David Norton, the coauthor with Robert S. Kaplan of *The Balanced Scorecard* book series, has stated that nine out of ten companies fail to successfully implement their business strategy.[3] Performance management addresses this with the integration of (1) strategy maps; (2) scorecards (for strategic objectives and their associated key performance indicators with targets); (3) dashboards (to cascade downward all measurements for operational actions); (4) incentives; and (5) analytics (to drill down to examine problem areas plus predict future outcomes).

- *Price optimization.* Pricing is too critical to be just a "thumb-in-the-air" intuitive feel for what price the market will bear. Performance management tools that optimize pricing include price elasticity analysis of consumer demand. This is incorporated into scalable forecasting and optimization routines that determine profit- and volume-maximizing price point, for example, for each retail stock-keeping unit at a store-specific level.

- *Product, service line, channel, and customer profitability.* Profit is calculated as sales minus costs, but few managerial accounting systems properly trace and assign consumed resource expenses into costs; they rely on antiquated broadly averaged cost allocations that distort true costs and profits. Traditional costing practices mask and hide costs of a product or service as a lump sum. Performance management's inclusion of activity-based cost (ABC) principles resolves these deficiencies. It is critical to have visibility and transparency of the contributing elements of costs—with accuracy—and to understand the many layers of profit margins.

- *Customer value management.* To determine the value of a customer, marketing staffs have traditionally relied on basic customer recency, frequency, and monetary spend data (the RFM triad). That data is not enough. Today there is a much greater need for customer intelligence that measures psychodemographic information of customers as well as to apply customer lifetime value metrics to answer the key questions, "What types of customer microsegments should we retain, grow, acquire, and win back? Which types should we not? How much should we spend with differentiated deals or offers on each microsegment so we do not risk overspending on loyal customers or underspending on marginally loyal customers who may defect to a competitor?" The more powerful and scalable performance management technologies answer these questions and enable the ultimate microsegmentation—to the individual customer or consumer.

Maximizing ROI is not accomplished by just growing sales, but rather by growing sales *profitably*—that is, *smart* revenue growth rather than growth at any cost.

3. *Operating expense savings.* The recent popular improvement initiatives of Six Sigma and lean management help the workforce learn *how* to think (and performance management provides more reliable and useful data for them, such as ABC information). But performance management provides information for *where* to think. Performance management brings focus. Improved productivity from business process improvements will reduce expenses, but there are diminishing limits, and breakthrough innovations stimulated by performance management information will inevitably be required. Warranty and service parts expenses are often loosely managed, and performance management addresses these with analytics that quickly detect minor problems before they escalate into major ones. Performance management also facilitates sourcing with supplier management and consolidation tools.

4. *Asset efficiency.* For product-based companies, a large portion of their working capital is inventory. Performance management's solution to reduce inventories leverages statistically based forecasts (updated periodically with demand history and potential influencing factors) to reduce uncertainty so a company can more confidently match its supply with demand. The objective is to minimize stockouts, shortages, and surplus unsold items. The resulting right-time and right-amount inventories increase inventory turnover rates that in turn improve the financial gross margin return on investment.

For fixed assets, a growing portion of an organization's expense structure is its information technology (IT) expenses. Performance management supports managing these infrastructure expenses with IT value management reporting. These are planning systems of capacity and usage for technologies, such as servers, software and laptop computers, as well as for associated workforce staffing level requirements.

5. *Cost of capital reduction.* The cost of capital has two components: (1) the amount required and (2) its composite rate. Performance management methodologies contribute to reducing both.

Performance management's "more with less" productivity actions optimize the *amount* of assets and resources required to fulfill customer orders and meet strategic initiatives. For banks, this means better control of their capital reserves. Performance management provides risk mitigation and reduced earnings volatility through powerful predictive analytics to reduce the cost-of-capital *rate*.

PERFORMANCE MANAGEMENT'S BONUS METHODOLOGY: ROLLING FINANCIAL FORECASTS

Capital market organizations hate surprises. Performance management cannot prevent surprises from fraud, ethics violations, or unexpected financial restatements (but performance management's analytics can provide earlier warnings). One surprise that performance management can reduce for capital market firms is an earlier alert that their acquired company will "miss its numbers." Today, the annual budget is arguably outdated as a financial control instrument in part because it is obsolete soon after being published. But worse, the annual budget is criticized for not effectively allocating resources to their highest returns. Performance management addresses these shortcomings by shifting the accountants' mentality from negotiating the next fiscal year's incremental percent spending changes with managers to a more logical approach. This approach models resource capacity planning, staffing levels, and supplier spending.

Imagine producing a budget 12 times a year. That is a nightmare for the accountants. Budgets are financial translations of nonfinancial operations. Performance management tools combine future volume-based demand drivers (e.g., sales projections) with funding for strategic initiatives. Since sales forecasts are constantly updated and because a strategy is dynamic, not static, then with constant adjustments, various performance management methodologies automate the translation of operations into rolling financial forecasts.

WHAT LEADS TO THE UNFULFILLED PROMISES OF ROI FOR CAPITAL MARKET FIRMS?

Capital market firms place high importance on executive leadership. And they should. From reading this chapter you may conclude that the performance management methodologies are like cog gears, and the executives with the best-in-class technologies that support performance management's methodologies can just push or pull the levers and pulleys and watch the dials. To achieve superior results, executive leaders must exhibit vision and inspiration. That is what a workforce responds to.

However, to fully achieve the highest potential in the lower-right side of Exhibit 28.1—Value of New Company—an enterprise cannot rely on a rudder-and-stick approach to get there. The executive team and their workforce need integrated business intelligence and performance management software for those gears to mesh and revolve at faster speeds. The premier software technology integrates performance management's suite of methodologies. Its underlying architecture is on a common data platform and its compute power is optimized for analytics—particularly predictive analytics. The resulting benefit is better, faster, cheaper—and smarter, by not just making processes more efficient but also prioritizing the ones most critical to creating higher value.

Enterprise resource planning (ERP) software is helping companies get operational control, but ERP software is not designed to transform transactional data into information needed for decision support. As the capital market firms influence (or require) their acquired companies to adopt and integrate performance management methodologies with their supporting technology, their desired ROI targets will be achieved and possibly surpassed.

NOTES

1. Deloitte Research, Economist Unit, M&A Survey, 2007.

2. Carol Bailey and Trevear Thomas, Deloitte Consulting LLP, "Mergers and Acquisitions: What CFOs Should Consider Asking Before the Deal Is Done," March 18, 2008, webinar.

3. David Norton, coauthor of *The Balanced Scorecard: Translating Strategy into Action*, at the Balanced Scorecard Collaborative Summit on November 7, 2006.

Chapter 29

Will Private Equity Funds Turbocharge Applying Performance Management?

In case you have not noticed, there is a sea change occurring in how the capital markets allocate financial capital to organizations to fuel growth and prosperity. Private equity funds are displacing public capital markets managed by international stock exchanges.[1] Widespread adoption of the performance management framework is increasing, but will the emergence of private equity funds accelerate the application of performance management methodologies?[2]

WHO ARE THE PARTICIPANTS IN CAPITAL MARKETS?

In order to understand why private equity funds are sprouting globally, here is a basic primer about capital markets.[3] There are three capital markets that profit-oriented organizations can tap to fuel their growth:

1. *Public capital markets.* These are the stock exchanges, such as the New York and London stock exchanges, where individuals like you and I as well as investment managers of mutual and pension funds and university endowments can invest along with others in publicly traded companies. Investors will always bear some risk, but broad participation by constant buyers and sellers typically moderates turbulence in stock price changes. Stock exchanges are also where new companies raise funding through initial public offerings.
2. *Internal capital markets.* This is where operating divisions within a parent company, such as Procter & Gamble, are provided cash by senior executives at the parent's headquarters. In effect, divisions compete for the parent's limited funding by submitting proposals supported by justifications that estimate the financial returns they can generate from the funds. In short, this is how financial resources are allocated within a conglomerate.
3. *Private capital markets.* This is the emerging player. You may recognize the four major types of participants as angels (primarily individuals), venture capitalists (investors betting on entrepreneurs), private equity funds, and hedge funds. One differentiator of private capital markets is they are not burdened by compliance with government and public stock exchange regulations and laws.

From these descriptions, you can see that managers of private capital markets are freer to identify investment opportunities and flexibly shift funds in those directions. As a result, they can more quickly produce higher financial returns than public and internal markets. Consequently, they are attracting insurance, university endowment, and retirement pension fund managers to supply them with capital. Global liquidity available for investing is at record-high levels,[4] and managers are chasing the highest risk-adjusted returns.

WHAT IS CAUSING THE EMERGENCE OF PRIVATE EQUITY FUNDS?

The emergence of private equity funds is being stimulated by the governance short-comings of the other two types of capital markets: public capital markets and internal capital markets.

Public capital markets will always be appealing to both investors and companies seeking funding. This is partly because a substantial pool of global financial savings is available, and, more important, because investments are highly liquid. That is, investors can easily enter and exit with their cash savings. And this efficiency with pooled, risk-shared, and liquid investments creates broad diversification that translates into a minimal extra price premium to purchase an equity position.

One shortcoming of public capital markets is that investment managers may behave impatiently and be somewhat fickle in choosing which stocks to buy and sell. Examples are the dot-com bust of 2000 and former Federal Reserve chairman Alan Greenspan's famous warning of "irrational exuberance." An impediment to full attainment of profit potential is the legal separation of a company's ownership from its management. Investment managers rarely have access to internal managerial information that the company's managers have. Yet, at the extreme, we observe young, recently minted MBAs at investment banking firms pressuring and influencing accomplished executives to make decisions favoring short-term financial results when relatively better decisions could result in much higher long-term financial outcomes. Finally, because recent Enron-like scandals have inspired regulatory burdens such as the Sarbanes-Oxley Act, publicly owned companies incur significant out-of-pocket expenses for regulatory compliance.

Internal capital markets can yield better financial performance because the executive leadership has access to internal information, marketing plans, return on investment analysis, and projections. On the downside, however, similar to public capital markets, internal capital markets also impede the ability to attain full profit potential and maximize a company's market value. But the explanation gives a different reason: corporate socialism. What I mean by this is that executives tend to patiently tolerate underperforming operating divisions. Further, they may be reluctant to starve an old colleague heading a division of his or her capital requests even though a sober and objective assessment would recommend it. Politics and personal favoritism are present. Strong divisions often subsidize weak ones.

In addition, executives tend to tolerate inefficiencies and fat that privately owned companies would be more ruthless to address and remove. They tend to universally apply standard performance measures that are not tailored to the unique traits of a division's industry. In short, some publicly owned company executives are simply too slow at restructuring or divesting a division that is not living up to its full potential.

PRIVATE CAPITAL MARKETS ARE FREE OF THE SHORTCOMINGS OF PUBLIC AND INTERNAL CAPITAL MARKETS

It is because private capital markets are not subject to the anchors and burdens of public and capital markets that they are capable of relatively higher performance. With a "barbarians at the gate" reputation, private capital managers reject internal capital allocation socialism in unleashing higher financial value from the tangible and intangible assets of their acquisitions. Among the four types of private capital market participants, private equity funds, such as the Blackstone Group and the Carlyle Group, are relatively more aggressive than angels and venture capitalists. With a buy-low-and-sell-high approach to investing, private equity funds have one goal: to transform and turn around the acquired company. Note that they always have an exit plan. In contrast, angels and venture capitalists are interested in helping the young companies they are funding to successfully blossom as a business, as did Yahoo! and Google.

Private equity funds do not necessarily acquire glamorous growth companies but often older ones in mundane industries. Similar to a hospital patient in an intensive-care unit, companies acquired by private equity fund managers have one purpose—to have their financial health improved and then be sold. However, the stakes and risks are large. In contrast to public and internal capital markets, with private equity funds, an investor's capital is locked up until the sale of the company—or until its parts are broken up and sold individually. There is a price premium for an illiquid investment, which places additional pressure on private equity fund managers to produce a high yield at the time of sale. (Because upon exit these acquired companies are frequently purchased by publicly owned companies, these assets are basically returned to the public capital markets. The intensive-care patient is returned to the traditional business model.)

There is a problem with private equity firms that performance management can resolve. The objective of a private equity firm can be summed up as follows: Buy a pig (or some pigs) with other people's money, spend a few years covering it with lipstick and starving it so it has a more elegant figure, and then sell the pig at a profit to someone who thinks it is Miss Universe. The key to the process is to be able to generate enough cash to pay for renting "other people's money" while at the same time being able to afford all the lipstick. There is nothing inherently evil in this process. The point is that the owners of a business managed in such a way appear to have little concern for the business's long-term success or even its continued existence after it is sold. Their goal is to pay for the interest and lipstick until they can sell the pig at a profit. Performance management aims at long-term sustained shareholder wealth creation.

WHY WILL PRIVATE EQUITY FUNDS TURBOCHARGE THE ADOPTION OF PERFORMANCE MANAGEMENT?

One question you may be asking is: What actions do private equity funds take that produce incrementally higher financial value in such short periods of time? The answer is simple. The managers of the private equity funds do three things:

1. They hire talented senior executives to transform the acquired businesses.
2. They have relatively higher performance targets and higher investment hurdle rates.
3. They equip these executives with the technology and tools that constitute and support the performance management suite of methodologies.

The third item is where the turbocharging is occurring. Both the private equity managers and their hired guns who operate the businesses—who have compensation reward packages tightly linked to improved financial and nonfinancial performance goals—are adopting progressive managerial methods. These include strategy maps, customized balanced scorecards, advanced managerial accounting systems to accurately measure and manage product and customer profitability and future value, rolling financial forecasts, customer relationship management systems, analytics-powered business intelligence tools for better employee decision making, and much more. All of these are mounted on an integrated enterprise information platform.

To be clear, the boards of directors of companies listed in public capital markets are not ignoring performance management. They are making the transition from a ceremonial role, entering into a new era of activist boards that more seriously accept their corporate governance responsibilities to represent shareholders.

Today's building contractors would never expect their workers to manually excavate a foundation with shovels; they equip their employees with industrial-strength power tools. The same goes for most companies—at least those aware of the shortcomings of spreadsheets and other nonintegrated information systems that are limited in supporting control, analysis, and decision making.

NOTES

1. In 2006, private equity funds accounted for 35% of global acquisitions, which was double the prior ten-year average of 17% (PricewaterhouseCoopers study).

2. To learn the basics about the performance management framework, read "The Tipping Point for Performance Management," at www.dmreview.com/article_sub.cfm? articleId=1027292.

3. For more information, Google Professor Jayanth R. Varma, Indian Institute of Management, Ahmedabad, India, who inspired this chapter.

4. See http://usmarket.seekingalpha.com/article/22629.

Environmental Performance Management

Being a good corporate citizen has never been so challenging. Companies have long been under public scrutiny for practices ranging from recruitment to workplace safety, from attitudes to overseas investment to environmental pollution. The emergence of climate change as a mainstream political issue, however, has served to drive home the breadth of ethical issues with which firms must now grapple. The business—and societal—implications of how companies address these are so far reaching that a new area of management practice has come into being to manage them, known by many as "corporate sustainability."

> —Dr. Paul Kiestra,
> *Doing Good: Business and the Sustainability Challenge*,
> Economist Intelligence Unit

Going green and demonstrating sustainability have arrived as requirements for all organizations. Exhibiting social and environmental responsibility is no longer an option. Organizations have reached the tipping point from moral introspection and complacent recognition of the green and sustainability movement to taking actions. The issues of oil, carbon-dioxide emissions, and global warming now impact any organization's social and environmental performance and its financial health. This is characterized by the term *triple bottom-line reporting—profit, people, and planet.*

Part Nine begins with a description of how going green and pursuing sustainable policies and practices can also create economic value. The concluding chapter in this part of the text is an interview with myself about how chief financial officers, typically responsible as guardian of assets, can contribute to helping their organization go green and embrace sustainability.

Chapter 30

Social and Environmental Performance Management

The new focus on corporate social responsibility (CSR) and environmental management is real; these are no longer just hollow words in an annual report or a public relations "me-too" message. Terms like *sustainability* and *going green* are surfacing throughout the business media. In the past century, free-market capitalism has done a lot to raise the economic prosperity of citizens in developed nations. Now capitalism appears to be accepting an advanced mission—to help and possibly save our planet. For example, with escalating carbon dioxide (CO_2) emissions globally, we have been running an uncontrolled experiment on the only home we have. Can we fix it? Only our unborn great-grandchildren and their offspring will be able to judge whether capitalism succeeded.

In the April 15, 2007, issue of the *New York Times Magazine*, journalist Thomas L. Friedman, author of the popular book *The World Is Flat*, said about the United States:

> We don't just need the first black president. We need the first green president. We don't just need the first woman president. We need the first environmental president. . . . We need a president who is tough enough to level with the American people about the profound economic, geopolitical and climate threats posed by our addiction to oil—and to offer a real plan to reduce our dependence on fossil fuels.

Sustainability is a way of thinking and acting when making decisions, not a way of reacting after wrong decisions have been made.

HOW CAN WE HELP?

In the past, when I advised organizations, I restricted my discussions almost exclusively to focus on business topics like resource capacity management, alignment of processes with the organization's strategy, or product and customer profitability reporting—pure capitalism, pure enterprise performance management. However, with the realities of global warming, pollution, deforestation, and the dwindling of nonrenewable energy sources like oil, I am increasingly discussing *triple bottom-line reporting—profits, people, and planet* for social and environmental accounting.

I respect organizations that are committing to a CSR role and *greening* the global economy. These organizations consider the impact of their activities on customers, employees, shareholders, communities, and the environment. They feel an obligation to extend their behavior beyond legal compliance and to voluntarily improve the quality of life for employees, local communities, and society at large. This chapter focuses mainly on environmental and climate change responsibility; but other corporate social responsibilities such as consumer safety, health, and poverty reduction are also important.

Commercial organizations face a perceived paradox of simultaneously trying to manage social performance for the planet and financial performance for shareholders. This creates challenges to develop information systems to identify opportunities and support decisions. The appealing aspect is that actions commercial companies take to reduce carbon emissions do not necessarily mean incurring higher costs. They can be both green *and* greedy—but greedy in a good way. Through innovative thinking, they can develop new methods that both increase revenues and reduce costs. And higher profits provide executives discretion to divert some of the higher retained earnings to more environmentally sound investments. Understanding the cost-versus-benefit ratio of sustainability initiatives will involve analytics similar to those used in performance management. The better an organization understands them, the better will be their financial performance.

A leader in promoting sustainability is Wal-Mart, which has created the position *vice president of sustainability*. Wal-Mart recently announced its partnership with the Carbon Disclosure Project to measure the amount of energy used to create products throughout its supply chain—many of which come from China—and reduce costs. For example, Wal-Mart has collaborated with Procter & Gamble to sell only higher-concentrated liquid detergent that requires less storage space and shipping costs and also less water usage in washing, less plastic, and less cardboard. In another example, materials destined for landfills are being replaced with new materials that disintegrate over time with no environmental impact.

There are now signs that political and business leaders are no longer saying "It's not my problem" or "This is their problem." This is a problem for humanity; and, fortunately, there are people of influence stepping forward who appear up to the multifaceted task of lessening our impact on our environment and mitigating the future risk of depleting our planet's natural resources.

Of course, a nagging concern is the question former Vice President Al Gore alludes to in his book and movie, *An Inconvenient Truth*: "Are we too late?" And if we're not too late, are we sufficiently serious about the costs, effort, and scale of change required to shift companies and countries toward being substantially emissions-free? Are there scalable technological solutions to blunt the most scary threat—climate change? How do we offset the tidal wave of truck and automobile purchases and dirty coal-burning energy generation in developing countries? It will take a lot more than replacing incandescent light bulbs with low-energy fluorescent ones.

WHEN DO YOU REALIZE ENVIRONMENTAL MANAGEMENT IS SERIOUS?

My own environmental awareness was inspired by a university student, Kristian Livijn, from the University of Arhus in Denmark. Livijn sought my advice regarding his master's degree thesis on the topic of environmental accounting. His message is that our environment is changing—and not for the better. Fixing matters will require a new way of life. All societies owe a tribute to our young people, who through their activism, such as protests, seem to sense there are needs and ideas for a better quality of life for everyone.

Livijn's belief is that an effective way to aid government policy makers is to develop monetary reporting mechanisms that expand a company's financial balance sheet to include planet Earth. His vision is that by introducing quantitative methods that represent all global assets, not just the financial assets worshiped at the altar of the capital markets, humankind can price and trade resource consumption to minimize waste. The joint exchange of carbon-traded credits and debits is one example of creating such a market economy. More important, quantitative methods and analytical tools can assist managers with identifying the sources of change and what might be the impact of change. He pointed me to the book *Activity-Based Cost and Environmental Management: A Different Approach to ISO 14000 Compliance,* by Jan Emblemsvag and Bert Bras.[1] The book expands on cost accounting to monetize an organization's consumption of energy and creation of waste.

MEASUREMENTS: A USUAL PROBLEM BUT HUGE OPPORTUNITY

Assessing the impact of changes that will affect the environment confronts a classic problem: *what* to measure and *how* to measure it. Fortunately, there has been much progress in identifying what to measure. Emblemsvag and Bras describe two categories of what they term *sustainability indicators*:

1. *Environmental performance indicators.* These include managerial measures about management's efforts to influence environmental performance (such as number of projects and allocated budgets as well as operational measures about results like usage rates of energy and water).
2. *Environmental condition indicators.* These report information on the condition of the environment. These are subdivided into two dimensions: (1) natural resources and environment (e.g., acidification, hazardous waste, ozone layer depletion); and (2) social environment (e.g., housing, health, education, security).

Global standards, such as the Global Reporting Initiative G3 guidelines[2] and ISO 14000 certification standards, are evolving that provide suggested measures to make organizations think beyond not only complying with the law, but becoming proactive rather than reactive to environmental concerns. This is where introducing rigorous and robust data measurement comes in. Hopefully, unlike financial regulations for financial reporting (e.g., U.S. generally accepted accounting principles and Financial Accounting Standards Board rules or international financial reporting standards), which are often of little value for internal decision making, the evolution of environmental standards such as for cap-and-trade programs will be logical and drive the necessary behavior for humankind to get a grip on this sometimes-overwhelming problem. One accepted set of standards comes from the Greenhouse Gas Protocol (GHG Protocol),[3] sponsored and developed through collaboration by the World Resources Institute and the World Business Council for Sustainable Development.

Good progress is being made in the area of greenhouse gas carbon footprint modeling. For example, Cisco, the large technology supplier, has taken commercial activity-based costing software and replaced resource spending in monetary units with carbon dioxide emissions, and displayed results and visibility tracing the source quantities through the locations, equipment, and assets (e.g., buildings) all the way to the outputs that consume the CO_2 equivalents. This provides robust information to determine where to initially focus as well as to project the impact of changes.

Hopefully, market-based capitalism can be mobilized to facilitate greenhouse gas management, monitoring, and reduction. There is a price that can be placed on CO_2 and other environmental factors. This needs to be done and put in a market context. Our climate-energy-pollution situation is an opportunity disguised as a problem.

PERSONAL REVELATIONS

My personal revelation from Livijn, Emblegsvag, and Bras is that performance management does not need to be restricted only to enterprises; it can be expanded to serve as global environmental performance management. However, Emblegsvag and Bras noted in their book's conclusion that technology alone cannot overcome this challenge; instead, we must discipline ourselves and overcome the imbalance between our need and greed. They quoted Mahatma Gandhi:

> There is enough in the world for everyone's need;
>
> There is not enough for everyone's greed.

NOTES

1. Jan Emblemsvag and Bert Bras, *Activity-Based Cost and Environmental Management* (Dordrecht, The Netherlands: Kluwer Academic Publishers, 2001), www.wkap.nl.

2. www.globalreporting.org.

3. www.ghgprotocol.org/.

Chapter 31

How Is a Chief Financial Officer Affected by the Sustainability Movement?

At a minimum, the corporate social responsibility (CSR) movement will involve external reporting that falls within the normal role of the chief financial officer (CFO). Reporting is one thing, but making positive changes is another. In this interview with myself, I share my opinions as to how CFOs might be affected.

Question: How does the current sustainability and green movement impact the CFO's duties and responsibilities?

Answer: Commercial, not-for-profit, and public sector organizations must now deal with the same compelling issues that consumers are acknowledging—a permanent high price of oil on the financial side with climate change and reduction of poverty on the social side. Social and environmental responsibility is no longer an option. Organizations have reached the tipping point from complacent recognition of the sustainability and green movement to taking actions. The issues of oil, carbon-dioxide emissions, global warming, and poverty impact any organization's social and environmental performance and its financial health. This has led to the term *triple bottom-line reporting—profit, people, and planet.*

The CFO's organization has traditionally been responsible for collecting data, validating the data, and reporting the data as information. The sustainability and green movement will extend this fundamental role to nonfinancial and nonoperational information. For example, the economic dimension for sustainability deals with the organization's impacts both on economic conditions of its stakeholders, such as its investors, and on economic systems at local governmental, countrywide, and global levels. Therefore, an extended financial performance aspect involves sustainability measures that extend reporting beyond the traditional measures of performance and quality.

Another example, greenhouse gas reporting, will introduce new data sources and data collection methods, but the discipline of reporting that accountants are trained in will be similar.

Question: What are the key issues and challenges for the CFO's organization?

Answer: A key challenge for CFOs will be balancing the organization's emphasis on complying with new and unfamiliar reporting and assisting their
organization to make good decisions as to where they should put their
efforts to improve. With accounting, CFOs balance external *financial
reporting* (e.g., generally accepted accounting principles) for investors
and regulatory stakeholders, mainly for economic valuation, with internal *managerial accounting* for internal decision making to create value.
If they primarily focus their energy on compliance reporting, then they
deny their managers and employees help with managerial information
to improve their organization's performance. Similarly, with social and
environmental reporting, if CFOs become too focused on only compliance reporting, such as with the popular Global Reporting Initiative
G3[1] standards, then they contribute little to helping their managers understand and determine the optimal ways to reduce the organization's
carbon footprint. In other words, weighting the indicators for the three
different aspects (i.e., finance, environmental, and social) will become
an important issue for the CFO function to optimize performance for
their organization in a sustainability context.

    In short, CFOs will need to facilitate their organization in formulat-
ing its sustainability and green strategies at the same time they are supporting enterprise performance management initiatives. There is an
emerging connection between adopting sustainability and green practices and successful long-term economic growth.

Question: What does the sustainability and green movement portend for the future
role of the CFO?

Answer: A concern that CFOs may have is a further increase in their reporting
workload. New laws, such as Sarbanes-Oxley, have already caused
extra work for them. However, the longer-term shift in CFOs' organizational role from reporter of history to strategic and operational advisor
has increased their value with the executive team. (It is no longer just
counting beans, but helping to *grow* the beans.) The sustainability and
green movement will provide the CFO's organization an opportunity
not just to focus on reporting but more important to provide
the analysis to identify in economic terms which sources of carbon dioxide and greenhouse gases can be reduced. Organizations have
little experience with such analysis.

    CFOs are now gaining competencies with performance measure-
ment scorecards and operational dashboards. They are recognizing that
leading indicators measured *during* a time period have causal and
correlated relationships with lagging indicators, such as the financial
results, reported *at the end* of the time period. Environmental reporting

will result in the emergence of CSR and green scorecards, including measures on key success areas, shortcomings, and operational and organizational risks. As an example, SAS, a leader in business intelligence and analytics software, offers software solutions for sustainability performance management.[2] But similar to business performance management reporting, the key will be not just *monitoring* the dials but taking actions to *move* the dials based on analyzing information, forecasting trends, and identifying gaps.

Question: What skills, adaptations, and so forth may be required in the future for the CFO, and why?

Answer: The monitoring of carbon dioxide, water, and power usage will have surprisingly similar accounting practices as with monetary currencies—such as expense reporting and product and customer cost reporting. That is the good news. Obviously, CFOs will need to learn about the science of carbon dioxide inputs and greenhouse gas emissions.

A challenge for CFOs will be to shift their mentality from debit and credit thinking to modeling. For example, activity-based costing is widely accepted as consistent with the cause-and-effect accounting principle to transform resource expense spending into calculated costs of outputs, such as a product cost, that consume the resources. Costing is basically modeling. However, many CFOs retain the traditional practice of allocating indirect expenses using broad averages that produce misleading costs. Advanced organizations have already demonstrated that their ABC modeling software can substitute carbon dioxide equivalents for money and quantify how much and where their energy inputs convert to specific outputs, such as buildings or products. That is, carbon-footprint modeling provides organizations with visibility and transparency to trace the carbon-footprint quantities of their products and services back to the sources. Other CSR methods include Life Cycle Assessments (LCA) and Design for Environment (DfE) for performance and process evaluation. CFOs will need to adopt these types of progressive methods, or else their managers and teams will need to guess at where the best trade-offs lie.

Question: Currently, are CFOs embracing the sustainability and green movement? Why, or why not?

Answer: The answer depends on one's interpretation of the term *embrace*. I believe most CFOs are personally cognizant of the new era we are all in and do not wish to push the problem that our current and past generations have created onto our children's children. But *embracing* the sustainability and green movement will likely require regulations, standard reporting, and cap-and-trade market forces to bring traction. This is in its infancy stage now. The European Union is a step ahead of the United States, but one could argue that they have just begun this journey.

Question: What advice do you have for CFOs in dealing with the ever-increasing sustainability and green landscape?

Answer: I would immediately advise CFOs to realize and accept that this movement is accelerating. Most CFOs can sense this by just observing the increased media attention, such as the number of news articles being published and radio and television broadcasts on the topic. That's the easy advice. My next advice is to start thinking of their organization's social and environmental responsiveness as an asset and opportunity, not as a liability and extra costs.

Implementing CSR must become a journey from a cost focus to a value creation focus where LCA, carbon-footprint modeling, and DfE will become strategic tools for managing the bridge from cost to value. This will be a strategic process that will challenge CFOs to support their organization in making new types of decisions based on new information. Not all of this information will be classic numbers that can be easily consolidated. Therefore, the CFO should help build a knowledge management organization that can calculate company performance, including unstructured environmental, climate, and social parameters.

When reasoned actions are taken, they can favorably result in improved processes, innovations, improved reputations, and increased financial profitability. Investing in sustainable practices can deliver a positive financial return for shareholders.

Question: What resources do you recommend for the CFO who wants to get up to speed on the topic?

Answer: A Google search will produce a landslide of information. I suggest understanding the guidelines reporting of the Global Reporting Initiative that more than 1,000 organizations are now voluntarily complying with. I would also read the *McKinsey Quarterly* article (2008, No. 2) titled "Business Strategies for Climate Change" and the executive summary of "The Prince of Wales Accounting for Sustainability Project."[3]

Question: Anything else you'd like to bring up?

Answer: Embracing the sustainability and green movement can help organizations achieve the accepted objectives of enterprise performance management—the trifecta of innovation, profitable customer satisfaction, and workforce retention.

NOTES

1. www.globalreporting.org.

2. www.sas.com/presscenter/london08/.

3. www.princeofwales.gov.uk/.../the_prince_of_wales_s_accounting_for_sustainability_
   project_1286619552.html.

Part Ten

Conclusion

No facts that are in themselves complex can be represented in fewer elements than they naturally possess. While it is not denied that many exceedingly complex methods are in use that yield no good results, it must still be recognized that there is a minimum of possible simplicity that cannot be further reduced without destroying the value of the whole fabric. The snare of the "simple system" is responsible for more inefficiency . . . than is generally recognized. . . .

—Alexander H. Church,
"Organization by Production Factors," 1910

The concluding part of this book begins with a magic-wand fantasy of mine, my letter to Santa Claus. The next chapter is my imagining of future diary entries written by a fictitious executive team in 2015.

I conclude the book by expressing a little frustration that I have had with the gradual (not fast enough) rate of adoption of performance management's methodologies, which I believe are solidly logical and which all managers and employees deserve to have.

Chapter 32

Christmas Gift Letter to Santa Claus

TO: SANTA CLAUS, The North Pole

Dear Santa,
I have been a good boy this past year. I believe that qualifies me for 100% order fulfillment of my Christmas gift requests, which follow. (And I promise there will be no returns and exchanges like I did last year.)

My top Christmas gift choice is that the marketplace will begin to view performance management as being much broader than the narrow chief financial officer–driven approach of merely financial reporting, budgeting, and unconnected dashboard dials. Those are important, but performance management includes so many more integrated methodologies.

If you can't deliver on that top choice, I beg of you to deliver this next request. I ask that the marketplace understand that the focus of performance management has shifted from historical reporting to forecasting and predictive analytics. This does not mean that there is no valuable information that can be gleaned from historical data; there are tons (kilograms, Santa, if you use European standards) of information. There is even an entire software industry of business intelligence (BI) based on this need for decision support. But BI is a subset of performance management (see Chapter 10, "How Do Business Intelligence and Performance Management Fit Together?"). Decisions must anticipate expectations of the future, including efforts to reduce uncertainty and mitigate risk.

My final request involves how companies interact with their customers and potential prospects on behalf of their shareholders. My Christmas gift wish is that you will make companies realize that how much they spend on customers—to acquire, retain, grow, or win back—is an *optimization* problem. That is, when it comes to serving customers, they should tailor the level of services in an *optimal* way. A company should not want to underspend on marginally loyal customers and risk their defection to competitors. Conversely, a company should also not want to unnecessarily overspend on already highly loyal customers with deals, offers, and price breaks where the incrementally higher service level won't really change anything—except waste spending to the detriment of shareholders.

Santa, you have been a pretty good guy these past years. Keep up the good work. I realize you have an emerging and huge problem related to protecting planet Earth. So, if giving out "green and sustainability" presents to others is a higher priority for you this year, I won't mind waiting until next year to receive my requests as noted above.

Very truly yours,
Gary Cokins

Chapter 33

Performance Management from Future Diaries

I recently read a newspaper column describing pretend future diary entries written by politicians.[1] It inspired me to conjecture what executive C-suite officers might write in their future diaries. My crystal ball is crystal clear. From the year 2015, with perfect hindsight, here are the personal diary entries from the executives of a fictitious corporation reflecting on their experience implementing the performance management framework. The final diary entry, written by the chief executive officer (CEO), was most surprising.

VICE PRESIDENT, SALES

Dear Diary of Sales Commissions,

Recalling 2008, I did not believe our CFO's claim that some of our long-term customers were very unprofitable to us. But then I saw the facts in her customer profitability reports. I also could not believe that our customer with the highest sales volume was much less profitable than our midsize customers. But then she proved that all the extra work we did for that No. 1 customer substantially dragged down our profit. When the CEO and CFO ganged up on me to change our sales force's commissions and bonuses to also include targets for customer profits, I thought they had flipped out. Everyone knew the name of the game was sales growth. Now I realize the goal is growing sales *profitably*—smart growth. You live and learn.

VICE PRESIDENT, OPERATIONS

Dear Diary of Chaos,

I remember, back in 2008, when my solution to wrestling with our volatile and dysfunctional operations was to standardize our processes to reduce our costs. But as the years progressed, I realized that our marketing research and engineering product and services development was increasingly tailoring differentiated products and services to each customer segment—and they kept microsegmenting our customer base and future sales prospects! The continuing customized services became a huge tsunami wave that standardization of processes could not overcome. Now I am thankful we shifted our efforts to attaining much higher forecasting accuracy. The better our forecasts, the less uncertainty we have experienced—and the better our scheduling and capacity planning. What was I thinking back then?

VICE PRESIDENT, MARKETING

Dear Diary of Spray-and-Pray Advertising,

My MBA marketing courses taught me the current fads of the time: Put your budget money in branding, take your big customers golfing, and use gimmicks to retain existing customers and acquire new ones. But fortunately, I then discovered that the secret to maximizing the yield from my budget money was through understanding the unique preferences of our individual customers and targeting new customers with traits similar to our most economically valuable customers. My big *aha!* was when I saw how powerful analytics of all flavors—statistics, segmentation, forecasts—provide us answers. At first I feared that the cost and effort to collect, understand, and apply all the necessary data would be galactic and that I would have to replace my street-smart marketing staff with PhD geeks. But then I saw my team gain competency with precision targeting of their marketing campaigns and optimizing deals, offers, and service levels based on the new intelligence we gained about our customers and their desires.

VICE PRESIDENT, HUMAN RESOURCES

Dear Diary of Employee Turnover,

My staff and I reminisced today about how proficient we were back in 2008, processing paperwork for exiting employees and stacking inbound resumes in piles. I am so glad those days are over. The big breakthrough in our mind-set was when we seriously applied workforce analytics to retain employees by predicting which were most likely to next quit so we could optionally intervene to prevent them from resigning—and also to hire new employees who would truly fit our current and future needs as well as our culture. Now my challenge is growing our employees' brains to accelerate their pace to innovate.

CHIEF FINANCIAL OFFICER

Dear Diary of Jail Prevention and Bean-Counting,

When we built our second cafeteria in 2008 just for the on-site external auditors, I thought then that any aspiration for me to actually help improve our business would be consumed by a life of compliance and governance duties. Thank you, thank you, thank you for the software systems that have made those responsibilities just a minor part-time job. I now recall my excitement these past years to use my freed-up time in a much more value-adding way to help our workforce and executives improve our profit performance. This new twist has been a rewarding surprise. Also, I love my expanded role contributing to the green and sustainability movement to enable my organization to achieve a negative carbon footprint with money to spare to reduce global poverty. We are now only a year away. Yesterday, my kids told me they want to grow up just like me. I'm a hero in their eyes.

CHIEF INFORMATION OFFICER

Dear Diary of Spreadsheet-itis,

I still laugh about the CIO I replaced in 2008, who got fired when our business nearly collapsed from the week that all of our spreadsheets converged into an infinite closed-loop system. All our laptops kept endlessly calculating and calculating. No new data could be input or information reported. Our company logo could have been replaced with the hourglass symbol. Spreadsheets are a disease, but I cured it with business intelligence systems. I wish I could laugh today about the dwindling size of my IT department—all the line and staff departments now do what we used to do for them. I guess buggy-whip makers somehow found new careers. I'll survive.

CHIEF EXECUTIVE OFFICER

Dear Diary of Relentless Pressure,

My fellow CEOs in 2008 dreamed that boards of directors would return to those ceremonial jobs for which you just showed up at quarterly board meetings to pick up your director's check. In contrast, my board was certainly an activist one in 2008. I vividly recall trying to turn around my sagging business by training everyone in Six Sigma quality and lean management techniques. With hindsight, I am glad I shifted our attention to strategy execution and our culture to embracing measurements with accountability. Those strategy maps, scorecards, dashboards, and other perform-ance management systems saved my tail. I realize now that Six Sigma and lean programs, though relevant, are limited in that they merely teach employees *how* to think, but our strategy management methods and enabling software technologies taught us *where* to think. Better yet, they gave us the focus, traction, torque, and yield regarding *what* actions to take to continually optimize to dynamic change. My next challenge? Grow my people. I hope my VP of human resources is thinking about that, too.

With perfect hindsight, these diary entries could be true ones. With imperfect foresight, these C-suite executives would probably have far less successful events to relate. To sustain long-term success, embracing the full vision of the performance management framework is not optional—it is essential.

NOTE

1. Todd Domke, "The Political Word from Future Diaries," *International Herald Tribune*, March 1, 2008, p. 5.

Chapter 34

A *Dear-CEO* Advice Column You Might Want to Read

Self-help books and newspaper advice columns, such as the famous Ann Landers column, are prevalent for issues involving relationships, money, or etiquette. What if there were an advice column for chief executive officers (CEOs)?

Dear CEO:

I am a relatively capable midlevel manager in my mid-40s. I have worked for my employer for ten years. During the past few years our company has been losing market share and declining in profits. Our executive team tries to talk a good game with quarterly town hall meetings with employees, but they appear to show no interest in implementing any of the core methodologies of an enterprise performance management framework, such as strategy maps, customer profitability analysis, or driver-based budgeting. Some of our executives openly ridicule these managerial techniques and say that real managers just need good old common sense and instinct, not fact-based information. What can I or my coworkers do to encourage our executives to be more innovative?

—Confused and Dismayed

Dear Confused and Dismayed:

Executive teams are one of the more interesting social groups to research and study their behavior. Even the most talented executive teams fail to reach their full potential due to their lack of trust and confidence in one another and the inevitable conflicts, reduced commitment, and avoidance of accountability that result from mistrust.

Sometimes you just have to figure out how to manage your bosses. Resistance to change is often the root of their problem. This is understandable because resistance to change is human nature—people like the status quo. I have relied on a simple formula to overcome resistance to change. It is $(D \times V \times F) > R$, where R stands for resistance. Do not underestimate how large the R is; it can be enormous. Therefore, in the equation, if D, V, or F is zero or small, then their combination will not exceed R.

You will need all three factors in great abundance. You are now asking what D, V, and F stand for.

- D is dissatisfaction with the current state. Unless people have discomfort, they will not be interested in changing anything.

- V is a vision of what "better" looks like. When people see a different view of their circumstances that can lead to an improved condition, they will consider changing.

- F is often neglected—it stands for "first practical steps." Some may think that a lot of dissatisfaction (D) with a solid vision (V) is sufficient to overcome that large resistance (R) variable. Large amounts of D and V are not enough. If people think the vision is overly theoretical, complicated, costly, or impractical, they will not pursue changes to realize that vision. You need F to make the vision attainable.

So how do D, V, and F apply to influencing your executive team? Most enthusiastic and well-meaning managers try to promote their vision. They get excited about implementing enterprise performance management techniques, such as strategy maps for critical projects and initiatives and with identified core business processes that need to be improved. My advice from experience is to first focus on the D. Here is why.

Change will result only when people feel compelled to change. Having high levels of dissatisfaction and discomfort, the D, is your best lever to influencing your executives. But dissatisfaction is often latent, not overt. You will need to create the discomfort in them. My suggestion is to use the Socratic method of questions, named after the classical Greek philosopher Socrates, who stimulated rational thinking and illuminated ideas by posing questions to his students, such as Plato.

- Do you have the nerve to start asking your executive team questions like these?

- Are your largest customers presumably your most profitable ones?

- Are any of them so demanding that the extra costs erode your profits? How do you know?

- Do all your managers and employee teams understand your strategic objectives?

- How do they know that what they do each week and each month contributes to achieving your strategy?

- Are the performance measures you monitor more weighted toward lagging, after-the-fact reporting that you react to?

- Or do you monitor leading key performance indicators (KPIs) that enable you to make proactive decisions? If it is the latter, how well do the leading KPIs correlate with the lagging ones?

- How do you know which types of customers to acquire, to retain, to grow, or to win back?

- How much is optimal to spend on each customer type with deals, offers, and promotions to acquire, retain, grow, and win back those customers?

- Won't any spending amount above or below the optimal for each customer type lead to destroying shareholder wealth?

In many cases, the executives may not have good answers. That is when you can hit them with the knockout-punch questions. Ask them, if they do not know the answers,

"Is that a good thing? How long can we keep making decisions without knowing these answers?" If you ask these thought-provoking and deliberately disturbing questions in the right way, you will not need to spend much time on promoting your vision (V) of the equation, the variable that many managers prefer to begin with. By converting and exposing latent problems into ones evident to your executives, the solutions become more obvious and understandable.

And what about the F in the equation—the first practical steps? Many organizations embarking on the journey of adopting enterprise performance management struggle with how to get started. Consider pilots and rapid prototyping with iterative remodeling techniques to demonstrate value and prove concepts. These accelerate learning and will get more buy-in.

Always remember that in the absence of facts, anybody's opinion is a good one. And usually the biggest opinion wins—which is likely to be that of your boss or your boss's boss. So to the degree your executives are making decisions on intuition, gut feel, flawed and misleading information, or politics, your organization is at risk. Write me again in few months and update me on how you are progressing. You can make a difference.

Chapter 35

From Nag to Wag: Why Performance Management Now?

If you have been reading my blogs, articles, and books, or researching what other advocates of applying performance management are saying, you probably detect a common theme—*start integrating now; do not postpone it.* Some of us performance management advocates are growing tired of *nagging* organizations to adopt performance management and are now *wagging* our finger to get them going. Why are we so passionate about this topic? One explanation is because advocates like myself have observed organizations that have integrated performance management components enjoy tangible and sizable benefits. And on the flip side, we have seen that organizations that continue to defer integrating suffer adverse consequences.

Of course, many of you are insisting "Name companies that have failed. Tell me the return on investment (ROI) on performance management." For the answers, we start by pondering the question, "How many of the original Standard & Poor's (S&P) 500 list originally created in 1957 are on that list today?" Answer: 74—just 15%. Of those 74, only 12 have outperformed the S&P index average.[1] That is pretty grim. My belief is that when it comes to considering whether to implement and integrate the various component methodologies that constitute performance management, there are actually two choices: to do it or not to do it. Many organizations neglect the fact that to *not* act, which means to continue with the status quo and to perpetuate making decisions the way they currently are, is *also* a decision.

And what about this need to prove that it is worth it to act by calculating an ROI for performance management?

THE OBSESSION WITH ROI JUSTIFICATIONS

Consider how you would measure the impact of having better performance measures from a strategy map and balanced scorecard system to drive employee behavior. Or consider how you would measure the impact of better decisions resulting from having more accurate and explanative information from an activity-based cost management (ABC/M) system. You will eventually conclude that the many parallel improvement and change initiatives that organizations pursue (e.g., total quality management, business process engineering) are occurring simultaneously.

As a result, it is nearly impossible to trace benefits, such as cost savings or future cost avoidance, directly back to any individual change program. This is like trying to put a broken egg yolk back together again.

One step removed from this ROI measurement challenge is to measure the effect of having better information, such as from using an ABC/M methodology, serving as an enabler to turbocharge the effect of all of these improvement programs. This further complicates quantifying the financial returns from the contribution of each change initiative program.

I am not big on making decisions based on faith, but there are some managerial concepts that just seem to be the right thing to do. Completing the full vision of the performance management framework is one of them. Take action or do not take action. Both choices have an ROI; and with performance management, my belief is that the former is positive and the latter is negative.

Life, business, commerce, and government are a continuous process of making choices. Strategy, which I have described as of paramount importance, is all about making choices. When making choices and decisions, conflicts are naturally competing, and they are weighed among options when the final decision is made. Computers, data management, quantitative analysis, and analytical theory have made huge strides that facilitate making performance management pay off. Performance management provides managers and employees clear direction and the computational horsepower to measure and weigh the trade-off decisions to always point to the highest value creation.

DID BEETHOVEN PAVE THE WAY FOR PERFORMANCE MANAGEMENT?

As I mentioned in the Preface, I was educated as an industrial engineer. Engineers are not perceived as very worldly or sophisticated. They are often pictured wearing a pocket protector stuffed with ink pens. But some engineers, like me, do have appreciation for the performing arts. For example, I appreciate classical music. In particular, I admire and am in awe of the great classical music composers. How did Tchaikovsky and Mendelssohn transcribe such beautiful music as notes from their brain to a page of musical score for so many instruments? (*Hint:* I do not think they had a BlackBerry or e-mail to distract their concentration.)

I believe that in the next few years, the adoption rate for performance management (as I have been defining it broadly) will accelerate similar to the effect that Ludwig van Beethoven's masterpiece, his third symphony, *Eroica*, had on the future of classical music. After *Eroica*, Beethoven's universally memorable fourth to ninth symphonies followed, and other great composers followed Beethoven's lead. What connection am I making between classical music and performance management?

Before going further, do you ever hear much about Beethoven's first or second symphonies? They do not seem to be played as often. That is because at the point of *Eroica*, his third symphony, was where Beethoven himself is quoted as saying

"I will now take a new path." It was a radical change in music composition. *Eroica*, inspired by Beethoven's admiration for Napoleon as a world leader, had true melody. Prior to *Eroica*, Beethoven's music compositions followed tradition where melody was subordinated within certain constraints. He complied with the conventional rules of what tasteful music for the elite should sound like. His earlier music was influenced by the previous masters, such as Bach and Haydn. But Beethoven had a strong urge to break free from tradition of the Classical era of music to evolve to the Romantic era. With *Eroica*, symphony music was changed forever. Symphony music compositions that followed were influenced by *Eroica*.

The evidence of the *"Eroica* effect" is this: How many billions of people, including you and me, will die with little trace of remembrance generations from now but a tombstone? But the works of Beethoven, Mozart, Rossini, Sibelius, Grieg, and others, along with Bach and Haydn, will be listened to for millennia to come.

Are we now at a point in time where the implementation of performance management's suite of integrated methodologies, like *Eroica*, will also "take a new path"? Yes. This is because tradition increasingly gives way to change—and organizations are slowly and gradually learning not just to manage change but to drive change. I hope this book has convinced you of this.

THE FUTURE OF PERFORMANCE MANAGEMENT

People are what matters, so I honor and respect the importance of applying the principles of behavioral change management. However, my love for quantitative analysis influences me to conclude with a short quote by the great Princeton University mathematician and Nobel Prize winner, John Nash. Nash introduced a theory describing how rational human beings should behave when there is a conflict of interests. In the Academy Award–winning movie about Nash's life, *A Beautiful Mind*, he said:

> I like numbers, because with numbers truth and beauty are the same thing. You know you are getting somewhere when the equations start looking beautiful. And you know that the numbers are taking you closer to the secret of how things are.

The executive management teams with the courage, will, caring attitude, and leadership to take calculated risks and be decisive will likely be the initial adopters of fully integrated performance management systems and will achieve its full vision. Other executive management teams will follow them.

NOTE

1. Gary Biddle, University of Hong Kong, Presentation at *CFO Connections* conference, September 11, 2007, Beijing, China.

Index